AFFECT AND AMERICAN LITERATURE IN THE AGE OF NEOLIBERALISM

C000151689

Rachel Greenwald Smith's *Affect and American Literature in the Age of Neoliberalism* examines the relationship between American literature and politics in the twentieth and twenty-first centuries. Smith contends that the representation of emotions in contemporary fiction emphasizes the personal lives of characters at a time when there is an unprecedented, and often damaging, focus on the individual in American life. Through readings of works by Paul Auster, Karen Tei Yamashita, Ben Marcus, Lydia Millet, and others who stage experiments in the relationship between feeling and form, Smith argues for the centrality of a counter-tradition in contemporary literature concerned with impersonal feelings: feelings that challenge the neoliberal notion that emotions are the property of the self.

Rachel Greenwald Smith is an assistant professor of English at Saint Louis University. Her work has appeared in journals such as *American Literature, Twentieth Century Literature, Mediations*, and *Modern Fiction Studies*.

AFFECT AND AMERICAN LITERATURE IN THE AGE OF NEOLIBERALISM

RACHEL GREENWALD SMITH

Saint Louis University

CAMBRIDGE
UNIVERSITY PRESS

University Printing House, Cambridge CB2 8BS, United Kingdom

One Liberty Plaza, 20th Floor, New York, NY 10006, USA

477 Williamstown Road, Port Melbourne, VIC 3207, Australia

314-321, 3rd Floor, Plot 3, Splendor Forum, Jasola District Centre, New Delhi - 110025, India

79 Anson Road, #06-04/06, Singapore 079906

Cambridge University Press is part of the University of Cambridge.

It furthers the University's mission by disseminating knowledge in the pursuit of education, learning and research at the highest international levels of excellence.

www.cambridge.org
Information on this title: www.cambridge.org/9781107479227

© Rachel Greenwald Smith 2015

First published 2015
First paperback edition 2021

A catalogue record for this publication is available from the British Library

Library of Congress Cataloging in Publication data
Smith, Rachel Greenwald, author.
Affect and American literature in the age of neoliberalism / Rachel Greenwald Smith,
Saint Louis University.
pages cm
Includes bibliographical references and index.
ISBN 978-1-107-09522-9 (hardback)
1. American literature – 21st century – History and criticism.   2. Literature and society –
21st century – United States.   3. Emotions in literature.   4. Affect (Psychology) in literature.
5. Neoliberalism – United States.   6. American literature – 20th century – History and
criticism.   7. Literature and society – 20th century – United States.   I. Title.
PS229.S65   2015
810.9'355–dc23   2014038215

ISBN 978-1-107-09522-9 Hardback
ISBN 978-1-107-47922-7 Paperback

For my parents

The emotion of art is impersonal.

– T. S. Eliot

Contents

Acknowledgments

This book calls into question the notion that we own our own feelings. Likewise, writing this book has been a persistent reminder of how little we own our own thoughts. The ideas enclosed here are not in any way exclusively mine: they were fostered, challenged, and refined by the brilliance of those with whom I came into contact during the process of its evolution. Most of all, this book is a reflection of the intellectual culture of my family, in which my mother's insistence on the importance of political critique was answered by my father's interest in the ability of works of art to access the strange, intuitive, and unknown. In this and in so many other ways, this book would not have been written without the unceasing support and inspiration of my parents, Marta Greenwald and Gary Mac Smith, and my sister, Sophie Smith.

In practical terms, this project began with a dissertation that served as a testing ground for some of its central claims. While no actual material from that project appears here, I am greatly indebted to my mentors at Rutgers who helped me in my early efforts to think through questions of politics, affect, and literary form. Thanks particularly to my advisor, Richard Dienst, who not only tolerated but improbably encouraged my propensity toward manifesto writing, and to Marianne DeKoven, John McClure, and Harriet Davidson for their guidance. Thanks also to my cohort at Rutgers, particularly Paul Benzon and Cornelius Collins, for helping me learn what it meant to be both an academic and a human being; to my friends in New York – Aram Jibilian, Christa Parravani, Jacob Steingroot, and Helena Ribeiro – for cocktails, brunch, warmth, and wisdom; and to my bandmates Boshra AlSaadi, Nicole Greco, Rich Smalley, and Robbie Overbey, for putting up with the inconveniences of my double life. And I am endlessly grateful for the friendship and collaboration of Sean Grattan and Megan Ward, both of whom read substantive parts of this manuscript along with much of everything else I have written, and who have been rare and enduring sources of sanity throughout my academic development.

I feel very lucky to have found a home at Saint Louis University, where the vitality of the English department has been a source of great stimulation. Thanks particularly to the two department chairs who served during the completion of this project, Sara van den Berg and Jonathan Sawday, and to the rest of the faculty – Toby Benis, Ellen Crowell, Ruth Evans, Devin Johnston, Georgia Johnston, Paul Lynch, Jen Rust, Nathaniel Rivers, Joe Weixlmann, Phyllis Weliver, and many others – whose friendship and counsel have been invaluable. Thanks too to my friends in the English department at Washington University – Musa Gurnis and Melanie Micir, as well as Maggie Gram and Dan Grausam – for making Saint Louis such a vibrant and welcoming place to live and work. I am particularly grateful to one of these friends, Vincent Sherry, for first bringing my work to the attention of Ray Ryan at Cambridge University Press. It has been a great pleasure to work with Ray, as well as Caitlin Gallagher. Their work, along with the rigorous and thoughtful readings of Michael Clune and Steve Belletto, has given this project greater shape and scope.

Portions of this book have benefited from the feedback of the audiences and participants of the Post45 Symposium at Stanford University, the Northeast Americanist Colloquium at Brown University, the Americanist group at the University of Illinois, Urbana-Champaign, and the English department's Faculty Research Symposium at the University of Missouri, Columbia. Thanks to Michael Szalay, Mark McGurl, Deak Nabers, Jennifer Lozano, Benjamin Bascom, and Alex Socarides for their hospitality during these events. I am also exceptionally grateful for the community of scholars associated with the Association for the Study of Arts of the Present, most of all Andy Hoberek and Mitchum Huehls, both of whom offered substantive comments on this project and have offered their support from its earliest stages.

In a book that takes seriously the claims that nonhuman beings and things have upon us, it seems apt to express my gratitude to those that made writing this book feel even remotely possible. Thanks to Remi and Mosley, my furry companions, who refuse to let me take myself too seriously. Also thanks to the egg sandwiches at Bloc 11 in Somerville; the electricity generator (and the air conditioner it so industriously powered) at Costa Coffee in New Dehli's GK2 district; the creepy and beautiful lagoon at the Art Library at the University of Iowa; the cormorants who migrate every winter to the river on which my parents' house boat is moored; and the 300-pound orange tank desk in my home office in Saint Louis that makes my work space, if not my work itself, feel substantial.

This project was financially supported by two Mellon Faculty Development Grants as well as a Vice Presidential Faculty Leave Grant, all through Saint Louis University. Kathryn Grundy, Ludwig Weber, and Emily Philips offered essential research assistance. Kay Kodner provided an early copyedit on the manuscript. A version of Chapter 2 and a portion of Chapter 4 originally appeared in *American Literature* and *Twentieth-Century Literature*, respectively. I am grateful to the editors of both journals and to Duke University Press and Hofstra University Press for granting permission for that material to appear here.

Finally, it is impossible to describe the impact that Ted Mathys has had on this project. From his patience in helping me clarify its thorniest claims, to his tireless reading and rereading of every one of its sentences, he has been my greatest inspiration, editor, critic, and advocate. And, when one year ago, Lucy Noa Mathys-Smith appeared in this world, he became my partner in navigating the most astonishing and wondrous affective terrain I have ever encountered. Thank you, Ted, for this.

Introduction
The Affective Hypothesis

This book is an argument against the ubiquity of what I call the *affective hypothesis*, or the belief that literature is at its most meaningful when it represents and transmits the emotional specificity of personal experience.[1] Like most commonly held beliefs, the affective hypothesis is so prevalent that it tends to function invisibly, silently supporting a range of critical practices: it lurks in reviews evaluating recently published novels, in critical appraisals of authors' hallmark styles, and in large-scale assessments of literary movements. And it is just as often employed by nonspecialists in literature, appearing in institutional appraisals of the value of literary study to a larger college curriculum and in justifications for the inclusion of literature departments in interdisciplinary initiatives. In all directions, among critics, scholars, administrators, and casual readers, there is an odd and unsettling consensus: We read works of literature because they allow us direct contact with individuals who are like us but not us; they allow us to feel what others feel; they provoke empathy; and they teach us how to understand what it means to be a unique human being.[2]

What could be wrong with that?

As it turns out, plenty. While the affective hypothesis is not a recent invention, it has found renewed support, particularly in scholarly circles, since the early 1990s. The contemporary prevalence of the affective hypothesis therefore coincides historically with the securing of neoliberalism as a political, economic, and cultural dominant in the United States.[3] Neoliberalism began as a set of economic policies in the late 1970s and early 1980s aimed toward unfettering domestic and global markets, dismantling social safety nets, and privatizing previously public institutions. With the end of the Cold War and the beginning of the Clinton presidency, neoliberalism began to look as if it could exist in perpetuity, uncontested from superpowers abroad or political parties at home.[4] As a result, neoliberal policy has become increasingly normalized, accompanied by a corresponding shift in the social expectations that are placed upon individuals. Neoliberalism's emphasis on the necessity of personal initiative, along with its pathologizing of structures of dependence, calls upon subjects to see themselves as entrepreneurial actors in a competitive system.

These subjective aspects of neoliberalism coincide startlingly with the assumptions underlying the affective hypothesis. While neoliberalism casts the individual as responsible for herself, the affective hypothesis casts feeling as necessarily owned and managed by individual authors, characters, and readers. Neoliberalism imagines the individual as an entrepreneur; the affective hypothesis imagines the act of reading as an opportunity for emotional investment and return. The neoliberal subject is envisioned as needing to be at all times strategically networking; feelings, according to the affective hypothesis, are indexes of emotional alliances.

Like any structure of belief that functions without contestation, the affective hypothesis is both totalizing and limiting, stuffing diverse literary practices into a single mold and excluding those that don't conform to its shape. Works of literature highlight, intensify, and transmit feelings in a wide range of ways. Yet when it comes to defining a work as warm or cold, emotional or flat, alive or dead, or determining whether it functions on the level of the heart or the head, the affective hypothesis shuts out the multiplicity of textual approaches to feeling.

This book argues that the feelings that are acknowledged under the affective hypothesis are largely what I call *personal feelings*. Personal feelings function like personal property. They are private, not in the sense of being secret or interior, but in the sense of being "privatized": they are personally controlled, even though they circulate outside the self; they are managed by the individual but they are augmented by connections with others; and ideally they enrich the individual through their carefully calculated development, distribution, and expansion.[5]

But there are also forms of textual feeling that tend to be overlooked in contemporary literary criticism because of the prevalence of the affective hypothesis. I call these *impersonal feelings*. Impersonal feelings do not straightforwardly conform to a market model, because they are not easily codifiable or recognizable; they do not allow for strategic emotional associations to be made between readers and characters; and they emphasize the unpredictability of affective connections. As a result, these modes of textual affectivity, if they are recognized and defined as forms of feeling, challenge the principles of subjectivity that underpin not only our aesthetic judgments but our economic, political, and social convictions as well.

Emotional Economies

In her study *Poetic Justice*, Martha Nussbaum makes an impassioned argument for the political importance of the novel form by appealing to its privileged emphasis on the personal. In one of the more exemplary moments of the affective hypothesis, she praises the novel's

> commitment to the separateness of persons and to the irreducibility of quality to quantity; its sense that what happens to individuals in the world has enormous importance; its commitment to describe the events of life not from an external perspective of detachment, as the doings and movings of ants and machine parts, but from within, as invested with the complex significances with which human beings invest their own lives.[6]

In this view, the novel form provides a focus on the individual that society as a whole lacks. This focus is anchored in the emotional provocations of fiction, wherein "readers of novels ... find themselves led by these works to fear, to grief, to pity, to anger, to joy and delight, even to passionate love."[7] For Nussbaum, the novel's attention to the emotional dimensions of human experience leads the form to be "profoundly opposed ... to the reductive economic way of seeing the world."[8] If economic assessments rely on cold data and rational actors, the argument goes, the novel's warmth and interest in nonrational experiences should counter the tendency to evaluate human needs according to economic logics. Emotions, in this reading, accentuate the specificity of individual experience, and the feelings triggered by the reading of novels allow for readers to ethically invest themselves in the emotional specificity of characters just as they "invest their own lives."

It may be true that traditional economic reasoning undervalues the role of emotions in decision making. And it may also be the case that certain forms of the novel do put great emphasis on individual emotional experience. But anchoring the political promise of the novel form in its ability to do so, as Nussbaum does, ignores the degree to which individualization is as key to how all forms of capitalism function as is rigid or unfeeling systemization.[9] As social institutions, from welfare systems to educational systems, and from media sources to public spaces, increasingly become personalized and privatized, neoliberalism amplifies this tendency for capitalism to individualize, casting individuals as exclusively responsible for themselves.

Despite this coincidence between the logic of neoliberal capitalism and an emphasis on the personal, the contemporary trend toward seeing literature as offering an education in the uniqueness of the individual through an experience of emotional connection has been on the rise over the past twenty-five years. A range of new subfields in literary criticism, while methodologically diverse, tend to see literature as socially beneficial insofar as it provides evidence of the centrality of individual emotions. These include ethical appeals to literature's capacity to insist on the importance of the individual over and above the faceless mass; neurobiological efforts to understand literature as literal brain training for the individual reader; and approaches within trauma studies that see works of literature as performative utterances that, when read for their gaps, breaks, and incongruities, reveal the psychological state of their authors or narrators. This notion also underpins a range of recent trends in literary production that are envisioned as compromises between modernist experimentalism and the representation of the feeling subject, including the emergence of neo-realism and post-postmodernism in fiction and the post-language lyric in poetry. The ubiquity of these schools and styles, along with a publishing and review culture that celebrates them, furthers the tendency for fundamental literary meaning to be equated with the production of recognizable emotional content.

The appearance since the 1990s of approaches like these, which see literature as a means to an ethical encounter with the specificity of personal experience, stems from several related currents: the waning of postmodernism as a formal practice and aesthetic dominant; skepticism toward poststructuralism and deconstruction along with a more general decline of the study of theory as an autonomous subdiscipline; and increasing interest in themes and approaches that are seemingly more anchored in what is imagined to be authentic human experience. The turn away from linguistic modes of analysis and the move toward ontological concerns in particular is often used to justify interest in works of literature that appear to represent human experience realistically – that is, without self-conscious aestheticization or other distancing effects.[10]

While the recent turn to ethical and ontological literary criticism is commonly attributed to changes within the discipline of literary studies, less commonly considered is the historical coincidence of this shift with the consolidation of neoliberalism.[11] Championed by the administrations of Ronald Reagan in the United States, Margaret Thatcher in the United Kingdom, and Deng Xiaoping in China, neoliberalism initially emerged as a set of domestic and global policies aimed toward developing what David Harvey describes as "an institutional framework characterized by strong private property rights, free markets, and free trade."[12] The fundamental neoliberal belief that "human well-being can best be advanced by liberating individual entrepreneurial freedoms and skills" has since underpinned many of the policy changes that have character-ized the past three decades, which include state-enforced limitations on the power of unions, the dissolution of social safety nets, the deregu-lation of financial institutions, the privatization of industry, and the development of international free trade agreements.[13] These practices and priorities in the United States have been relatively stable and secure despite dramatic changes in the party affiliations of presidential adminis-trations and congressional majorities, significant historical events includ-ing the 9/11 attacks and subsequent wars in Iraq and Afghanistan, and serial periods of economic recession and growth. This stability attests to the endurance and widespread acceptance of basic neoliberal beliefs in policy circles on both the right and the left.[14] The resilience of neoliber-alism despite these apparent challenges suggests that it is more than a set of policies aimed at responding to the needs of a given moment. Rather the foundational assumptions of neoliberalism have "become hegemonic as a mode of discourse," appearing in a wide range of institutional and personal practices.[15]

As a result, the consequences of neoliberalism extend beyond the par-ticularities of economic and political policy, affecting the assumptions that underlie political subject formation. As Jason Read argues, neoliberalism has been achieved "not by a transformation of *the mode of production,* a new organization of the production and distribution of wealth, but by the mode of subjection, a *new production of subjectivity.*"[16] The social effects of neoliberalism therefore go beyond what can be understood through a purely economic analysis of financial indexes, market instruments, and production processes.[17] This is because, as Wendy Brown explains, neo-liberalism's "effect on governance and the social is not merely the result of leakage from the economic to other spheres but rather of the explicit imposition of a particular form of market rationality on these spheres" such that previously nonmarket-oriented forms of life become under-stood as best functioning according to a market logic.[18] This form of mar-ket rationality transforms the subjective norms underlying liberalism, in which individuals were shaped on the one hand as citizen-subjects and on the other hand as economic subjects, with all of the tensions and contra-dictions that go along with this double role. Under neoliberalism, a model of the subject emerges that reconciles the contradictory commitments of democratic citizenship and capitalist competition by jettisoning the polit-ical demands of liberalism and retaining the economic imperatives of the liberal market.[19]

While the emphasis this places on individual success and self-care does contribute to the much-discussed rise of individualism over the course of the past few decades, the neoliberal subject is not individualistic in the traditional sense. Neoliberal society requires and encourages engagement with others: it is, after all, under neoliberalism that we see the rise of social media and the premium put on networking and the acquisition of "friends." But these forms of association are largely understood to lead to the enrichment of the self (as opposed to the company, family, or locality) such that the development of the self becomes the primary aim of social engagement. In this social context, emotions are increasingly understood as resources to develop and manage, rather than as instances of authentic experience that fall outside rational control. In the neoliberal context, recognizing the presence of emotions, in art, in other people, and in the self, does not challenge market-oriented thinking. Instead, feelings frequently become yet another material foundation for market-oriented behavior: emotions are acquired, invested, traded, and speculated upon.

Managing the Emotional Portfolio: The Case of *The Corrections*

The convergence of the economic and the emotional that occurs under neoliberalism appears thematically in a range of contemporary works of fiction. For instance, Jonathan Franzen satirizes the emotional consequences of neoliberal ideology in *The Corrections* through the character of Gary, a vice president of a local bank, who maps his mental health as if he were tracking stocks:

> Although in general Gary applauded the modern trend toward individual self-management of retirement funds and long-distance calling plans and private-schooling options, he was less than thrilled to be given responsibility for his own personal brain chemistry, especially when certain people in his life, notably his father, refused to take such responsibility. But Gary was nothing if not conscientious.... He estimated that his levels of Neurofactor 3 (i.e., serotonin: a very, very important factor) were posting seven-day or even thirty-day highs, that his Factor 2 and Factor 7 levels were likewise outperforming expectations, and that his Factor 1 had rebounded from an early-morning slump related to the glass of Armagnac he'd drunk at bedtime. He had a spring in his step, an agreeable awareness of his above-average height and his late-summer suntan. His resentment of his wife, Caroline, was moderate and well contained. Declines led advances in key indices of paranoia (i.e., his persistent suspicion that Caroline and his two older sons were mocking him), and his seasonally adjusted assessment

of life's futility and brevity was consistent with the overall robustness of his mental economy. He was not the least bit clinically depressed.[20]

Gary manages his emotional life as if it were his stock portfolio: tracking gains in his neurochemistry, keeping a watchful eye on the "key indices" of his responses to those around him, and warding off any existential musings that might challenge the "robustness of his mental economy."[21] His feelings are figured as personal assets, such that his responsibility for himself is understood to require the proper management of those assets. Gary, whose interest in the stock market is motivated by personal competitiveness as much as it is by economic necessity, is particularly prone to seeing his own neural portfolio as reflecting his moral character more than it does the contingencies of his environment or social context. While his emotions do stem from his relationships – he suffers throughout the novel from conflicted feelings about his nuclear family – those emotions are understood to be solely his responsibility to manage. Resentment is therefore seen as a threatening factor to be contained, rather than the result of an interpersonal dynamic that could change depending on a shifting external situation. Similarly, depression is seen not as a variation of emotional experience but as evidence of improper management of emotional resources; it is characterized as shameful evidence of unwise decisions and moral failings. This personalization of emotional life is consistent with Brown's argument that neoliberalism "carries responsibility for the self to new heights: the rationally calculating individual bears full responsibility for the consequences of his or her action no matter how severe the constraints on this action."[22] Consequentially, unhappiness and other emotional difficulties, regardless of their causes or contexts, are seen as evidence of an irresponsible abdication of responsibility for the self.[23]

Franzen's satire of the culture of psycho-pharmaceuticals and neurology reflects how major technological and cultural changes in popular approaches to psychology have led to beliefs about mental health and psychology consistent with neoliberal assumptions. Central to the many changes in psychology that have occurred since the 1980s have been the development of more sophisticated neural imaging tools,[24] the emergence of a new generation of antidepressants,[25] and the growth of the self-help industry.[26] All of these factors have led to a shift in psychological theory and practice, in which the therapeutic model that dominated much of the twentieth century is increasingly replaced with the fantasy that individuals, armed with a pop-scientific knowledge of the brain, a Prozac prescription, and a pull-yourself-up-by-your-bootstraps attitude, might take full personal control of their emotional lives. Neoliberal policies have, in turn, supported this view by allowing for greater flexibility in the advertising of drugs to potential consumers. The FDA's 1997 deregulation of Direct to Consumer (DTC) advertising by pharmaceutical companies allowed prescription drugs to be advertised in broadcast and print media, which is likely to have contributed to a rise in psycho-pharmaceutical use. These advertisements often call upon individuals to seek out their doctors to obtain prescriptions for particular drugs rather than representing doctors as responsible for properly diagnosing and treating patients.[27] Prescription drug use since this ruling has therefore been based more directly on the model of commodity and consumption. In addition, neoliberal reforms in health insurance delivery in the 1980s and 1990s led to a rise in health management organizations (HMOs), which tended to restrict reimbursements for long-term psychotherapy. This perpetuated the rise of prescription-only, and thus often primarily self-monitored, mental health practices.

The Corrections includes moments of scathing writing on these and other emotional consequences of neoliberalism. Yet the parallels between personal experience and the economic logics that underlie neoliberalism extend beyond these satirical passages to the structure of the novel itself. In this aspect, the critical posture disappears, and what remains is an apparent acceptance of the notion that the economy and the personal function in tandem. While the title of the novel has valences that range from the penitentiary system (correctional facilities) to generational change (making corrections in the behavior of one's parents) to revision (the endless corrections that Chip, one of the main characters, makes to his doomed screenplay), the metaphor that looms most dramatically over the novel is that of the market correction, the dip that often occurs in the stock market after a dramatic rise. The market correction that Franzen addresses most directly in the novel is the end of the dot-com bubble in the NASDAQ, which caused most major market indices to slip beginning in the spring of 2000 and to continue to lose ground after the attacks of September 11, 2001, hitting a cyclical low after the publication of *The Corrections* in October 2002. Calling this dive, which was in progress and certainly not resolved at the time of the novel's publication, a "correction," as Franzen implicitly does, betrays the fundamental assumption that, in the long term, U.S. financial markets will function as they have for more than a century and continue to rise over time. This has historically been the case, even despite substantial losses like those that accompanied the Great Depression. In other words, what looks like a catastrophe in the short term, if the market functions as it has since the beginning of the twentieth century, becomes in the long term a mere momentary adjustment to otherwise predictable and steady growth.[28]

The Corrections takes place immediately before the end of the dot-com bubble – the NASDAQ crash occurs only in the final section of the novel that serves as an afterword of sorts – but the shape of the market correction provides a foundation for the plot arcs of the lives of each of the Lambert children. Chip, Gary, and Denise, each with their own separate story told through their own primarily separate part of the novel, all start out moving upward in their lives according to most traditional standards of success. Chip is an assistant professor at a prestigious liberal arts college about to go up for tenure, Gary is a father of three with a lucrative job and a skyrocketing stock portfolio, and Denise is a star chef receiving local and national publicity. Over the course of the novel, each undergoes a major episode of degradation. Chip goes on a three-day drug-and-sex binge with an undergraduate and is fired from his academic job; Gary becomes so paranoid when his wife and children believe he is depressed that he gets drunk, serves the family raw meat, maims himself with hedging shears, and ultimately has to confess to a depression he may or may not in fact suffer; and Denise is caught in a double affair with both her boss and his wife. The three characters' lives each begin on a steep rise and then appear to plummet disastrously. By the end of the novel, however, each has, through a renewed commitment to wise self-management, reversed the trend and is on the way back up, albeit having undergone a "correction" toward more modest forms of success. Chip is married and expecting a child; Gary has a less robust financial profile but he is uneasily reconciled with his family; and Denise moves to Brooklyn and finds a job at a new, less flashy restaurant.

The fates of the three characters, in other words, mimic the behavior of the market under the assumption that it will, if properly managed, continue to rise over time. This reinforces the notion that any loss of value – whether in life or finance – is part of a natural process of growth and not a fundamental hindrance to the accumulation of greater value. Unlike the obvious satirical tone of the economic terms with which emotions are understood in Gary's section of the novel, the collapsing of life and finance in the overall structure of the novel is not self-reflexively critical. In fact, the degree to which the narrative structure of the work matches prevailing market expectations affirms the inevitability of those expectations and leaves the novel entirely subject to their logic. In other words, the comedic structure of *The Corrections* is dependent on its acceptance of a vision of the workings of both finance and human life consistent with the ideological bases of neoliberalism: the notion that independently generated upward movement is ultimately achievable and that problems along the way are likely to merely signal the end to an unusual bout of euphoria and a return to less spectacular but more predictable progress.

Not only does this reflect the belief in the self-moderating market that is foundational to the neoclassical economic theories that underpin neoliberalism, but when applied to characterization and plot it has the double effect of making the emotional lives of each individual appear to function like that self-moderating market – as working autonomously from the effects of the others who surround them. Many of the most humorous moments of the novel stem from the irony generated by each character's unawareness of every other's desperation. Early in the novel, for instance, Chip is so determined to impress his parents during their visit to New York that he steals expensive fillets of fish by putting them in the crotch of his leather pants while, unbeknownst to him, his mother is so preoccupied with her own overwhelming shame over her husband's creeping dementia that the quality of Chip's meal is the last thing on her mind. These moments of irony signal that the overall emotional story of the novel is the struggle each person goes through alone to "correct" themselves despite the various factors – familial, social, economic, and intellectual – that press upon them. In this sense, Sam Tanenhaus is right in his glowing assessment of *The Corrections* when he writes, "even as [Franzen's] contemporaries had diminished the place of the 'single human being,' Franzen, miraculously, had enlarged it."[29] Yet the consequence of this enlargement of the single human being in the novel is the diminishment of the network of associations that inform the relative successes and failures of each individual member of a family. The result is a novel that depicts the lives of individuals with specificity, represents their emotional lives in depth, and offers a plot that follows a familiar path of despair and renewal; yet at the same time it remains strangely tonally detached.[30] Tanenhaus's claim that the novel "cracked open the opaque shell of postmodernism, tweezed out its tangled circuitry and inserted in its place the warm, beating heart of an authentic humanism" therefore relies on an odd conception of what "authentic humanism" entails. The assumption seems to be that a focus on the individual as a discrete actor is so paramount to the generation of "warmth" that it can be the litmus test for what it means to write novels that engage authentically with the human experience, even if that experience is highly scripted within prevailing economic narratives, and even if it neglects to engage with the contingency, context, and indeterminacy that tends to accompany emotional relationships.

If *The Corrections* is complicit with the logic of neoliberalism, in other words, it is not merely because, as James Annesley suggests, the novel's cynicism "closes off the possibility that [it] may have a dialectical relationship with the conditions" of contemporary capitalism.[31] It is also because, in its shaping of narratives of emotional life as if such narratives adhere to market norms, it participates in a process of affective training that runs in accord with the emotional expectations that accompany the neoliberal moment. It is not simply that the novel seems to describe emotional separation as inevitable; it is also that it formalizes that separation, produces identification with it, and therefore habituates readers to look for it elsewhere. For this reason, it may not matter whether the novel merely represents the contemporary status quo as inevitable or if the darkness of the novel, as Colin Hutchinson puts it, points to "the need for some form of transgression against oppressive orders."[32] Through the apparent naturalness of its patterning – the rise and fall of its characters, the separation of points of view, and the vision of the market that informs both – the novel trains readers to see those patterns in their daily lives. The novel can therefore be read as affectively reinforcing neoliberal norms as a result of its formal operations.

A Brief History of Impersonal Feelings

It is a central argument of this study that assessments of contemporary literary aesthetics that appear politically neutral should be read in the context of the ways neoliberal discourse bleeds over into the formal, as well as thematic, mechanisms of literature.[33] When James Wood celebrates "novels that tell us not 'how the world works' but 'how somebody felt about something,'" for instance, this might be seen not only as an aesthetic indictment of the social novel but also as a reinforcement of the affective hypothesis that, in turn, reinforces neoliberal subjective norms.[34] Yet while there is a lengthy history of the notion that textual emotion lies in the representation of characters' personal feelings, there is an equally long but largely unrecognized history of literary scholarship that sees the relationship between aesthetics and feelings as one that destabilizes the connection between the emotional and the personal. I call these literary affects "impersonal feelings," and argue that the neoliberal moment makes the recuperation and operationalization of their history particularly urgent, as such approaches might drive a wedge between neoliberal assumptions about the self and critical assumptions about emotional dynamics in literature.

This history even appears at times, albeit *via negativa*, in articulations of the affective hypothesis. This occurs, for instance, when Wood ventures a history of the split between novels that value the "single human being" and those that do not, tracing the former to the work of Henry James and the latter to the work of Charles Dickens. He argues that contemporary novelists turn to Dickens because his mode of characterization "offers an easy model for writers unable, or unwilling, to create characters who are fully human." As opposed to "the recessed and deferred complexities of … Henry James's character-making," Dickens's characters "are, as Forster rightly put it, flat but vibrating very fast. They are vivid blots of essence. They are souls seen only through thick, gnarled casings. Their vitality is a histrionic one."[35] For Wood, the liveliness of these flat characters is merely decorative and gestural, existing on the surface rather than residing in the recesses as with the round characters of James. Because it does not emanate out of a clearly defined person, their vitality appears to be generated mechanically, like electricity. Yet reading Wood against the grain, this sense of liveliness can be understood to index a different form of literary affect – not the representation of an individual character's feelings but a tonal intensity that emerges from the tensions generated out of the association of narrative elements in the prose. This affective charge comes at the expense of character depth, but it indicates the amplification of a general affectivity that relies on externalization rather than internalization.

In suggesting that flat characters "vibrate," Wood's analysis recalls an earlier moment of interest in the relationship between emotion and form by referencing E. M. Forster's use of the work of Dickens to define flat characterization in his *Elements of the Novel*. While Wood categorically objects to what we might call "the vibration effect" in experimental fiction, Forster argues that it is precisely this formal mode in Dickens that gives his novels texture:

> The case of Dickens is significant. Dickens' people are nearly all flat…. Nearly every one can be summed up in a sentence, and yet there is this wonderful feeling of human depth. Probably the immense vitality of Dickens causes his characters to vibrate a little, so that they borrow his life and appear to lead one of their own…. Those who dislike Dickens have an excellent case. He ought to be bad. He is actually one of our big writers, and his immense success with types suggests that there may be more in flatness than the severer critics admit.[36]

Forster offers little by way of explanation as to why Dickens is good when he should be bad, other than the suspicion that somehow it is Dickens's own vitality that moves through his prose in lieu of that of his characters.

And ultimately Forster does see a form of literary perfection in the composition of round characters that he does not see in even the very best examples of flat characterization. Yet all of this does not limit his praise of Dickens, or of H. G. Wells for that matter, who, he argues, writes characters that, while flat, are "agitated with such vigour that we forget their complexities lie on the surface."[37] Forster therefore admires the best writers of flat characters, who, as he puts it, "are very clever at transmitting force" through their prose, generating a kind of diffuse energy through the movement, connection, and friction of their characters' surfaces.[38]

In seeing felt literary effects as achievable through the play of formal surfaces rather than merely through representational depth, Forster's work is characteristic of the general preoccupations of the pre–New Critical moment in the 1920s. In his *Principles of Literary Criticism*, for instance, I. A. Richards argues that the representational content and the affective consequences of a literary image can be almost entirely separated from one another in terms of their effects:

> The sensory qualities of images, their vivacity, clearness, fullness of detail and so on, do not bear any constant relation to their effects. Images differing in these respects may have closely similar consequences. Too much importance has always been attached to the sensory qualities of images. What gives an image efficacy is less its vividness as an image than its character as a mental event peculiarly connected with sensation.... An image may lose almost all its sensory nature to the point of becoming scarcely an image at all, a mere skeleton, and yet represent a sensation quite as adequately as if it were flaring with hallucinatory vividity. In other words, what matters is not the sensory *resemblance* of an image to the sensation which is its prototype, but some other relation, at present hidden from us in the jungles of neurology.[39]

Richards is interested in how abstracted images still manage to produce cognitive effects that give rise to sensation. The affective response to an image is, he concludes, not necessarily linked to its representative content but to "some other relation," one that, he argues, would require advancements in neurology to discover.[40] Moreover, for Richards the social value of literature is to be found not in the "pleasure or ... poignancy" that it inspires during the process of reading but "in the readiness for this or that kind of behaviour in which we find ourselves after the experience," or in the attitudinal and orientational changes that are catalyzed in the body by exposure to a work of literature causing what he calls "permanent modifications in the structure of the mind."[41]

In the two major interests motivating his argument – the desire to separate form from content in the analysis of literature's effects and the belief that there is an impersonal component to aesthetic experience – Richards's project is exemplary of work on feeling and form that prevailed from the late nineteenth century up through the early twentieth. These twin concerns motivated a range of intellectual projects of the period, including inquiries into the neurological bases of sensation by Henri Bergson,[42] experiments in phenomenology outside the conventional constrains of subjectivity by Martin Heidegger and Jacob von Uexküll,[43] and work on cinema and shock by Walter Benjamin and Sergei Eisenstein.[44] Many of these projects draw from an impersonal understanding of emotion that saw its most dramatic articulation in the late nineteenth-century work of William James, who famously reversed the typical cause-and-effect trajectory of emotional experience to argue that "we feel sorry because we cry, angry because we strike, afraid because we tremble, and not that we cry, strike, or tremble because we are sorry, angry, or fearful, as the case may be."[45] James found that "the trouble with the emotions in psychology is that they are regarded too much as absolutely individual things" and that it was only in novels where emotions were conveyed in ways that were shareable and went beyond being "merely descriptive."[46] But he was mocked for much of the twentieth century for his presumed crudeness in putting bodily expression ahead of conscious feeling. It has only been recently that his legacy has been recuperated through developments in neuroscience.[47]

Indeed, for most of the mid- to late twentieth century, these kinds of approaches to aesthetics were subordinated: first to New Criticism, with its assertion that to analyze feeling was to commit the affective fallacy and substitute the ephemerality of subjective emotion for the universality and permanence of the work itself;[48] and later to linguistic and historicist theories, both of which saw the invocation of the physiological as indicative of undertheorized positivism. In addition, psychoanalysis became the branch of psychology that was seen as best suited to literary studies, with its focus on representation and interpretation over direct physical stimulation.[49] In the process, feelings became understood as fodder for a range of textual practices – ideology critique, historicization, and deconstruction – rather than as material products of works of art. Yet at the same time, historicism, poststructuralism, and deconstruction were laying the groundwork for a reconsideration of the relationship between text and feeling. Jacques Derrida's work on performativity,[50] Raymond Williams's addition of the concept of "structure of feeling" to the Marxist critical vocabulary,[51] and perhaps most of all Gilles Deleuze's suggestion that works of art produce sensations with material effects on the world at large all provided a basis for what Patricia Ticineto Clough would dub, by the beginning of the twenty-first century, "the affective turn" in the humanities and social sciences, but which more accurately might be called, given its roots in the intellectual climate of the 1910s and '20s, "the affective *return*."[52]

Deleuze in particular has been a pivotal figure in the development of a return to the study of the relationship between bodily aspects of feeling and art. Perhaps surprisingly consistent with the aims of New Criticism, his interest in affect stems from an effort to get away from readings of art that focus on either the artist or the audience. Together with Félix Guattari in their final collaborative work, *What Is Philosophy*, he defines the most important products of art as impersonal:

> Percepts are no longer perceptions; they are independent of a state of those who experience them. Affects are no longer feelings or affections; they go beyond the strength of those who undergo them. Sensations, percepts, and affects are *beings* whose validity lies in themselves and exceeds any lived. They could be said to exist in the absence of man because man, as he is caught in stone, on the canvas, or by words, is himself a compound of percepts and affects. The work of art is a being of sensation and nothing else: it exists in itself.[53]

The relationship between the subject and feeling is reversed in this view. Perceptions and affections do not belong to a preexisting subject; the subject is instead composed of the material of percepts and affects, which themselves exist independently of any given subject. To read affectively according to this model is not to commit the affective fallacy if, as W. K. Wimsatt and Monroe Beardsley suggest, the problem involved when reading for affect is that "the poem itself, as an object of specifically critical judgment, tends to disappear."[54] For Wimsatt and Beardsley, reading for affect means attending to the experience of the particular reader over and above the formal properties of the work. In contrast to Forster's suspicion that it is the intensity of Dickens himself that is channeled through his characters, on the one hand, and Richards's interest in the reader's physiological response as a site for the affective implications of literature, on the other, in Deleuze and Guattari's view the work itself is foregrounded by attention to the sensory material it is understood to produce, material that exists apart from both the writer and any individual reader. Characters, too, are not imaginary subjects who possess perceptions and affections; they are the vessels of new affects, producing them through their transformations. As Deleuze and Guattari explain, "A great novelist is above all an artist who invents unknown or unrecognized affects and brings them to light as the becoming of his characters."[55] Affects are therefore not the cause or effect of changes in individual lives; they index the possibility of change itself.

In seeing affects as realized through processes of change, Deleuze and Guattari draw from a lineage that extends from Baruch Spinoza through Friedrich Nietzsche and Bergson for whom affects are understood to be the result of encounters among human and nonhuman actors.[56] Spinoza defines affects (*affecti*) as "the affections of the body by which the body's power of activity is increased or diminished, assisted or checked, together with the ideas of these affections."[57] As bodies interact with other bodies, creatures, and things, those bodies change. As a result, "the human body can be affected in many ways by which its power of activity is increased or diminished," and the ideational counterparts to these changes are affects.[58] Crucially, these transformations occur in both mind and body – the Spinozist affective paradigm is therefore not, as some critics contend, crudely physical – but the mental and physical realms for Spinoza run parallel to one another. The former therefore often loses track of the latter, even as they coexist in each and every action a body undertakes. Problems arise when we believe that the mental controls or wills the physical, when in fact, for Spinoza,

> mental decision on the one hand, and the appetite and physical state of the body on the other hand, are simultaneous in nature; or rather, they are one and the same thing which, when considered under the attribute of Thought and explicated through Thought, we call decision, and when considered under the attribute of Extension and deduced from the laws of motion-and-rest, we call a physical state.[59]

An affect is therefore the result of an event of change registered under the attributes of thought and extension, as both mental and physical alterations. When Deleuze suggests that works of art create new affects, then, he argues that works of art catalyze bodily and conceptual change and lead to the registration of that change in both physical and mental terms.

Reading literature affectively according to this trajectory has origins in American and English materialist philosophies; the aesthetics of James, Richards, and Eliot; and the continental figures in the Spinozan-Deleuzian genealogy. This type of reading differs substantially in its methodological assumptions from the way literature is read affectively in much of the existing work on literature and feelings. The subfield of affective criticism in literary studies has been dominated by projects that see literary works as holding evidence of the historicity of certain emotional states that are legible primarily through the emotional qualities of characters and poetic speakers. These projects are largely interested in seeing the representations of specific emotions in literary texts as signs of the emotional relationships that would have existed between texts and certain readerships. They therefore take up several aspects of emotional experience: the degree to which emotions signal social and political positionings, the tendency for some emotional states to be used as forms of control, and the possibility that the cultural transmission of certain less socially sanctioned emotions might offer modes of resistance to the prevailing emotional expectations of a given time and place.[60] Drawing from the insights of trauma theory and queer theory, this approach to the question of affect complicates the personal/political divide, demonstrating that emotions are as public as they are private. Nevertheless, feelings in these studies are anchored primarily in representations of individuals. Emotion is endowed with political significance only insofar as there are clearly articulated individual people – albeit people influenced heavily by their sociopolitical climates – to do the feeling; and only insofar there are feelings that can be named, isolated, and traced historically through their cultural representations.

The most significant critique from within recent literary studies of this methodology is Sianne Ngai's foundational work, *Ugly Feelings*. Ngai locates literary feelings in the formal characteristic of tone, or "a literary or cultural artifact's ... global or organizing affect, its general disposition or orientation toward its audience and the world."[61] Because tone resides primarily in the art object itself, attention to tone places critical focus on the objective aspects of feeling. Ngai argues that this focus on the objective status of literary feeling is an essential corrective to most studies of affect in literature, which have "predominantly centered on the emotional effects of texts on their readers" through methodologies that are "predominantly historicist."[62] She explains:

> What gets left out in [the] prevailing emphasis on a reader's sympathetic identification with the feelings of characters in a text is the simple but powerful question of "objectified emotion," or unfelt but perceived feeling, that presents itself most forcefully in the aesthetic concept of tone.... Tone is never entirely reducible to a reader's emotional response to a text or reducible to the text's internal representations of feeling.[63]

What is useful in the concept of tone, for Ngai, is precisely its inability to be located in either subjective experience or specific objective features of a text. "For we can speak of a literary text whose global or organizing affect is disgust without this necessarily implying that the work represents or signifies disgust, or that it will disgust the reader," she writes. "Exactly 'where,' then, is the disgust?"[64] Ngai is interested in this particular paradox: tone tends to be readily recognizable, but difficult to pin down because it is neither entirely objective nor entirely subjective. The central aim of her work is to trace these palpable but messy feelings, and, in her more recent work, the aesthetic judgments that accompany them, in order to demonstrate how they function both aesthetically and ideologically.

This study is indebted to Ngai's work, particularly her insistence that aesthetics and affect are intimately linked: "nearly every canonical work of aesthetic philosophy," she reminds us, "depends, at some initial stage, on an act of careful affective discrimination."[65] Yet the impersonal feelings I am interested in here might be thought of as the inverse of the tonal categories that Ngai outlines. The tone of a work of art as Ngai describes it is almost universally recognizable, but difficult to locate in terms of the specific formal techniques that give rise to it: we all know when a work is disgusting, but we don't know where the disgust is coming from. Impersonal feelings, on the other hand, often go unrecognized on an intuitive level and become visible only when traced in particular formal gestures. Many of the works I examine here have been critically deemed numb or cold; others have been judged to be simply confusing. Yet looking at these works closely reveals that there is more to their coldness than a simple lack of affect: what feels cold is, instead, a feeling produced from the very act of withdrawing, in very specific ways, from the project of representing and transmitting easily recognizable sentiments. As a result, whereas Ngai is interested in taxonomies, from a set of minor affects (envy, disgust, animatedness, and so on) in *Ugly Feelings* to what she argues are the fundamental aesthetic categories of late capitalism (the zany, the cute, and the interesting) in *Our Aesthetic Categories*, this book does not offer such a taxonomic structure. This is precisely because of its interest in the distinction between two different types of literary feeling, one that can be more easily felt, described, and therefore traded and valued, and another that is less immediately palpable and codifiable.

The notion that feeling can be split into two types, one that is recognizable within existing categories and one that is more indistinct is most thoroughly explored in Brian Massumi's *Parables for the Virtual*, which argues that "emotion and affect ... follow different logics and pertain to different orders."[66] For Massumi, an emotion is "a subjective content, the sociolinguistic fixing of the quality of an experience which is from that point onward defined as personal" while affect is an entirely preconscious, virtual substrate to human experience.[67] While my definitions of personal and impersonal feelings are influenced by this aspect of Massumi's work, by using the more capacious term "feelings" for both personal and impersonal qualities of literary experience, I hope to underscore that the distinction between these qualities is not one that I see as absolute, nor is it one that I understand to be fundamentally cognitive in nature. Rather than investigating how the brain and body respond to works of art, this study examines how works of art envision, enact, and transmit their specific effects. While some works fall in line with prevailing cultural expectations as to how emotions work, others highlight the aspects of feeling that run askew of these expectations. Like Massumi, I see the latter forms of feeling as offering greater potential for catalyzing experiences that are challenging to the status quo, but rather than seeing the presence of those feelings as signaling something different happening on the level of the brain, I see them as signaling something different happening on the level of literary form.

What I call affect in this study could therefore be defined more broadly as "effect," in the sense of what perhaps the twentieth century's greatest emotional skeptic, Bertolt Brecht, calls "estrangement effects."[68] Estrangement effects, when implemented in the theater through techniques that disrupt the audience's suspension of disbelief, produce a situation where "the spectator is prevented from feeling his way into characters."[69] Whereas most critics see Brecht as working toward the categorical abolition of affect in his work, I would define the kind of dynamic Brecht is interested in creating as an affective one, even if the point is precisely to estrange the audience from their sentimental attachments. In his experiments with estrangement effects, Brecht cultivates a particular kind of affective relationship to a work of art: the feeling of being drawn away from the feelings one customarily expects from the theatrical experience.

Brecht ultimately aspires to a situation where the response to a work of art could be "placed in the conscious realm, not, as hitherto, in the spectator's subconscious," and therefore become a primarily rational experience.[70] The impersonal works I explore here, like Brechtian drama, reject the primacy of personal experience, but they part ways with this model insofar as they also have explicitly affective stakes. For instance, Richard Powers is notoriously skeptical of sentimental narratives – he goes so far as to collapse the distinction between human characters and versions of a computer server in his *Galatea 2.2* by naming both solely with individual letters – but he has also argued that his aim is to "rearrange ... readers viscera" with his novels.[71] And Ben Marcus, whose early work experiments with a nearly total absence of characters and plots, is nevertheless explicitly interested in making literary experience "a possibly biological event" that might "light literal fires in the heads and homes of ... readers."[72] Despite this interest in affective experience, however, neither author sees the cultivation of individual taste or sentiment as central to his project. And both, rather than focusing on the formal strategies that we might associate with the cultivation of emotion, those that appeal to the lives of individuals, are interested in forms and structures as such: Powers is drawn to narrative "patterning" and Marcus is drawn to "systems" of language.[73] These works explicitly aim to undermine the personalization of aesthetic experience by withdrawing from typical ways of producing emotional responses in readers. But they are not categorically anti-affective, because they are interested in feelings that are unsettling insofar as they fall outside existing sociopolitical codes for what a feeling is understood to be. These impersonal feelings – those that are not yet "owned and recognized" – are potentially destabilizing insofar as their presence defies the prevailing notion that feelings only exist insofar as they are the property of the individual.[74]

Impersonal Connections: The Case of *Tropic of Orange*

This definition of impersonal feelings can be illustrated through a reading of a work that withdraws from customary techniques of emotional provocation and instead addresses both thematically and formally the various systems – social, economic, ecological, and textual – that inform individual experience. Karen Tei Yamashita's novel *Tropic of Orange* is rigorously patterned, consisting of seven sections, one for each day of the week during which the novel takes place. Each of the seven days is divided up into seven smaller sections that are told from the perspective from each of seven central characters. The artificiality of this structure and the flat form of characterization that it entails is highlighted by the inclusion of a "HyperContexts" table, which, as a supplement to the traditional "Table of Contents" that precedes it, maps the novel as a whole in a spreadsheet-like manner detailing each day's sections, their central concerns, and their settings. The HyperContexts page makes it clear to a reader even before beginning the novel that each character's sections will have a particular form of perspectival unity: hardworking American dreamer Bobby's sections have titles like "Benefits," "Car Payment Due," "Second Mortgage," and "Life Insurance"; while TV anchor and news-obsessed Emi's sections have titles like "Weather Report," "NewsNow," "Live on Air," and "Prime Time."[75] And indeed, the diction of each of these sections accentuates these very singular qualities of each character. Traditional Rafaela's chapters are pastiches of recognizable works of Latin American magical realism. The word choice is elemental, the sentences snake-like, and the descriptions hover between realism and an easy acceptance of miracle. Bobby's passages are staccato, fast-paced, packed with full stops and mostly devoid of commas. Hard-boiled Gabriel's are in the first person, with a heavy noir self-consciousness. The tonal peculiarity of each perspectival shift contributes to the flatness of the character from whose perspective the section is narrated. Rafaela's connection to the earth, Bobby's compulsive movement, and Gabriel's narcissism are all defining qualities underscored by their corresponding prose styles. Unlike *The Corrections*, in which the sectioning off of characters' points of view is pronounced but casual enough to seem natural, the partitioning of the narrative into character perspectives in *Tropic of Orange* is so clearly artificial that the very nature of separation among the characters is exposed from the start as a narrative construction rather than as reflecting an established fact of individual experience.[76]

Following a form that has become a hallmark of turn-of-the-twentieth-century film, drama, and fiction, the seven seemingly unrelated characters in *Tropic of Orange* meet as the novel progresses through unlikely circumstances, demonstrating how apparently distant elements of a complex society affect one another in unpredictable ways.[77] A Chinese-born, Spanish-speaking janitor who is mistaken for a Vietnamese refugee; a Mexican housekeeper; a performance artist who may have been traveling through South America for upward of five hundred years; a Chicano human-interest news reporter with a love of film noir; a Japanese American TV producer with a hatred of multiculturalism; and a madman who conducts imaginary symphonies on an LA overpass improbably find themselves connected through the unlikely plot of the novel, which involves the unintentional distribution of a truckload of oranges spiked with cocaine; the revelation of a transnational black market trade in infant organs; a Mexican wrestling match; two catastrophic traffic accidents; and the warping of time and space that occurs when the line that marks the Tropic of Cancer is pulled northward, tethered to a California orange that grows, in spite of all odds, in the yard of a vacation home in Mazatlán. Given this wild profusion of highly unlikely collisions, it is easy to be sympathetic with Wood's claim about works like Yamashita's, when he says that "what above all makes these stories unconvincing is precisely their very profusion, their relatedness."[78] It is indeed the novel's chaotic profusion that leads to the diminishment of the importance of any individual character: just as one character's perspective begins to take on a sense of subjective authority, another character intervenes from a dramatically different context, putting the former central character into the position of a supporting cast member. As the novel revolves, this structure functions as a foregrounding and backgrounding machine, demonstrating the degree to which narrative perspective informs the highlighting of any given set of concerns or the life of any given individual.

But the lack of depth of interiority in the novel does not lead to a general lack of feeling in the text despite the almost mechanical structure of the work as a whole. Instead, the revolving door of character centrality signals a transformation in what kinds of feelings readers can expect from a novel. In *Tropic of Orange*, deep identification with any individual character is interrupted – by the flatness of the characters to begin with, by the mapping of their fates and concerns in advance, by the stock quality of their diction, and by the brevity with which each takes center stage before being interrupted by another – yet the novel constructs a world that despite its glaring artificiality has depth in its plenitude of situations and tones. As Caroline Rody contends, the novel does not merely represent multiplicity, it performs it through the development of this tonal plurality and lack of clear narrative hierarchy. She writes, "Yamashita has accustomed her readers to a novelistic project that [oscillates] between the intimate and the historic, fusing individual plots of quest with mass-scale developments of enormous consequence." The novel's major achievement is therefore affective, as this oscillation produces "a certain readerly … pleasure," a "giddy enjoyment of the sheer piling up of life."[79]

Crucially, the novel establishes the primacy of relation over identification without sentimentalizing the commodified forms of connectivity that were beginning to solidify in the late 1990s: the commercialized Web, shallow senses of "globalization," and cable news–generated information culture.[80] In *Tropic of Orange*, commodified ways of feeling connected are satirized throughout the novel and ultimately shed in favor of forms of intimacy that exceed existing structures for the management and maintenance of connections: Buzzworm, who earns his moniker by listening to the radio at all times, unplugs his earphones; Gabriel flirts with total submersion in the Web but realizes that the connections he wants to trace cannot be found in chat rooms and news groups; and Bobby, whose globalized subjectivity is literalized in the end of the novel when he finds himself being pulled apart by the severed line of the Tropic of Cancer, the ends of which he holds in his left and right hands, finally lets go and embraces his family instead. These gestures privilege forms of immediate, and often inconvenient, contact over sanctioned forms of interconnectivity. Importantly, the overall structure of the novel also prevents this valuing of intimate contact from descending into a valuing of the personal. Because of the flatness of the characters and the brevity with which they are addressed, the emotional displays each of the characters make remain solely gestural rather than being deeply sentimental, and their parallels are so grossly obvious that they lose the particularity that might otherwise make them seem individual. When the novel ends with Bobby hugging his family and the words, "Embrace. That's it," it does so not to place the domestic domain over the urgencies of the political. "Embrace" is instead declared as a more generalized imperative, reverberating as it does among all seven characters and scenarios that resolve in the final pages of the book.

At times, *Tropic of Orange* takes this emphasis on the impersonality of forms of connection one step further, suggesting that the novel itself might be read as an inorganic mediator between human and nonhuman actors and natural and artificial structures. This possibility is articulated in one of Manzanar's traffic-conducting sections, in which he envisions his work as a conductor of the music of cars and traffic as being in disturbing tension with his previous work as a doctor. He muses:

> To envision the automobile as an orchestral device with musical potential was an idea lost upon the motorist within. In moments such as these, the mechanical and the human elements of Manzanar's orchestra became blurred. The car became a thing with intelligence. He envisioned the person within as the pulpy brain of each vehicle, and when the defenseless body emerged, for whatever reason, he often felt surprise and disgust. A memory was triggered, and he was once again a masked surgeon, cutting through soft tissue. He remembered intimately the geography of the human body, and that delicate, complex thing within each car frightened him.[81]

Both the individual within the car and Manzanar are revealed to have limited capacities to perceive where the music Manzanar hears comes from and what it is capable of producing. While the drivers cannot imagine the crude material of an automobile as contributing to something as moving as music, Manzanar cannot conceive of the raw physicality of the human as a component of what makes the cars do what they do. The novel's answer is that the music Manzanar conducts both emerges out of and surpasses the people responsible for the movement of the automobiles. Insofar as the meditation on music as emerging from both individual humans and artificial structures can be read as a metafictional comment on the novel as a similar organic-artificial hybrid, it is possible to read this scene as a comment on the medium of fiction. In this case, the passage suggests that the novel, too, might be understood to be an artificial container for a nonspecific, impersonal, yet fully human expression of feeling. Feeling in the novel is therefore posited, like the symphony that issues forth from the traffic while being to some degree separate from each individual driver, as a property of the text. It is connected, but not subject to, the people who produce and read it. At the same time, the novel thematizes that affective dynamic, exposing the apparent conflict between attention to interconnection and embodied commitment to the particular as a false tension, reconcilable through the awareness that interconnection is registered on the level of the specific body and that the demands systems make upon us are as singular as they are expansive.

In its interest in how feeling might emerge out of relationships among formal materials of art rather than through the representation of the feelings of a given character, narrator, or artist, *Tropic of Orange* responds to neoliberalism in ways that go beyond its satirical jabs at NAFTA and its interest in the centrality of informal labor to the workings of global capitalism. Unlike *The Corrections*, its politics extend to its form, calling into question the core neoliberal assumption that the individual is affectively responsible for herself.[82] While neoliberalism, through its positing of the human as *homo economicus* in all spheres of life, takes evidence of the body's situatedness in complex human and nonhuman ecologies and rescripts it as a scene for personal development, *Tropic of Orange* refuses to locate value in the personal, formally refiguring feelings as unpredictable forces that are modified, intensified, and transmitted through interpersonal and interobjective relationships that exceed the capacities of any individual to manage them.

From the Impersonal to the Ecological

Tropic of Orange demonstrates how some works of contemporary literature intervene in the consensus behind the affective hypothesis, reinterpreting feelings not as evidence of the primacy of the self but rather as evidence of the persistence of ecological interconnection. Throughout this project, I use the term "ecological" to reference the presence of both human and nonhuman actors in the systems in which humans are situated. The term is not intended to prioritize a sense of nature as separate from the world of technology, artifice, and other human constructions.[83] Instead, it functions as a reminder that human social relationships are themselves constituted in relation to nonhuman beings and things. As Timothy Morton argues, thinking ecologically means simply "the thinking of interconnectedness."[84] But as I use it here, the term "ecology" not only refers to connections among human and nonhuman, living and nonliving things. Because ecosystems are notoriously difficult to manage, the term also signals the displacement of individual agency in relation to those connections.[85] Indeed, it is perhaps this implied challenge to the intentional management of networks that draws so many of the impersonal works addressed here toward ecological themes. While environmentalism is a specific focus of the works I discuss in Chapter 4, many of the works taken up elsewhere in this book, like *Tropic of Orange*, place nonhuman actors at the center of their plots. And insofar as "ecological art, and the ecological-ness of all art, isn't just *about* something (trees, mountains, animals, pollution, and so forth" but rather "*is* something, or maybe … *does* something" ecological, this book argues that reading ecologically involves reading both formally and affectively: reading for what literature does, not simply for what it says.[86]

My use of the term "impersonal feelings" itself has direct ecological antecedents, as it echoes Jane Bennett's description of "impersonal affects" in her work *Vibrant Matter*. She explains, "organic and inorganic bodies, natural and cultural objects … *all* are affective."[87] While her interests are particularly anchored in examinations of nonhuman agency within biological and geological processes – she explores the role of nonhuman actors in the consumption of food, the composition of minerals, and the effects of worms on human culture, among other situations – I find that Bennett's argument that nonhuman and even inanimate objects can possess as well as transmit affects has ramifications for the study of literature. Using this definition of impersonal affectivity, works of literature themselves can be understood to work affectively, catalyzing and modulating human attitudes and orientations toward other humans and their environments. Reading affectively is therefore reading ecologically in a more specific sense: reading for affect means reading for the ways works of literature themselves act in larger systems.[88]

Along with this shift from affects understood as personal property to affects understood as evidence of interconnection comes another critical shift: from seeing feelings as political, insofar as they are evidence of political structures that give rise to them as symptoms, and seeing feelings as political insofar as they contribute materially to social systems. The distinction between these two critical perspectives involves a movement away from the notion that literary criticism's mandate is to demystify, uncover ideological assumptions, and expose the real relations behind those structures and toward a notion more sympathetic to Bruno Latour's concept of compositionism. For Latour, while critique as a demystifying practice has "run out of steam," intellectual activity retains the capacity to affect social and political structures insofar as it is able to trace and construct systems of association that often run counter to prevailing beliefs as to how systems function, through what agencies, and to what ends.[89] Seeing the literary intensification of affects as material effects of the relationships among textual elements within works, as well as effects of relationships among texts and readers, suggests that a critical practice of tracing affects in literary texts might form a literary counterpart to Latour's intervention in the social sciences.

Among the most destructive discursive consequences of our neoliberal present is the prevailing tendency to see all systems as functioning like market systems. We have become accustomed to applying the rules of capitalism – the primacy of competition, the relationship between supply and demand, the notion of investment and return, and the belief that circulation follows patterns of consumption – to participatory systems ranging from education to democratic politics. The notion that literary circulation ideally functions this way is equally on the rise today.[90] Yet attending to the participation of nonhuman actors like books within systems of human and nonhuman beings and things presents an alternative to the market model for the conceptualization of literary circulation. If literary circulation is understood to function on the model of the ecosystem rather than on the model of the market, then the various people who come into contact with a book – writers, readers, booksellers, or reviewers – are not merely instigators and consumers of emotional value. Instead, works of literature can be understood to materially influence those with whom they come into contact in ways not entirely circumscribed by the various roles of buyer and seller that inform that contact. A work of literature, in this view, is itself an active participant in an ecosystem, a participant that is the result of human activity and that has effects primarily on humans, but that once unleashed in the world can have unpredictable effects on those with whom it comes into contact.

The Chapters

This study begins with one of the primary consequences of the tendency to see the affective dynamics of literature as mirroring the dynamics of the market: the belief that a reader's investment in a novel should be met with an emotional return. The first chapter argues that the critical and commercial success of Cormac McCarthy's novel *The Road* is in part the result of its construction of a simple and elegant emotional economy between text and reader, in which the reader's emotional investment in the hero of the novel provides an emotional return in the form of a highly personal feeling of hope for the perseverance of the singularly good individual. The emotional intimacy of the story, along with McCarthy's autobiographical disclosure that he wrote the story about his young son, has led critics to read the story as apolitical despite its postapocalyptic vision. Yet I argue that the effects of *The Road*'s are anything but apolitical, cultivating an emotional commitment to the survival of the individual regardless of the social context or costs, a commitment consistent with the aims and practices of neoliberalism. In contrast, Paul Auster's *The Book of Illusions*, a work often criticized for being emotionally cold, self-consciously distances its affective operations from specific characters, speakers, or readers construed as unique individuals. *The Book of Illusions* has highly emotional stakes – it opens with its central character having just undergone the loss of his wife and children – but unlike *The Road* it offers little in the way of opportunities for identification, personal investment, or empathy. Reading *The Book of Illusions* as engaging inventively with the relationship between emotions and aesthetics, despite its refusal to produce an emotional payoff for the reader, I argue that it is when works appear coldest that they may be doing the most transformative work, coding feelings that are not yet recognizable for subjects who have been trained to read emotions as exclusively personal.

The second chapter explores the distinction between personal and impersonal literary feelings in the context of 9/11 and its aftermath. I argue that the cultivation of feelings of personal and national trauma in the days and weeks following the attacks justified the further implementation of controversial neoliberal reforms already under way well before the events took place. This political consistency, which looked like historical novelty, is reflected in the tendency of many of the early novels about 9/11 – including Jonathan Safran Foer's *Extremely Loud and Incredibly Close* and Don DeLillo's *Falling Man* – to insist on the rupturing force of the events while representing its emotional effects in surprisingly conventional terms. In contrast, Laird Hunt's strange experimental noir of the same period, *The Exquisite*, which takes place in Lower Manhattan in the immediate aftermath of the attacks, replaces the notion of sudden traumatic rupture with weaker attitudinal shifts of uneasiness and discomfort through the development of a highly unstable analogy between the destruction of the World Trade Center and the abuses of the international fishing industry. This metaphorical confusion produces a sense of disconcertedness, a feeling that Sianne Ngai defines as "a feeling of confusion about what one is feeling," which affectively engages with the complexity of the global systems out of which the events of 9/11 emerged.[91]

Since the mid-1980s, Fredric Jameson's concept of cognitive mapping has provided one of the most prevalent theories for imagining what a politically engaged aesthetic looks like in the context of late capitalism. Jameson argues that works of art should respond to the disorientations of contemporary life by offering readers opportunities to locate themselves in world systems and therefore to claim agency in relation to them. In the third chapter of this study, I argue that the emphasis on the cultivation of agency in this approach does not take into account the degree to which neoliberalism appropriates the notion of individual freedom as a form of control. As a result, a work like Dave Eggers's *A Heartbreaking Work of Staggering Genius*, which appears to offer readers a position of agency through its paratextual disclaimers and metacommentary, can be understood to reflect the neoliberal dynamics by which the feeling of agency grants the illusion of freedom while control is maintained over the outcomes of that freedom. In contrast, Ben Marcus's short story collection, *The Age of Wire and String*, which establishes itself as a "catalogue of a culture," produces not orientation but instead a sense of the strangeness of the basic materials of life we take for granted: weather, wind, water, cloth, animals, leather, and metals. Marcus's collection demonstrates how tracing a subject's in a system might be registered through affects of disorientation and estrangement rather than through the cultivation of feelings of freedom and autonomy.

As we have seen, in the neoliberal context, most systems of association, circulation, and production are interpreted and realized on the model of the capitalist market. Yet, as I argue in the book's fourth chapter, ecosystems remain surprisingly stubborn to this interpretation, resisting easy codification into market terms despite attempts at rampant greenwashing, corporate sustainability campaigns, and the literal commodification of atmospheric gases in the service of carbon markets. Lydia Millet's novel *How the Dead Dream* illustrates how the awareness of the centrality of nonhuman beings to human survival exposes the single-minded entrepreneurial pursuit of profit as disastrous for humans and nonhumans alike. Yet the novel also performs its own futility in the face of the attempt to represent nonhuman experience, as it ultimately deteriorates into clownish pastiche and fragmented aphorism once its central character comes to this realization. Richard Powers's *The Echo Maker*, on the other hand, imagines the ecological work of fiction not as representative, but as performative. *The Echo Maker* maps the structure of the novel itself onto the seasonal migration patterns of birds, and it connects both to the circulation of a mysterious note that demands that its recipient do something both instinctive and altruistic. This narrative patterning signals the centrality of not only impersonal but also nonhuman, temporalities, perspectives, and impulses to the process of textual circulation, figuring the circulation of feeling in literature as occurring on the model of the ecosystem rather than on the model of the market.

At a time when the study of literature itself is increasingly made subject to a cost/benefit analysis, it is tempting either to retrench by appealing to the traditional literary value of individual emotional experience or to capitulate and allow the importance of literature to be evaluated in market terms. Yet literature is neither an inert vessel for the representation of individual consciousness nor does it offer predictable rewards for those who consume it. Though works of literature are the result of human activity, they nevertheless possess their own dynamism and produce unforeseeable effects. For this reason, while I am sympathetic to the views of those who see attention to so-called subjective states as complicit with the cultural logic of neoliberalism, I do not see critical attention to feeling as always symptomatic of self-concern.[92] Instead, I argue that such conclusions are themselves results of the pervasiveness of the affective hypothesis: they begin with the assumption that reading for feeling in works of literature involves reading for subjective qualities. It is true that when attention to feeling is equated with attention to the individual, attention to feeling often aligns with the logic of neoliberalism. And it is equally true that impersonal feelings are far from being challenging by default; they can and often do support the status quo. But the very strangeness of impersonal feelings also suggests their potential to diverge from our expectations. These feelings affect readers in ways not entirely recognizable as individually owned emotions. The results are unstable, multivalent, and far from utopian. But at their most provocative, impersonal feelings point toward alternative paths of circulation and heighten the presence of nonmarket-oriented forms of collectivity, signaling the potential for nonhuman objects to lead humans in unpredictable directions, catalyzing attitudinal states that suggest alternatives to the apparent permanence of the neoliberal status quo.

Personal and Impersonal: Two Forms of the Neoliberal Novel

In his 1884 essay, "The Art of Fiction," Henry James diagnoses a condition among his contemporaries that we might recognize, albeit in a slightly altered way, in our own era. He laments that, for most readers, "literature should be either instructive or amusing, and there is in many minds an impression that ... artistic preoccupations, the search for form, contribute to neither end [and] interfere indeed with both." James finds that most readers seek practical outcomes from works of fiction as either didacticism or amusement. Experiments in form serve neither of these two aims, leading to works that are deemed "too frivolous to be edifying, and too serious to be diverting."[1] Experimentation and readerly payoff, in other words, are seen as being at odds with one another. Readers want what is familiar to them; but for James, if fiction is to be successful as an art form, it should seek out the unfamiliar. In sketching out this dissonance, James draws two opposing paths for the future of the genre: one that sees fiction as essentially conservative, reinforcing the expectations and desires of an existing readership; and one that sees fiction as essentially disruptive, challenging those expectations through aesthetic invention.

James's defense of the latter path is based primarily on his interest in capturing previously unacknowledged forms of perception, sensation, and feeling. He maintains that the literary representation of life is not achievable through stock plots, nor is it reflected in familiar character types. Fiction's aspiration should rather be the production of what he calls elsewhere "felt life."[2] This is a discontinuous, unpredictable sense that highlights "the strange irregular rhythm of life," the pursuit of which "is the attempt whose strenuous force keeps Fiction upon her feet."[3] This pursuit goes beyond everyday perceptions, narrative conventions, and historical assumptions to animate works of fiction, which are understood to succeed precisely to the degree to which they depart from readerly expectations.

James wrote his essay at a pivotal moment between the golden age of realism and the advent of modernism. For him, any friction that exists between the effort to produce "the illusion of life," associated with the former era, and the emphasis on formal novelty, associated with the latter age, is productive, not divisive. Novelty, difficulty, and experimentation, in James's view, are crucial to literary efforts to reflect human experience; without them, what is achieved is not the vibrant feeling of life transmitted in prose but a tired, mechanical repetition of commonplaces and clichés. If pursuing that vibrancy means thwarting his readers' desires, there is no question where James's allegiances lie. In this sense, his approach to fiction exemplifies a modernist posture that would expand and flourish over the following decades.

Since the end of the twentieth century, which saw a schism between camps that perceived themselves as realist on the one hand and those that self-identified as committed to formal novelty on the other, it looks as if we have returned at last to an uneasy reconciliation of these two impulses in literary fiction.[4] If modernism and postmodernism tipped the scales away from the attempt to accurately render life as it is and toward formal and theoretical play, the fiction of the past decade or so seems to have struck a gentler balance. Once again critics and novelists alike are interested in real people and real places, but the experiments of the twentieth century linger in these accounts, providing a degree of aesthetic interest.[5] Or at least this has been the general consensus among scholars interested in the literature of the late twentieth and early twenty-first century by authors raised on postmodernism and, in one way or another, skeptical of its distancing effects. As Robert McLaughlin describes it:

> Many of the fiction writers who have come on the scene since the late 1980s seem to be responding to the perceived dead end of postmodernism, a dead end that has been reached because of postmodernism's detachment from the social world and immersion in a world of nonreferential language, its tendency, as one writer once put it to me, to disappear up its own asshole. We can think of this aesthetic sea change, then, as being inspired by a desire to reconnect language to the social sphere or, to put it another way, to reenergize literature's social mission, its ability to intervene in the social world, to have an impact on actual people and the actual social institutions in which they live their lives.[6]

It is this interest in the possibilities for literature to have meaning for "actual people" that, for most critics, separates contemporary writers from their forebears. In poetry, this turn has been reflected in what Stephen

Burt has dubbed "ellipticism," another compromise between formal play and the concerns of real people. "Elliptical poets," Burt explains,

> try to manifest a person – who speaks the poem and reflects the poet – while using all the verbal gizmos developed over the last few decades to undermine the coherence of speaking selves. They are post-avant-gardist, or post-"postmodern": they have read (most of them) Stein's heirs, and the "language writers," and have chosen to do otherwise.... They want to entertain as thoroughly as, but not to resemble, television.[7]

In both poetry and prose, such movements express an interest in preserving the formal gains achieved under the modernist and postmodernist dominants of the twentieth century while reconnecting with the personal in such a way that might be appealing to a larger group of potential readers, such as those who find narrative sustenance from television rather than books.[8] There are pronounced variations among the contexts and cures posited by each of these movements. But one feature they share is a belief that the interest in the materiality of language associated with earlier experimental movements can be retained, even as it merges with an attempt to represent the human subject in a recognizable form: as a discrete, feeling entity.[9]

While this aesthetic shift suggests the development of a project that we might recognize as recalling the aims of James and his immediate contemporaries – one that sees formal interest and engagement with reality as compatible – the ground for these attempts has been altered as the qualities by which cultural objects are assessed have changed since the late nineteenth century. The value of the novel in James's moment, as he describes it, was largely understood in terms of either its social value or simply its capacity to entertain. The growth of neoliberalism, however, has meant that these systems of valuation have undergone a transformation to conform to an economic matrix of investment and return. Moral instruction and amusement might still be seen as desirable effects of literary engagement, but their desirability is measured by how much morality or amusement is understood to enrich the life of the individual, according to the individual's wants and needs. While in the past these may have been social goals subject to collective definitions of appropriate behavior, today they are more likely to be understood as individual goals subject to an assessment of usefulness to and advancement of the individual subject. In other words, literary fiction is figured less as a public or social intervention and more as an individually consumable resource.

This chapter takes up the intersection of these two shifts: the contemporary formal compromises that allow for the resurgence of emotional content in fiction, on the one hand, and the use of an economic logic as the primary basis for assessments of literary value, on the other. I will argue here that the appearance of these two phenomena in the 1990s and their strengthening through the present moment is not merely a result of the march of literary history, but rather that it reflects the growth of neoliberalism during the period. Beginning with an examination of how economic models are applied to the assessment of literary value and the ways such models reflect liberal and neoliberal paradigms, I turn to Cormac McCarthy's novel *The Road* as a case study of what happens when emotional circulation and economic circulation are conflated within a work of fiction. I then examine Paul Auster's *The Book of Illusions*, a novel that invokes emotional subject matter only to refuse its anticipated emotional payoff. Both *The Road* and *The Book of Illusions* are stylistically interested in compromising between experimental and realist techniques, and both are of the neoliberal era. But drawing from the distinction between these two exemplary texts, I argue that there are forms of feeling produced by contemporary novels that productively call into question the assumption that emotion is an owned resource that circulates from individual to individual. Ultimately, this chapter posits the coexistence of two major strands in works of contemporary literary fiction that seek a compromise between aesthetic novelty and emotional grounding: one sees contact between formal innovation and reality as necessitating a move toward the representation of recognizable emotional subjects; and one sees such contact as most thoroughly achievable through the provocation of feelings that are not as easily identifiable as such to readers trained to look for emotional payoff for their readerly investments.

The Value of Fiction

Jonathan Franzen famously confronted anxieties about the relationship between popular readability and formal interest when his novel, *The Corrections*, was offered a spot in Oprah's Book Club. Franzen found himself caught between concern that association with the Book Club would diminish the work's prestige as high art on the one hand, and not wanting to alienate Oprah's vast audience on the other. This ambivalence led to a series of comically impolitic statements on Franzen's part and a much-publicized feud that culminated in Oprah rescinding her invitation to have Franzen on her show. Soon after, Franzen published "Mr. Difficult," an essay that begins with an overview of the hate mail Franzen received during the controversy. One letter in particular troubles him because of its suggestion that not only did the author hold himself apart from mainstream readers in his criticism of the Oprah franchise but also that the form of *The Corrections* itself was unfriendly to those readers. "Who is it that you are writing for?" a Mrs. M – reportedly said in this letter. "It surely could not be the average person who just enjoys a good read."[10] Franzen reports being paralyzed by letters like Mrs. M – 's because of his adherence to two divergent models of literary value. Like James before him, Franzen still sees some credence in the argument that fiction writing is an art form that should not be subject to the demands of a general readership. In this model, he muses,

> the best novels are great works of art, the people who manage to write them deserve extraordinary credit, and if the average reader rejects the work it's because the average reader is a philistine; the value of any novel, even a mediocre one, exists independent of how many people are able to appreciate it. We can call this the Status model. It invites a discourse of genius and art-historical importance. (*MD*, 100)

Evident in the dubbing of this model as "Status" is a critique of its basis in setting the novelist above the public. In the Status model, Mrs. M – is left behind to puzzle over "words like 'diurnality' and 'antipodes'" while her imagined opposites, "the elite who are beautiful, thin, anorexic, neurotic, sophisticated, don't smoke, have abortions tri-yearly, are antiseptic, live in lofts or penthouses," hold sway over U.S. literary culture (*MD*, 100). The alternative, Franzen argues, is a model in which "a novel represents a compact between the writer and the reader, with the writer providing words out of which the reader creates a pleasurable experience. Writing thus entails a balancing of self-expression and communication within a group." Explaining his increasing sympathy with this approach to literature he writes:

> Every writer is first a member of a community of readers, and the deepest purpose of reading and writing fiction is to sustain a sense of connectedness, to resist existential loneliness; and so a novel deserves a reader's attention only as long as the author sustains the reader's trust. This is the Contract model. The discourse here is one of pleasure and connection. (*MD*, 100)

Whereas James saw something like a Status model (although he would not have chosen to describe it that way), running counter to a prevailing demand for fiction to be socially recognizable as either morally edifying or pleasurable, Franzen's alternative to the Status model has no clear social definition. Instead, he invokes the metaphor of the contract to stipulate that writers should deliver on their promises, whether they are educational, aesthetic, moral, or recreational, and that readers should hold them to these promises.

At the heart of the concept of the contract itself is a dual inheritance: early theories of political liberalism on the one hand and the economic basis of capitalism on the other. The former gives the Contract model its emphasis on connection and communication; the latter gives it a different cast, the more problematic side of which Franzen acknowledges:

> Taken to its free-market extreme, Contract stipulates that if a product is disagreeable to you the fault must be the product's. If you crack a tooth on a hard word in a novel, you sue the author. If your professor puts Dreiser on your reading list, you write a harsh student evaluation. If the local symphony plays too much twentieth-century music, you cancel your subscription. You're the consumer; you rule. (Ibid.)

Most of us who have experienced the increasing tendency for college students to see themselves as consumers and for administrators to envision themselves as CEOs recognize this problem as one that Contract writing shares with the corporate model of the university. Both take an activity that was once understood in terms that were if not entirely distinct from then at least somewhat in tension with those of the market, and make it unproblematically subject to an entirely market-based logic. This tendency to understand activities once seen to some degree as extra-economic as obeying the logic of the market is not restricted to academic and artistic circles; it is one of the hallmark qualities of neoliberalism in general. Such beliefs, for instance, provide the very foundation for neoliberal policies aimed at privatizing previously public or collectively administered institutions under the assumption that if such institutions are already understood to best function *like* corporations they are most effectively run *by* corporations.

Such innovations are traditionally understood to be value-neutral: they change how an institution is run but not what it produces. But crucially, the Contract model does not lead to a value-neutral approach to the question of form. Franzen explains:

> As the decades pass, the postmodern program, the notion of formal experimentation as an act of resistance, begins to seem seriously misconceived.
> Fiction is the most fundamental human art. Fiction is storytelling, and our reality arguably consists of the stories we tell about ourselves. Fiction is also conservative and conventional, because the structure of the market is relatively democratic (novelists make a living one book at a time, bringing pleasure to large audiences). (*MD*, 108)

The belief that the author/reader relationship is one that can best be understood through the model of the market provides the foundation for the two significant formal arguments of this passage: first, that it is a misconception that formal experimentalism constitutes an act of resistance; and second, that fiction's form is essentially "conservative and conventional." These two claims about literary aesthetics have provoked the most vocal responses to Franzen's essay, notably Ben Marcus's defense of experimentalism published in *Harper's* a few years later.[11] But these responses have largely failed to acknowledge the degree to which Franzen's aesthetic arguments are reliant on his positing of the literary relation as one that is appropriately understood to function on a market model. In this passage, fiction is conservative and conventional because of the structure of the literary market. The formal assessment hinges on the economic assessment.

In other words, what appears to be an essay about literary form – about the relative value of experimentalism, difficulty, identification, and aesthetic pleasure – turns out to be an essay that foregrounds the degree to which contemporary assessments of the value of fiction are based on subordinating literary experience to the logic of economic investment. Because in the end, the aim for Franzen and his imagined cohort of Contract readers is not the abolition of formal difficulty per se as much as it is the need to subject aesthetic innovation to a cost/benefit analysis. He explains:

> Like many other Contract-minded Americans, like the literary societies of a hundred years ago, like the book clubs of today, I understand that the Contract sometimes calls for work. I know the pleasures of a book aren't always easy. I expect to work; I *want* to work. It's also in my Protestant nature, however, to expect some reward for this work. And, although critics can give me pastoral guidance as I seek this reward, ultimately I think each individual is alone with his or her conscience. As a reader, I seek a direct personal relationship with art. The books I love, the books on which my faith in literature rests, are the ones with which I can have this kind of relationship. (*MD*, 111, emphasis in original)

Ultimately, the essay gives no rigorous definition of what constitutes frivolous difficulty and what merely requires the Protestant get-up-and-go that Franzen eagerly volunteers. Instead, in defining the practice of Contract reading, he posits a model in which readerly investment of energy needs to be justified by the return of readerly reward or pleasure. Of course, this is not the only option: there is always recourse to the Status model with its own modes of assessing literary value. But this imagined alternative requires a return to the bad old days of academic elitism, ivory tower privilege, and the discourse of genius.[12] It is as if a reader has only two mentors to choose from when deciding how to assign value to literary art: Paul Volcker on the one hand and Harold Bloom on the other. The apparent dead end of this choice, however, ignores the complexities of literary experience and what it means to produce collectively engaged works of literature. As I will argue later in this chapter, connection, social engagement, and emotional meaning, all qualities Franzen attributes to Contract writing, may in fact be developed in ways that fall outside the market model Contract writing assumes. And these qualities can hinge on narrative forms associated with the very kinds of novels to which Franzen objects: those that do not follow through on their promises.

The Liberal Novel and the Neoliberal Novel

In his argument that literature should offer a clear return for effort expended, Franzen's Contract model reflects the form of the subject that appears with the advent of neoliberalism. Unlike previous iterations of *homo economicus* in which an economic rationality was brought to bear only on situations with possible economic outcomes, the neoliberal subject is entrepreneurial in most spheres of life, taking on activities seemingly divorced from economic transactions as modes of enterprise. Education, health services, and even personal associations are sought on the basis of investment and return, aimed to cultivate a bigger, better, more lucrative self. As Wendy Brown explains, "Neoliberalism normatively constructs and interpellates individuals as entrepreneurial actors in every sphere of life. It figures individuals as rational, calculating creatures whose moral autonomy is measured by their capacity for 'self-care' – the ability to provide for their own needs and service their own ambitions."[13] The successful neoliberal individual therefore mirrors the successful corporation by being capable of consistent growth, effective competition, and flexible adaptation. As Michel Foucault puts it, the neoliberal subject can therefore be understood as "an entrepreneur of himself ... being for himself his producer, being for himself his own capital, being for himself the source of [his] earnings."[14] In other words, neoliberalism, with its expansion of market rationality to nonmarket activities, leads to a situation where individuals are encouraged to see themselves as the outcome of a range of investments and returns.

The Contract model's reader therefore evolves out of a situation where reading is not merely understood as a form of consumption; literary experience is expected to be productive of a more thoroughly realized self.

Foucault explains that with the advent of neoliberalism, "We should think of consumption as an enterprise activity by which the individual, precisely on the basis of the capital he has at his disposal, will produce something that will be his own satisfaction."[15] We might add to this emphasis on satisfaction a host of other possible productive outcomes of consumption: physical health (in the case of organic foods and fitness equipment), productive capacity (in the case of tablet computers and smartphones), and emotional well-being (in the case of yoga classes and self-help books). Franzen confesses a similar tendency when he describes himself taking on the project of reading William Gaddis's encyclopedic novel *The Recognitions* for the first time: "As if [I was] planting my feet on a steep slope, climbing," making "a regular job, with regular hours, out of climbing the mountain" (*MD*, 102). He reports feeling particularly wholesome after finishing the novel, seeing himself as "virtuous, as if I'd run three miles, eaten my kale, been to the dentist, filed my tax return, or gone to church" (ibid., 103).

While in general the notion that reading can be a form of self-improvement is not new, neoliberalism ushers in a shift as to precisely what reading fiction is imagined to offer the individual. Whereas liberal self-improvement was more likely to be seen as necessitating processes of self-realization that in turn required separation from structures of attachment, neoliberal self-improvement is more often understood to necessitate strategic alliances with others. As a result, the neoliberal novel is envisioned as having value for its capacity to provide a feeling of emotional connection rather than merely for its focus on the interior life of a discrete individual. For instance, in Ian Watt's famous analysis of the relationship between the eighteenth-century novel and the advent of modern capitalism, he identifies Daniel Defoe's *Robinson Crusoe* as exemplary of the individualism associated with traditional economic liberalism. For Watt, because it emerges alongside bourgeois liberalism, the novel puts thematic stress on the well-being of the individual over and above the individual's emotional attachments. As a result, he says:

> Emotional ties ... and personal relationships generally, play a very minor part in *Robinson Crusoe*, except when they are focused on economic matters.... Only money – fortune in its modern sense – is a proper cause of deep feeling; and friendship is accorded only to those who can safely be entrusted with Crusoe's economic interests.[16]

The mark of economic liberalism is the subjection of emotional bonds to the cold world of commerce, the erasure of irrational sentiment in favor of the rational *homo economicus*. We see this eschewal of emotion in the eighteenth-century novel because, with the rise of liberal individualism, as Watt explains, "the hypostasis of the economic motive logically entails a devaluation of other modes of thought, feeling, and action." As a result, he continues, "the various forms of traditional group relationship, the family, the guild, the village, the sense of nationality – all are weakened."[17] In a novel like *Crusoe*, this weakening is shown in the attention devoted to an individual character over and above his attachments. But this focus on the individual also extends to the form of the novel itself, which requires that the plot be "acted out by particular people in particular circumstances, rather than, as had been common in the past, by general human types."[18]

Among the strategies used for characters in novels to appear "particular," the representation of interior emotional lives has been paramount. In other words, while the liberal novel tends to represent individuals as separate from their emotional ties to the degree that they appear to be fully individuated, it also represents emotional interiority with great intensity. The development of characters with specific interior lives therefore mirrors the emergence of bourgeois individuals by minimizing the emotional charge of external connections, communities, and networks and intensifying the emotional charge of the owned, personal, and interior.

The innovation of the technique of developing "round characters" is central to this development. For while characters remain flat, the emotional quality of a work of fiction remains to some extent distributed.[19] As we saw in the introduction to this study, E. M. Forster's definition of flat characterization rests on the notion that such forms succeed in "transmitting force" without that force being contained within a discrete individual. But for Forster, the more "perfect" authors are those who construct fully enclosed individuals, creating round characters that have clearly demarcated insides and outsides. The primary force of the very form of the novel, in this view, emerges out of the social fact of emotional interiority. In *Aspects of the Novel*, Forster writes:

> In daily life we never understand each other.... We know each other approximately, by external signs, and these serve well enough as a basis for society and even for intimacy. But people in a novel can be understood completely by the reader, if the novelist wishes; their inner as well as their outer life can be exposed. And this is why they often seem more definite than characters in history, or even our own friends; we have been told all about them that can be told; even if they are imperfect and unreal they do not contain any secrets, whereas our friends do and must, mutual secrecy being one of the conditions of life upon this globe.[20]

Emotional isolation in the form of internal secrecy sets the stage for the emotional work of the liberal novel. The belief that people hold hidden interiors is what makes it compelling to turn people inside out and reveal their innermost workings. Round characters, those who are "capable of surprising in a convincing way,"[21] are those who give the illusion of this primary interiority by offering in glimmers and moments the full expression of its content.

One of the cardinal features of neoliberal individualism, as opposed to traditional liberal individualism, is its inclusivity of the very forms of collective attachment that liberal individualism eschewed. This leads to a qualitative shift not only in the relationships figured in neoliberal novels but also in the relationships cultivated between those novels and their readers. This inclusion of attachment within the logic of entrepreneurial advancement is possible because engagement in interpersonal domains is seen as achievable in ways that are consistent with the logic by which one engages in the market. In the neoliberal context, one can invest energy in the upbringing of one's children, for instance, not as an activity that distracts from economic priorities but rather as an activity that is consistent with economic goals. Foucault explains:

> We know that the number of hours a mother spends with her child, even when it is still in the cradle, will be very important for the formation of an abilities-machine, or for the formation of a human capital, and that the child will be much more adaptive if in fact its parents or its mother spend more rather than less time with him or her. This means that it must be possible to analyze the simple time parents spend feeding their children, or giving them affection as investment which can form human capital.[22]

Time spent developing emotional attachments within the family is here figured as an activity that can be undertaken with an entrepreneurial spirit and offer the possibility of material capital gains.[23] Neoliberal individualism is therefore expansive enough to include relationships – as long as those relationships do not violate the aims of entrepreneurialism in general. The logic of neoliberalism in this case piggybacks on the emergence of a general turn to biopolitical understandings of productivity. As control continues to be manifest in the daily lives of many U.S. subjects less and less as prohibition and more and more as production, the individual's economic autonomy is not seen as threatened by affective ties. Instead, these ties themselves are invested with an economic imperative.[24]

As a result, in neoliberal novels, there is less emphasis on the dramatic revelation of the inner emotional lives of characters. Rather than positioning the individual as secretly emotional in their interior life while being relatively free of attachments beyond the self, in neoliberal novels attachments to others are seen as themselves constitutive of the individual's full realization. With the rise of neoliberalism, we therefore see the waning of the kind of plot that pits the autonomous individual against a monolithic society. There is a dropping away of such characters as Randle McMurphy in *One Flew Over the Cuckoo's Nest*, Janie Crawford in *Their Eyes Were Watching God*, and Dean Moriarty in *On the Road*. Instead, we get pairs, families, and ensemble casts characterized by pronounced intimacy: the residents of the Enfield Tennis Academy and Ennet House in *Infinte Jest*; the interlocking lives of six New Yorkers in *Let the Great World Spin*; the women of the convent in *Paradise*.[25] Individualism as a value does not disappear in the neoliberal novel, but its qualities are transformed. Rather than figuring the individual as preexisting her attachments and as a potential location of resistance from mass structures, these novels see the individual as something that is produced through affective vectors. They are novels in which the individual's contours are refined through contact with others. The line that gets drawn is not between the private individual and public society, but between spheres of connection, in which individual success hinges on contact with others, and spheres of alterity, in which others are either of no consequence or a threat to the individual. The makeup of these spheres can be surprising, as with the loosely connected strangers of *Let the Great World Spin;* or it can more closely resemble traditional identity delineations, as with the women of *Paradise*. But in both cases there is a general movement away from the individual protagonist and toward the construction of emotionally bound groups. Characters that appear round persist; yet today what makes them seem real is not their capacity to surprise from the depths of their interiors but their capacity to grow and develop through their connections with others.[26]

Contemporary novels are increasingly concerned with communities and groups, so they can appear to signal a growing interest in collectivity that runs in opposition to capitalism's emphasis on individual competition. However, this collective emotional intimacy does not in and of itself run in opposition to the primacy of the entrepreneurial individual. The selves in neoliberal novels are often enriched by their relationships with others. Thus their capacities for self-development are not limited by their ties; they are expanded. It is as if the characters in some neoliberal novels could measure their success in terms of what one might imagine their Facebook profiles would look like: 6 friends! 200! 800! To be a loner is no longer understood as the height of individual achievement. One wants to be connected, but connected in such a way that serves one's own interests. In this model, emotion is not sublimated in favor of economic rationality; it is recast as a product of exchange. By the same token, literary invest-ment is understood as most appropriately met with emotional return, based not on the revelation of secret interiors but on the advancement of the reader's self.

The contemporary Contract model of literary investment, then, is not merely one in which readers generally expect to be rewarded for the time they put into reading a book. Instead, it is one in which readers expect reading to be productive of a specific kind of affective value: the value of connection with others that allows for the growth and enrichment of the self. Just as characters in neoliberal novels develop and grow out of con-tact with other characters, readers too expect emotional development and growth out of contact with the people who populate the narratives they consume. For a novel to follow through on its promises, in this context, it has to offer means for this connection: through identification, a sense of alliance, and emotional enrichment.

Emotional Scarcity: The Case of *The Road*

One of the clearest recent examples of a work of contemporary literature that follows through on this kind of promise is Cormac McCarthy's *The Road*. The novel tells a brief, brutal story of an unnamed man and boy as they try to survive in a horrifying postapocalyptic landscape. The reader never finds out what caused the disaster that blotted out the sun and left the land stripped of life; like the omission of the main characters' names, it doesn't seem to matter. What does matter is that the world of the novel is blanketed in ash, grey-skied, and almost entirely devoid of nonhuman life. The humans who have managed to survive the extreme resource depletion following the catastrophe have largely associated through "blood cults": cannibalistic slave societies with a distinctly tribal aesthetic that have made it through the postapocalyptic years by cultivating and feed-ing on human slaves and children. The man and the boy, however, have refused to join the cults and instead head down a vacant highway, pushing their belongings in a shopping cart, hoping to find a more forgiving habi-tat farther south. Along the way, they experience a host of close calls with dangerous people; they find goods and lose them; they experience terror and joy; and after the father dies of a sickness that he knows throughout the novel is likely to kill him, the boy finds a family that promises to take him in and nurture him.

Among *The Road*'s most-talked-about features is its minimalist style. The novel itself is slim, its sentences are largely simple, its vocabulary mostly straightforward – a significant departure from the winding sentences and grand diction that characterize much of McCarthy's earlier work.[27] Some critics have read this minimalism as signaling *The Road*'s interest in elemental or transcendent structures.[28] The fact that the characters are unnamed, according to this reading, gives rise to the notion that this boy could be any boy, this man any man, and that their fates, by extension, could be universalized beyond their specific character figurations. The spareness of the prose can additionally be understood as an attempt to shed the kind of personal voice that might develop a narrative consciousness as a particular interiority. The setting, characters, and diction are all seemingly nonspecific, and therefore they are potentially applicable to a range of circumstances. In this reading, *The Road* deploys formal and thematic extremity that recalls the experimental gestures of Samuel Beckett. Minimalism, in this view, is deployed to create a story that functions like allegory or even like scripture: it offers a scenario so radically decontextualized that it resonates in ways that have nothing to do with the particularities of the people who happen to play out that scenario. Yet it isn't at all clear that the primary effect of McCarthy's minimalism, insofar as it exists at all, is universalizing. *The Road* rejects a range of formal and thematic features such as quotation marks, variation in landscape, the presence of living things, other humans worthy of engagement, subordinate clauses, society, politics – and even the mother in the story, who is potentially the most powerful threat to the father-son bond – in order to exclude elements that might detract from the novel's primary relationship. This results in an intensified particularization of emotional cathexis between the reader and the two central characters and cleaves away other possible sites for attention. That the man and the boy are described and developed as "each the other's world entire" further heightens this emotional concentration.[29] The man survives for the boy and the boy for the man; the reader, having no external point of reference for the value of survival, inevitably participates in this tightly circulating emotional economy.

In other words, the novel's minimalism allows for the development of two seemingly contradictory emotional dynamics. On the one hand, it departicularizes time and space enough to broaden the sphere in which a given reader might relate to the pair. Many fathers are able to identify with the concern the man has for his son – they need not necessarily be of a certain generation, from a given region of the country, or of a specific class background. On the other hand, the novel's style intensifies emotional investment in the specificity of the man and the boy by crystallizing an event of historical, ecological, even geological proportions into the tiny lowercase words of the protagonists' meditations and, by extension, into the small personages of the man and the boy. The reader is made to care less about what environmental or global factors led to the apocalyptic backdrop of the novel and more about where the pair will find their next meal. The novel therefore offers the opposite scenario of *Robinson Crusoe*: instead of the presentation of the biographically and historically specific man, cut loose of all emotional ties, whose survival epitomizes the achievement of rational economic choice, we have the appearance of the biographically and historically undefined pair whose fate is the object of intense emotional engagement and whose survival epitomizes the payoff of specific emotional investment.[30]

The Road supports the notion that the material of emotional investment is a finite resource to be managed shrewdly. Crusoe's compulsive accounting does not disappear in this neoliberal iteration, it only morphs into a less recognizable form. Feeling – not land, money, or livestock – is the scarce but valuable resource that makes the difference between survival and death in *The Road*, and its circulation is managed with as much rigor as any other resource. For instance, early in the novel the pair tracks a single man as he wanders ahead of them on the road, not knowing if he is a threat. When they catch up with him, they find that he is in worse shape than they are:

> They followed him a good ways but at his pace they were losing the day and finally he just sat in the road and did not get up again. The boy hung on to his father's coat. No one spoke. He was as burntlooking as the country, his clothing scorched and black. One of his eyes was burnt shut and his hair was but a nitty wig of ash upon his blackened skull. As they passed he looked down. As if he'd done something wrong. His shoes were bound up with wire and coated with roadtar and he sat there in silence, bent over in his rags. The boy kept looking back. Papa? he whispered. What is wrong with the man?
>
> He's been struck by lightning.
>
> . . .
>
> Cant we help him? Papa?
>
> No. We cant help him. There's nothing to be done for him.

> They went on. The boy was crying. He kept looking back. When they got to the bottom of the hill the man stopped and looked at him and looked back up the road. The burned man had fallen over and at that distance you couldnt even tell what it was. I'm sorry, he said. But we have nothing

to give him. We have no way to help him. I'm sorry for what happened to him but we cant fix it. You know that, dont you? The boy stood looking down. He nodded his head. Then they went on and he didnt look back again.[31]

The man's justification, "we have nothing to give him," relies on one of two explanations. One possibility is that the man sees the burned man as needy only of material goods – clothing, food, or shelter. In this case, the demands of survival leave the man and boy helpless in the face of the burned man's needs. The other possibility, however, is that the burned man is needy of a range of other, less tangible, resources: emotional, spiritual, and interpersonal. This second possibility is the one supported more thoroughly by the rest of the novel, with its focus on morality, on "carrying the light" as a reason for survival, and on care as a form of basic sustenance. In this reading, the man's explanation is more complex, and his later assertion that "we cant share what we have or we'll die too" suggests that these affective resources are subject, in the world of *The Road*, to the same logic of scarcity as food and shelter. Read this way, *The Road* reflects the fundamental beliefs underlying neoliberalism: that extra-economic activities obey the same logic as market activities. The result, for the man and the boy, is careful attention to where emotional resources are directed and to what purpose.

It is worth nothing that it is one of the various minimalisms of the novel – its restricted chromatic scheme – that formally serves to justify the abandonment of the burned man more than the man's verbal explanations.[32] The monochromatic color palette of the novel allows for the plausibility that someone "as burntlooking as the country" might literally fade into the environment to the point where "you couldnt even tell what it was."[33] By extension, the burned man also fades into the background of the novel's plot soon after he disappears into its grey background as does character after character, event after event, giving the novel an overall sense of episodic groundlessness that consolidates readerly attention on the only persistently vivid elements of the novel: the man and the boy. The novel therefore stages not only an intense bond between the man and the boy but also, and perhaps more powerfully, it produces a pronounced emotional intensity between the characters in the novel and the reader. This construction of emotional intensity is particularly important in the case of *The Road*, where readerly interest could easily fall away in the face of the repetitive and episodic nature of the novel's plot. The reader's full and exclusive emotional investment in the central characters is crucial for the novel to function dramatically. Looked at structurally, the narrative of *The Road* is shockingly dull and repetitive, as undifferentiated as the grey setting that dominates it, unbroken by chapter headings, churning through square prose blocks, unhampered by initial indentation. If the novel avoids being unbearably boring, it does so because of its capacity to generate such pronounced interest in the fate of the characters that the monotony of its plot can be overlooked, greyed out like the landscape, the other characters, and history itself.

In other words, if *The Road* constructs a contract with the reader, it does so not by producing an engaging plot, or offering much in the way of concrete and applicable forms of instruction, but by eliciting intense emotional engagement out of readers and returning to those readers a sense of emotional connection with two particular, unreplaceable people. This is paradoxically all the more effective in the novel because the little boy and the man are so nonspecific. Or to put it another way, what is specific about the man and the boy are their emotional surfaces rather than any particular character traits, context, or histories. They have no secrets to tell, their interiors are blanks, but they are not flat. They are constructed through their emotional significance to one another and, vitally, through their emotional connection to the imagined reader of the novel. This is one possible explanation as to why readers see the primary emotional thrust of the novel as familiar despite the setting's pronounced strangeness. For instance, Michael Chabon writes:

> *The Road* is not a record of fatherly fidelity; it is a testament to the abyss of a parent's greatest fears. The fear of leaving your child alone, of dying before your child has reached adulthood and learned to work the mechanisms and face the dangers of the world, or found a new partner to face them with. The fear of one day being obliged for your child's own good, for his peace and comfort, to do violence to him or even end his life.[34]

Chabon's argument – that McCarthy taps into a universal paternal fear in his construction of the horror of *The Road* – is made all the more urgent through his use of the second-person pronoun. The appearance of "your" as both a stand-in for a personal possessive (a replacement for "my") and a general possessive (a replacement for "one's") in these final lines of his review attests to Chabon's recognition of the man's horror as his own while also implying that his specific horror is universal. This response is appropriate to the mechanisms of the novel, which manage to construct for the reader both a significant emotional investment in the specific fates of the man and the boy and a sense that there is something universal, contextless, and timeless about that investment.

The problem with all of this is that the cultivation of the very same emotional dynamic that Chabon identifies as universal to fatherhood is what motivates the fear of emotional scarcity in the novel and makes the novel's general antisocial vision seem itself to be appropriate and unavoidable. The degree to which this emotional bond justifies self-preservation over care for others should give pause. The novel seizes on emotions that are already recognizable to contemporary U.S. readers – the feeling, for instance, that a father would indirectly cause the deaths of others to protect his children – and heightens them rather than interrogating them or troubling them. Consider the sentiment of *The Road*, for instance, in relation to Annie Dillard's meditation on the very same impulse in an essay that attempts to take stock of the mass deaths of the twentieth century:

> "The atom bomb is nothing to be afraid of," Mao told Nehru. "China has many people... The deaths of ten or twenty million people is nothing to be afraid of."...
>
> Does Mao's reckoning shock me really? If sanctioning the death of strangers could save my daughter's life, would I do it? Probably. How many others' lives would I be willing to sacrifice? Three? Three hundred million?
>
> An English journalist, observing the Sisters of Charity in Calcutta, reasoned: "Either life is always and in all circumstances sacred, or intrinsically of no account; it is inconceivable that it should be in some cases the one, and in some cases the other."[35]

By asking this question, by pointing to its probable answer's brutality, and by noting the specificity of its cultural, emotional, and spiritual context, Dillard's essay does not let the question rest or allow her anxiety over her own answer provide any consolation. The answer *The Road* gives, on the other hand, is an unequivocal and hearty "yes," and its justification is made through the novel's form as much as through any specific moral arguments. The consolidation of emotional intensity on the man and the boy leaves, to borrow a phrase from the neoliberal ideologue Margaret Thatcher, "no alternative."[36] Without them, there is no story, nothing that emerges out of the grey; there is, indeed, no reason to go on. The novel offers a highly unbalanced choice: either the development of emotional investment and its return through the cultivation of clear ethical allegiances with the actions of the novel's characters or nihilistic acceptance of mere ash, repetition, horror, and suicide. In this way, *The Road* demonstrates how the cultivation of a situation in which readerly emotional investment is met with emotional return can have social consequences for the novel's readership. Whether or not we agree with the implied politics of the novel, simply by participating in its affective demands we participate in its social vision. When we invest ourselves in the urgency of the little boy and the man's plight to the exclusion of the masses of sufferers who provide the backdrop for the story, as we must if we are to care about the world of the novel enough to read it, our emotional attention is trained to zoom in on the needs of those with whom we already feel connected rather than the needs of a larger social or ecological system.[37] As a result, the novel and its affective incitements participate in the production of neoliberal subjects, prone to investing the self and those who help to sustain the self with emotional care, while strangers are seen as threats to a scarce emotional economy.

Generalizing this phenomenon allows us to see how works of literature that appear to merely describe what emotional experience is "really like" can be understood to be reinforcing a notion of the personal that has as much to do with the prevalence of certain social values as it does something inherent to emotion as such. *The Road* acts socially and politically regardless of its articulated opinion on any given issue. Its most seemingly apolitical aspect, the emotional family drama it narrates, is, in fact, perhaps its most politically relevant intervention. By amplifying the exclusive emotional connection between a man and a son in such a way that it positions any other potential relationship as diminishing that connection, and in so doing positing an emotional economy of scarcity, *The Road* helps to encourage the development of individuals who see emotional experience as governed by a market logic. Novels that follow through on their emotional promises, then, reinforce neoliberalism in two ways: they concede that literary dynamics can and should mirror market dynamics by allowing the contractual logic to proceed without question; and in obeying that contract, they often strengthen emotional beliefs that underpin neoliberal subjectivity.

Subtracting the Personal: The Case of *The Book of Illusions*

The Road is exemplary of the primary quality critics attribute to contemporary aesthetics: it has a keen awareness of the materiality of language but still manages to convey a crushing sense of emotional urgency. However, that emotional urgency is qualitatively conservative insofar as it intensifies already-existing emotional tendencies in the neoliberal reading populace, including the tendency to see emotional connections as obeying a market logic that necessitates careful investment decisions. The opacity of narrative form in the novel intensifies this effect, accentuating the specific value of the two central characters by minimizing all potentially competing vessels of attention – linguistic, environmental, or human. Yet for a work of literature to be both formally challenging and affectively engaging does not necessitate that it do so by intensifying familiar emotions. This need only be our conclusion if we believe that emotions are always recognizable, that we know when we are feeling something and when we are not, and that a text that is emotionally active will be all of the things we expect such a text to be: welcoming of identification, personal, and representative of familiar forms of connection.

The importance of this distinction can be seen in a work that articulates the dynamics of feeling as they relate to bodily impulse, self-conscious emotional experience, and art while itself withdrawing from a project of recognizable emotional payoff: Paul Auster's *The Book of Illusions*. Critics have often panned Auster's novels for this withdrawal, seeing it as an unintentional by-product of the author's interest in self-referential form and high concept. For instance, Brooke Allen writes of *The Book of Illusions*:

> Auster has always written from the head rather than the heart.... Characters are emblems as opposed to people; situations are created out of a feeling for dramatic symmetry rather than from the all-too-messy urgency of human passion. The results can be compelling, but they tend to be on the dry side.... *The Book of Illusions* is too allegorical to be emotionally affecting, and although it's perfectly readable, its prose is bland and undistinguished, its dialogue trite.... And, like all Auster's novels, it makes its careful architecture just a little too evident.[38]

Allen offers a series of binary oppositions typical of the affective hypothesis that many readers of contemporary fiction take for granted: head versus heart; emblems versus people; allegory versus emotional effect.[39] Her analysis rests on the notion that the "urgency of human passion," more than "dramatic symmetry," is the appropriate goal for literary fiction. But Auster is not merely faulted for his perceived coldness. A significant part of the difficulty this critic and others have with Auster's work is that it often takes on situations that have deep emotional consequences, but it refuses to render those situations through characters that seem to have emotional depth or with whom a reader can emotionally identify. As James Wood argues:

> What is problematic about [Auster's] books is not their postmodern skepticism about the stability of the narrative, ... but the gravity and the emotional logic that Auster tries to extract from the "realist" side of his stories. Auster is always at his most solemn at those moments in his books which are least plausible and most ragingly unaffecting.[40]

Auster, in other words, also participates in the contemporary trend of pairing formal play (in this case through complex metafictional architectures) with content that is clearly concerned with the real world and real people (in this case, serious emotional situations). Wood's indictment of this gesture in Auster's work has to do with the belief that he is so much a failure in the latter that he would do better to just stick with the post-modernist language play that gives distinction to his forms. Otherwise, he argues damningly, Auster ends up with "the worst of both worlds: fake realism and shallow skepticism."[41]

Yet evidence in the text itself suggests that the performance of the failure of the novel to convey an appropriate emotional tone or a believable emotional reaction is central to its innovative take on what it means to enter into a distinct state of feeling. *The Book of Illusions* begins after the main character, David, has lost his wife and children in a plane crash. This scenario does, indeed, seem to promise a novel of emotional intensity, one that will coax horror and a sense of awful sympathy out of its readers. But rather than offering the kind of emotional immediacy that we saw between the man and the boy in *The Road*, David's grief is articulated superficially, from a distance, as though Auster somehow never learned the fundamental creative writing credo, "Show, don't tell." As a result, "one never really believes in … David Zimmer's alcoholic grief" because it is reported so thinly and by a string of emotional clichés.[42] For instance, the narrator explains that he spent the days following the accident "in a blur of alcoholic grief and self-pity," in a past-tense use of the first-person point of view that reads as oddly removed from the events he describes. There is no effort to ground what that "blur of alcoholic grief" looks like in any specific action or interior revelation. And the grief-related action figured in the novel is not even remotely blurry. It is rather a very clearly articulated yet distanced account of how David connects with his deceased children by playing with their Legos:

> I wasn't able to think about them directly or summon them up in any conscious way, but as I put together their puzzles and played with their Lego pieces, building ever more complex and baroque structures, I felt that I was temporarily inhabiting them again – carrying on their little phantom lives for them by repeating the gestures they had made when they still had bodies.[43]

This gestural mode of connection is consistent with the prose style of the novel itself, which presents characters as being defined more by their bodily actions than by their specific motivations.[44] The emotional states of those who populate the book are reported in a self-conscious use of the past tense by a narrator who later is revealed to have died before the novel's publication. He is therefore represented as at a remove even from the self he describes in the core narrative of the book. The movements and actions of the central characters are also described from a detached perspective, preventing the realization of specific individuals with whom we might identify, sympathize, or feel connected.

And yet, David's repetition of the gestures of his children is clearly symptomatic not of cold detachment but instead of a deep physical attachment that extends across the seemingly impermeable barrier that exists between the living and the dead. As I will show, the project of *The Book of Illusions* echoes the ambition of this effort, constituting an experiment in how a novel might encourage its readers toward a similar posture of detached assessment of their own affective movements. For this reason, we might read David's building of "complex and baroque" structures as a comment on the physical impulses conveyed by the complex architecture of the novel's own plot. Through its metafictional descriptions of the relationship between works of art and their audiences, the text addresses the possibility that affective transmission could occur through a similar logic as David's gestural form of connection with his children, but at a greater remove through exposure to aesthetic forms that eschew the illusion of direct emotional connection.[45] Abstract as it might seem, *The Book of Illusions* chronicles and performs a form of affective investment that, while departing from common assumptions about what affective experience feels like and how it should be expressed, nevertheless indicates the possibility for intense forms of human relation that violate the cost-benefit logics of the Contract model and entrepreneurial connections more generally.

This possibility is posited first and foremost through Auster's metafictional reflections on cinema, a medium that acts as a stand-in for the medium of the novel in *The Book of Illusions*. As Timothy Bewes explains, the films chronicled in *The Book of Illusions* "turn out to be much more like novels than films."[46] And while "the attitude toward [cinema]" in the novel, in his view, "is deeply ambivalent," cinema is offered up as a corresponding narrative form to the novel that is distinct enough from it for it to be dealt with at relative remove.[47] This engagement with the novel form through representation of the mechanisms of cinema first appears early in the novel, when, catching a silent film on television during the height of his grief, David finds himself, to his surprise, laughing, much as he observes himself from a distance playing with Legos. He explains that the laugh "might not sound important, but it was the first time I had laughed at anything since June, and when I felt that unexpected spasm rise up through my chest and begin to rattle around in my lungs, I understood that I hadn't hit bottom yet, that there was still some piece of me that wanted to go on living" (*TBI*, 9). The laugh, like the Legos episode, is central to the emotional plot of the novel, but it is not narrated expressively. Instead, its physical properties, the spasm and the rattle, are chronicled in a clinical fashion, and the emotional meaning of those physical properties is represented as a conscious analysis made only after the fact. The dispassionate quality of the reporting of the incident is highlighted by its uncomfortable use of the faulty vocabulary of recovery, the concept of "hitting bottom" and the desire to "go on living" being stock phrases of precisely the kind of pop-psychological rhetoric that the book relentlessly calls into question. More accurately, David describes this moment as "an empirical discovery," which "carried all the weight of a mathematical proof" (10). This reconnection to the world that David ultimately experiences does not happen in a sudden surge of feeling. The experience is divided, occurring through preconscious bodily response on the one hand (the laugh) and rational assessment on the other (the "mathematical proof").

David's resulting feeling is not easy to put into a familiar emotional category; the laugh does not signal joy or happiness. Instead, the laugh catalyzes for David a recognition that he is capable of having a feeling – a meta-feeling – which might best be understood as the affective component of what Daniel Heller-Roazen calls "the sense of being sentient" or *aisthēsis*.[48] *Aisthēsis*, according to Heller-Roazen, is constitutive of a common trait of human beings that is at the same time not properly or exclusively human. He explains that in Aristotle's terms the feeling is

> the element that is left over in human beings once one has withdrawn from them what is particularly human: everything in man, for example, that remains after, or before, the life of reason, everything in him that cannot be said to owe its existence to the activity of thought. This is an element that persists in human nature without altogether coinciding with it.... [It] testifies to a dimension of the living being in which the distinction between the human and the inhuman simply has no pertinence: a region common, by definition, to all animal life.[49]

The feeling that one is feeling is one component of this sense, which Heller-Roazen explains has historically possessed sensory, perceptive, and affective valences. And because *aisthēsis* is precisely "the element that is left over" after the subtraction of reason, feeling is a crucial access point to that essential sense. The redemptive nature of artworks in *The Book of*

Illusions is therefore figured primarily as a function of their capacity to excite unqualified physical impulses, the recognition of which gives rise to a powerful yet often unrecognized feeling, a feeling that provides one aspect of the common ground of sentience as such.

David's description of the attributes of the silent film underscores the role of physical movement in an affective transmission that is at once impersonal and relational. He describes the force of the film as emanating not out of a believable representation of an individual but rather as emerging out of the mustache of the main actor, Hector. For David, "the mustache is a seismograph of Hector's inner states" as "a twitching filament of anxieties, a metaphysical jump rope, a dancing thread of discombobulation" (*TBI*, 29). The relationship between bodily movement and emotional transmission therefore runs both ways. David experiences his own emotion through a conscious recognition of a bodily change; he also recognizes Hector's inner world through the movements of his mustache, which "tells you what Hector is thinking, actually allows you into the machinery of his thoughts" (ibid.). The mustache therefore produces not a feeling of intimacy between screen character and audience member but rather an awareness of an affective possibility – the possibility that the movement of bodies on the screen might allow for feeling to be communicated. This emphasis on the materiality of forms of mediation, of course, intensifies the metafictional resonance between film and fiction in this scene. David explains:

> The intimacy of the talking mustache is a creation of the lens. At various moments in each of Hector's films, the angle suddenly changes, and a wide or medium shot is replaced by a close-up. Hector's face fills the screen, and with all references to the environment eliminated, the mustache becomes the center of the world. It begins to move, and because Hector's skill is such that he can control the muscles in the rest of his face, the mustache appears to be moving on its own, like a small animal with an independent consciousness and will … as the mustache goes through its antic gyrations, the face is essentially still, and in that stillness one sees oneself as if in a mirror, for it is during those moments that Hector is most fully and convincingly human, a reflection of what we all are when we're alone within ourselves. (*TBI*, 29–30)

Like *The Road*'s monochromatic setting, the close-up makes all environmental points of context fade into the background and heightens attention on a single point, in this case, the mustache. As Deleuze explains in *Cinema 1*, this is how the close-up achieves its affective power. He writes, "[The close-up has] the power to tear the image away from spatio-temporal coordinates in order to call forth … pure affect."[50] Yet whereas in *The Road* this type of heightened attention is profoundly personalizing, concentrating readerly attention on the specific fates of the man and the boy, in *The Book of Illusions* the close-up is depersonalizing. Rather than inviting a personal connection, its decontextualizing force extends beyond the twitching mustache to the person of Hector and "abstracts the face from the person to which it belongs."[51] What David experiences in connecting with the image of Hector's face can therefore not be understood to fall into any of our customary categories for emotional connection with fictional characters: he does not identify, feel sympathy, feel empathy, or feel as if Hector's character might be his fictional friend. The abstract language of the passage is crucial in conveying this distinction. David does not see himself in Hector's character. Instead, "one sees oneself as if in a mirror." The recognition one makes of oneself in the image is an abstract, impersonal recognition, one that relies on an essential stillness. In this way, Hector "loses his individuation, to the point where he takes on a strange resemblance to the other, a resemblance by default or by absence."[52] Where viewers are prone to looking for personal specificity in human faces, in the case of the close-up the face is represented as blank, general, and nonspecific, yet all the more "fully and convincingly human" for being so.

In one sense, the critical response to *The Book of Illusions* gets the book right: it is a novel that is primarily about novels, and as a result of that focus, it does not follow through on the promise of emotional depth that seems called for by the tragic scenario with which it begins. Yet while *The Book of Illusions* does not convey the kinds of feelings that would seem appropriate to the story it tells, it is far from being an unfeeling work. Through its nested, metafictional structure, the novel tells a series of stories that chronicle experiences of the loss of self, affective investments in works of art, and momentary connections with others. These stories are similar even though they are attributed to different characters: David, Hector, even one of Hector's fictional characters. In dispersing this story across a range of characters, all of whom are one way or another clearly established as narrative constructions rather than real people, the novel accomplishes something similar to Hector's close-up. While the characters act as depersonalized, self-consciously crafted twitching mustaches, conveying messages and themes, the novel itself is revealed to be a blank field of affective potential that is not unlike the face in the close-up. While it does not offer particular persons with whom readers might relate, it nevertheless allows for the cultivation of a feeling on the part of the reader that echoes the feeling David recognizes after his laugh: the feeling that one is feeling paired with the awareness that art can be the catalyst for this universal human capacity. This response is possible only in a work of art in which the ability to make strategic emotional alliances with characters is subtracted, because as long as that ability exists, readers will attribute their affective responses to narratives to the relationships they have forged with those characters. And this, in turn, reinforces the notion that emotional growth and well-being can be cultivated consciously through connections with the right people, real or fictional. The possibility that *The Book of Illusions* signals, on the other hand, is that the capacity for affective connection with others might be impersonal, contingent, and distributed throughout social systems and environments in ways that fall outside willful entrepreneurial investment.

Assessing Literary Affects

These two case studies, *The Road* and *The Book of Illusions,* share many of the traits we have come to see in attempts to define contemporary literary aesthetics. They both clearly draw their formal structures from modernist and postmodernist toolkits while gesturing to the possibility that novels might engage earnestly with the particularities of human experience in a way that is not entirely blocked by problems of linguistic reference, signification, and falsification. But the major difference between the two novels is subtractive. *The Book of Illusions* takes away the notion of specific interest that motivates the emotional investments readers are encouraged to make in the characters of *The Road*. There are particular reasons why readers should feel emotionally connected to the man and the boy rather than anyone else in the landscape of *The Road*: they demonstrate goodness, they remind us of ourselves, they don't eat babies, they have a nostalgic love of Coca-Cola that signals classic Americanness, and so on.[53] Emotional identification and alliance with the pair therefore allows readers to experience feelings that are familiar: pride, fear, love, patriotism, nostalgia. The invocation of these recognizable feelings acts as a payoff for readerly investment – it allows readers to feel more fully emotionally affirmed – while the feeling of connection with the man and the boy that is cultivated by the novel allows readers a sense of greater connection with others whose feelings resemble their own. All of these experiences are expected by readers when they choose to invest time in reading a novel. So in following through on those expectations, *The Road* pleases readers trained on the Contract model.

Why, on the other hand, should readers feel connected to David? At first, it might seem that the extremity of his loss should inspire empathy, calling up the same kinds of parental fears that *The Road* does and making readers want to befriend him. But the language of the novel works at cross-purposes to any attempts to forge these connections. It becomes apparent fairly early on in the novel that David will not be anyone's acquaintance or networking opportunity, nor will his experience allow for anyone to relate in ways that feel familiar. And given that the major connection that motivates the book's plot is forged between a live man and a dead man – as a result of the dead man's capacity to sculpt his gestures in highly unnatural ways – there are reasons to believe that any connection that exists between the reader and David will extend over an equally improbable distance through equally artificial means.

But the distinction between these two works and the two types of contemporary novel they exemplify is not, as many reviewers would suggest, summarizable in terms of the works' relative emotional power. It is not a matter of *The Road* being affecting and *The Book of Illusions* being cerebral and cold, although many readers would parse the distinction in precisely those terms. Instead, the difference between the novels' effects can be mapped onto a qualitative distinction within affective experience. If we concede that the dynamics of feeling include both the conscious and the preconscious, the physiological and the psychological, and that the recognizability of emotions depends, in part, on the development of a vocabulary for specific feelings, then we can imagine how feeling might mirror the dynamics of sight, where certain wavelengths are visible and others material but not as easily registered. In this view, *The Road* feels emotional because many of the feelings it produces fall into the emotional spectrum that is easily recognizable: it gives us red, yellow, and green. It would be odd to think that a novel, even one as apparently muted as *The Book of Illusions*, was fully devoid of feeling. Instead, we might say that its affective operations occur largely outside of our capacities for apprehension, in the infrared or ultraviolet range. The sight metaphor breaks down, however, when we consider that unlike our ocular physiology, our capacities for recognition and description shift with the cultural contexts to which we are exposed and the representative forms we invent. So if a given work of literature does operate largely in the ultraviolet spectrum, its affective impact is not doomed to be forever beyond our capacity to acknowledge it.

The Book of Illusions trains readers to regard forms of aesthetic experience as having affective power that they might not expect. It does so by staging a metafictional situation that mirrors the form of the book, using David's captivation by Hector's films as a comment on how a reader might be captivated by Auster's novels. The feeling both forms provoke is difficult to locate in our existing taxonomies of emotion. Indeed, *The Book of Illusions* is most interested in a feeling that is not only impersonal but also, insofar as it is nothing but the feeling of sentience, nonhuman – or perhaps more precisely, both essentially human and possibly exceeding its bounds. Whereas *The Road* heightens recognizable feelings out of the development of a familiar kind of relationship – the bond between a father and a son – *The Book of Illusions* is equally about connections with others – connections across time, across the borders of life and death, across the barriers of mediation – but it does not script those connections as either within individual control or generative of specific emotions. What is accentuated is the degree to which art forges these connections and the contingent yet affecting way it does so. *The Book of Illusions* is a work of art that both refuses to follow through on its promises and performs what art can do when it makes that refusal. Its dominant feeling is the feeling of recognizing in another human being the possibility for feeling. The novel thematizes the complexity of that recognition, and in doing so shows how experiences like it can propel individuals away from their prior lives and previous investments.

As I have argued in these case studies, there is not just one but at least two major trajectories within contemporary literary attempts to bring together formal experimentation and emotional impact: one that is committed to the specificity of the personal; and another that is interested in the potential of the impersonal. The distinctions between the two as exemplified in these case studies are outlined in Table 1.

At the root of these distinctions are three crucial points of departure: one formal, one affective, and one sociopolitical. First, whereas works of the personal variant see form as a vehicle for readerly interest, drawing from the innovations of modernism and postmodernism in order to entertain readers and position themselves in the literary market as novel commodities, those of the impersonal variant see form as the aspect of literature that carries its greatest potential to affect the world from which they emerge. There is therefore a greater modernist sympathy in the works that fall under this category, as they share modernism's optimism in regards to form even as they stop short of some of the more utopian modernist hopes for formal novelty. Second, works of the personal variant see the representation of recognizable feelings as an important, if not the most central, social role of literature. These works place a premium on the

Table 1. *Personal and Impersonal*

	Personal (case study: *The Road*)	Impersonal (case study: *The Book of Illusions*)
Form	Formal innovation for the sake of novelty; experiments in language give weight to sentimental connections.	Formal devices emphasize materiality of language; narrative and formal promises initiated and interrupted; art self-consciously posited as form of affective invention.
Tone	Immediacy.	Distance.
Feelings	The amplification of recognizable emotions.	The production of feelings that may not be recognized as such: second-order feelings (the feeling that one is feeling; the feeling of not knowing what one is feeling); physiological responses; temporal disruptions.
Emphasis on connections	Connections with characters motivated by specific interest on the model of networking.	Relations across time and space, emphasis on the role of mediation in forging connections, improbable and contingent contact with others.
Response to neoliberalism	Emotions figured as scarce resource; literature understood as productive form of consumption; participation in literary market understood as necessitating contractual fulfillment.	Affect figured as a commons; literature understood as productive of alternatives to the present; refusal to follow through on contractual promises.
Implied role of art	Art as chronicle of specific historical and personal circumstances.	Art as smeared across history; depersonalizing.
Relationship to modernism and postmodernism	Retention of modernist commitment to formal novelty; rejection of difficulty, rejection of notion of formal innovation as invention of new ways of life. Interest in return to an imagined premodernist or "realist" engagement with real life for real, everyday people.	Continued belief in form as the site of alterations in perception, affection, and forms of social engagement. Rejection of modernist belief in the separation between the aesthetic field and the demands of history, the environment, politics, and society. Rejection of postmodernist notion of language as merely empty signification.

cultivation of strong emotional relationships between readers and characters and provide tonal cues that deepen emotions readers have already experienced or believe they will experience in the future. The provocation of these emotional states is what makes these works seem connected to reality and appear to depart from the imagined coldness of their postmodernist predecessors. Impersonal works are equally committed to the notion that literature can be a site for the production of feelings, but the feelings they cultivate are not always or merely recognizable as emotions. Instead, these works see literary form as potentially provocative of feelings that aren't easily defined by existing psychological vocabularies.

These two major distinctions, formal and affective, are particularly urgent because of the third distinction between the two strands: the sociopolitical distinction. Because there has been an upsurge in literary works that seek compromise between experimental and emotional impulses that has been contemporaneous with neoliberalism, it is tempting to make the argument that such works constitute the cultural logic of neoliberalism, following Fredric Jameson's model in *Postmodernism, or The Cultural Logic of Late Capitalism*.[54] Yet this conclusion would ignore the varied landscape of contemporary literary fiction. As *The Road* demonstrates, the concerns of personal works are highly consistent with the assumptions of neoliberalism. Personal works follow the neoliberal shift toward the accumulation of entrepreneurial connections with others, offering up characters with whom readers can feel allied. And they obey the Contract model of reading, following through on their promises and thereby reinforcing the notion that literary experience can be represented by the logic of the market. Impersonal works reflect on neoliberalism differently, although it is important to emphasize that they are not necessarily explicitly or self-consciously critical of neoliberalism in any direct way. But the way they mobilize feeling complicates the fundamental expectations of neoliberalism by placing a focus on aspects of life that fall outside its structures. Impersonal works stage partial, inconvenient, and improbable connections across time and space and without regard for personal investment or return. The feelings that they construct are depersonalizing and therefore deindividualizing, calling into question the expectations that underpin the model of the neoliberal entrepreneurial subject. They do not follow through on their promises, and thus they are often not easily incorporated into a market model of literary production and consumption. They position themselves instead as existing within systems that themselves cannot be reduced to a market model: ecosystems, biological systems, and the contingencies of the circulation of art itself.

It is finally worth noting that my distinction between these two types of literary works could just as easily be applied to critical approaches to affect in literature. Indeed, in the chapters that follow, I argue both for greater attention to works that highlight impersonal feelings and for greater critical acceptance of models of affective criticism that allow for the recognition and analysis of impersonal feelings.[55] This is not to say that all forms of affective criticism that attend primarily to recognizable emotions are complicit with neoliberalism. Rather, I suggest that the relative emphasis within literary studies on such approaches forecloses opportunities for literary criticism to engage with the neoliberal dominant in such a way that, in refusing to rest solely on the protocols of ideology critique, engages more directly with the aesthetic and ontological assumptions that underpin the current state of affairs – assumptions that are cultivated perhaps most of all in cultural narratives and works of art.

2

Affect and Aesthetics in 9/11 Fiction

Don DeLillo's *Falling Man* begins with its central character, Keith, leaving the World Trade Center on the morning of September 11, 2001, blanketed in blood, as he emerges into "a world ... of falling ash and near night."[1] In shock, he wanders away from the towers, observing that, startlingly, "this was the world now," a world so suddenly changed that the image of something as seemingly banal as "office paper flashing past, standard sheets with cutting edge" is seen as one of so many "otherworldly things."[2] As Keith finds his way to a hospital, he learns that the total transformation of the outside world is only one possible consequence of what he has endured. His doctor warns, "Where there are suicide bombings ... In those places where it happens, the survivors, the people nearby who are injured, sometimes, months later, they develop bumps, for lack of a better term, and it turns out this is caused by small fragments, tiny fragments of the suicide bomber's body.... They call this 'organic shrapnel.'"[3] This metaphor literalizes what we tend to think traumatic events of this magnitude do: not only do they change the way the world appears, but they dramatically alter the very physical constitution of survivors, as fragments of the catastrophe continue to live and grow within them. The exposure to such horrifying events appears to involve an eerie permeability where the force of the experience radically alters the world, and with it the corporeal existence of its victims. And yet, despite the arresting horror of his experience, the doctor is able to take one look at Keith and declare, "This is something I don't think you have."[4]

This exposure to the transfiguring effect of the catastrophe is also something that *Falling Man*, along with many novels like it, lacks. As Richard Gray has argued of *Falling Man* and September 11 fiction in general, these novels insist upon the transformative force of the event even as they tend to "assimilate the unfamiliar into familiar structures."[5] It would seem as though DeLillo's typical narrative strategies would palpably strain to encompass the new world Keith envisions as he exits his building. Yet reviews of the novel consistently puzzle over the recycled feeling of DeLillo's prose and attest to the evenness of the assimilation of the event to existing formal possibilities.[6] In several places – in Keith's son's expansive fantasies about "Bill Lawton," a comfortably anglicized version of Bin Laden, for instance – the novel even seems aware of its own aesthetic armor – its capacity to assimilate the seemingly unassimilable. In this sense, the novel can be read as consciously attesting to the disturbing resiliency of narrative form in the face of the event that was supposed to change everything.[7]

This resiliency runs contrary to what many critics would like to see from September 11 fiction because of assumptions about what historical trauma does to literary form. Gray articulates those expectations:

> Trauma, as one theorist of the subject has put it, is a "mind-blowing experience that destroys a conventional mindset and compels (or makes possible) a new worldview." Recognition that the old mindset has been destroyed, or at least seriously challenged, is widespread in recent literature. We are still, perhaps, waiting for a fictional measure of the new world view.[8]

We look to trauma to produce opportunities for new ways of seeing and new ways of thinking, and we expect this upheaval in sensory, emotional, and intellectual experience to transform literature on the level of form. Major literary shifts are commonly understood to be consequences of violent historical change: this is why wars often serve as historical markers of aesthetic novelty. If September 11 novels do not appear to register the "new world view" aesthetically, it is tempting to conclude that there is something disturbingly amiss in the field of the literary.[9]

Yet the failure of many September 11 novels to reflect the breaking of the world in the breaking of form, as Gray and others would expect, is not merely a matter of faulty political perspective or lack of aesthetic ingenuity.[10] In what follows, I will show that the difficulty of channeling the traumatic force of September 11 in a way that encourages new ways of thinking, feeling, and creating is intimately linked to the historical conditions of the post–September 11 era. This period involved, among other things, a profound instrumentalization of the event at the service of neoliberal political and economic goals that were more ideologically continuous than disruptive. Through a reading of Jonathan Safran Foer's *Extremely Loud and Incredibly Close*, I will argue that novels that represent and articulate the events as world-changing while remaining formally familiar do indeed reflect the post–September 11 nexus of trauma, politics, and aesthetics with remarkable accuracy.

Turning to a lesser-known work of September 11 fiction, Laird Hunt's experimental noir *The Exquisite*, however, it is possible to see the appearance of a different affective relationship to the post–September 11 period. Hunt's novel produces a feeling of uneasiness that we might see as a way of registering affectively the embeddedness of the event within a web of complex geopolitical interactions. Whereas traumatic utterances are often understood to index the inability to fully comprehend an event that falls dramatically *outside* expectations and norms, this novel positions the events of September 11 as indicative of a different kind of incomprehensible situation: the widespread difficulty of coming to terms with our deep entanglement *within* political and social systems. The strange affects and uncomfortable feelings that this novel formalizes – importantly through images that tie the complexity of geopolitical systems to the complexity of ecological systems – suggest that literary works, despite their failure to reflect the trauma of the early twenty-first century, might still be sites for the production of challenging bodily attitudes and responses toward contemporary political realities.

Gray's claim that September 11 fiction should mirror the upheaval of the post-9/11 historical moment aesthetically is based on the now commonly held notion that literature emerging out of a traumatic context provides new ways of engaging with the world by formally transmitting to others the subjective fracturing constitutive of traumatic experience. Shoshana Felman's contention that in such testimonies "the breakage of the verse enacts the breakage of the world" therefore exemplifies the aesthetic analysis of many trauma theorists.[11] In this view, the formal breaking that we associate with traumatic testimony allows for the transmission of traumatic experience through form, so that, as Cathy Caruth suggests, "trauma may lead ... to the encounter with another" in such a way that "what is passed on ... is not just the meaning of the words but their performance."[12] In other words, the material force of language for Caruth does not lie in its capacity to represent, as trauma is precisely that which cannot be represented, but rather in its power to move, to produce affective responses, to make bodily demands.

Yet there are problems with this framework as it pertains to the relations among aesthetics, politics, and emotion in the particular context of the post–September 11 period. For one, as Ruth Leys points out, many theories of trauma either explicitly or implicitly posit the traumatic situation as entailing a fully integrated subject who is unexpectedly shattered by the intrusion of a shock from the *outside*. This perspective, Leys notes, "often gives way to ... the idea that trauma is a purely external event that befalls a fully constituted subject ... It depicts violence as purely and simply an assault from without."[13] In the aftermath of the events of September 11, the transmission of traumatic feelings through aesthetic means – as occurred, for instance, through televised coverage of the World Trade Center collapse – conferred victim status to the nation as a whole. This tendency to view a traumatic situation as a shock to a previously integrated entity from the outside was one of many contributing factors in the development of a new national myth, one that drew from therapeutic discourse to suggest that prior to the attacks, the United States was itself a fully constituted whole until it endured an unexpected and unidirectional assault from outside that spun it into chaos – a chaos it could only recover from by restoring its integral – and identical – wholeness.[14]

Sentimental Innovation: The Case of *Extremely Loud and Incredibly Close*

The relationship between contemporary literary form and this ideological development is perhaps best exemplified in Jonathan Safran Foer's novel *Extremely Loud and Incredibly Close*. The novel is told from the perspective of Oskar, a nine-year-old child who witnesses vicariously, through a series of phone messages, the death of his father in the World Trade Center collapse. Throughout the book, Oskar searches for clues as to what to make of his father's death, and Foer employs a wide range of experimental techniques to convey the hopelessness of this search for significance in the face of the devastating void of this traumatic loss. The book is littered with a variety of textual records – letters, newspaper articles, and video stills – as well as blank pages that attest to the inevitable gaps in significance. The epistemological uncertainty characteristic of the aftermath of trauma is thus reflected in formal innovation and fragmentation. The novel thrusts the reader into a textual morass that forces an identification with the confusion and devastation of its central character.

In the final pages of the book, Oskar, who has been compiling a folder of 9/11 evidence, examines a series of video stills of a man falling from one of the towers.

> Was it Dad?
> Maybe.
> Whoever it was, it was somebody. ...
> I reversed the order, so the last one was first, and the first one was last.

When I flipped through them, it looked like the man was floating up through the sky.

And if I'd had more pictures, he would've flown through a window, back into the building, and the smoke would've poured into the hole that the plane was about to come out of.

Dad would've left his messages backward, until the machine was empty, and the plane would've flown backward away from him.[15]

This vision continues its backward motion until Oskar's dad ends up securely in bed, and the novel ends with a single mournful sentence: "We would have been safe."[16] This final passage suggests that the temporal mechanisms of textuality might be restorative – if the forward movement of a novel's plot can be reversed, then the devastating inevitability of the tragedy can be undone, if only for a moment, in the literary experience. In case the reader misses the implication that literary narratives might allow for this backward movement, the backward flipbook is reproduced in the final pages of the book, which, when flipped, animate the upward flight of a falling man.

Despite what appears to be an unleashing of the possibilities of literature in the face of trauma, this device ultimately leads to a reading of the event that is compatible only with a highly limited historical outlook, one that sees the events of September 11 as isolated from any larger geopolitical frame. The narrative perspective of Oskar is so compelling and vulnerable, and the formal operations of the novel so effectively performative, that most readers would have a difficult time not longing with him for this ultimate temporal reversal and restoration of order. But not only is Oskar's vision disturbingly regressive, the use of the first-person plural pronoun in the final sentence of the book limits the powers of textuality to the restoration of safety only for those who can be counted as victims of the World Trade Center collapse. For most of Oskar's daydream, it is his father who is moving backward away from his death, but in the final line of the novel, an undefined but central "we" becomes the subject of the reversal – the "we" who would have been safe if only time could go in reverse. But who is the "we" who would be safe at the end of this process? This line literally seems to refer to Oskar and his family, but it might also extend to others who were in the World Trade Center or lost loved ones on that day. Pushed further, it could be read as an even more expansive "we," a "we" that represents anyone who identifies as a victim of the attacks – perhaps a Western "we," perhaps a capitalist "we," perhaps a secular "we" – but given the fact that the "we" envisioned in the novel "would have been safe" on the night of September 10, 2001, its inclusive force has definite limits. Because time cannot spin backward far enough for the "we" of the final line to expand to include victims of other tragedies, tragedies that might have had complex relationships with the attacks, the appeal to safety produces a clear line between the intolerable deaths of September 11 victims and the much more complicated geopolitical context of the event.[17]

Crisis and Continuity

The strange coincidence of formal experimentalism that appears to reflect the discontinuity of post–September 11 experience and what turns out to be a formal argument in favor of retaining a consistency of U.S.-centric values and experience in *Extremely Loud and Incredibly Close* seems less puzzling in light of the parallel coincidence of traumatic form and consistent content in the historical aftermath of the event. Just as trauma is understood to entail a sudden break with the subject that one once was, catastrophes are understood to entail a sudden break with history. They have, as a result, often provided opportunities for the institution of new forms of authority. As David Harvey has shown, many neoliberal policies were cultivated in catastrophic contexts, created or accidental, through interventions in debt crises, coups, and recessions.[18] Chicago School economist Milton Friedman's insistence in the 1982 preface to his 1962 bestseller *Capitalism and Freedom* that the kind of restructuring necessary to support the institution of free-market practices requires that the existing political system of a society be in chaos, and that "only a crisis – actual or perceived – produces real change," anticipated and undoubtedly informed the practice of seizing on moments of crisis in order to consolidate neoliberal institutions and policies.[19] Yet, as Naomi Klein shows in her work on the relationship between catastrophes and neoliberalism, the mass panic, fear, and disorientation in the post–September 11 period that contributed to the granting of unprecedented executive power to George W. Bush allowed for the extension of existing policies already working toward the privatization of previously public institutions – policies that began under the Reagan administration and extended throughout the 1980s and 1990s – rather than the qualitative transformation of the underlying logic of U.S. economic or political governance. Klein writes, "The mantra 'September 11 changed everything' neatly disguised the fact that for free-market ideologues and the corporations whose interests they serve, the only thing that changed was the ease with which they could pursue their ambitious agenda."[20] The increased privatization of the U.S. military through the use of corporate contracts, for instance – already a stated goal of Donald Rumsfeld early in the Bush presidency and highly controversial not only among the left but also among conservatives and the military itself – was accomplished largely by seizing upon the prevailing sense that the world as we once knew it was destroyed and that anything therefore was possible, even though it merely applied the same logic to the military that had been previously applied to all manner of other public services that now take for granted the presence of "public/private partnerships," including local infrastructure, social welfare services, and, of course, education.[21]

Our present moment is therefore characterized by a surprising intimacy between seemingly world-changing catastrophes and the expansion of existing political policies. This historical condition runs parallel to the intimacy we see in Foer's work between seemingly innovative formal experimentation and the creation of sentiments that support the emotional and political status quo. Alain Badiou responds to this precise situation in his 2003 manifesto and accompanying lecture, "15 Theses on Contemporary Art," which is framed as a critique of the privileging of formal innovation in the context of global capitalism. If art is to be politically effective, Badiou argues, it must first withdraw from any projects that merely "contribute to the invention of formal ways of rendering visible that which Empire already recognizes as existent."[22] This is the problem, he suggests, with the tendency to embrace the new for its own sake even as "capitalism itself is the obsession of novelty and the perpetual renovation of forms" (*CA*). Such beliefs tend to substitute formal novelty for conceptual novelty and substitute experiments in representing what exists for the creation of what does not yet exist. This confusion between saying what exists in new ways and creating what does not yet exist aesthetically finds an analog in the operations of global capitalism itself. Badiou argues that the contemporary economic order entails a paradox when it comes to the status of possibility: on the one hand, "all is possible because we have a big potency, a unity of the world … we may speak of everything"; while on the other hand, "everything is impossible, because there is nothing else to have, the empire is the only possible existence, the only political possibility" (*CA*). In constructing a particular idea of liberty envisioned as an alternative to authoritarianism, global capitalism allows for an unprecedented sense of the openness of possibility. At the same time, because there is increasingly less evidence of any significant challenge to the logic of the global capitalist system, possibilities are perhaps now more than ever entirely limited to those offered up by capitalism. Badiou emphasizes this point, maintaining that in "activities of circulation, communication, the market and so on, we have always the realization of possibilities, infinite realization of possibilities. But not creation of possibility" (*CA*).

Understanding the difference between the realization of existing possibilities and the creation of possibility is central to Badiou's contention that art might be a venue for the emergence of political change. He explains:

> Today art can only be made from the starting point of that which, as far as Empire is concerned, doesn't exist. Through its abstraction, art renders this inexistence visible. This is what governs the formal principle of every art: the effort to render visible to everyone that which for Empire (and so by extension for everyone, though from a different point of view), doesn't exist. (*CA*)

Because of its access to abstraction, to the production of invisibility as well as visibility, art today might be a privileged seat of politics, given that "politics truly means the creation of a new possibility. A new possibility of life, a new possibility of the world" (*CA*). It is important to note, however, that this political role for art has nothing to do with the articulation of a specific political position, nor does it emerge out of the specificity of a particular subject position vis-à-vis global capitalism. Badiou's contention is compelling precisely because it links aesthetics to politics through form without falling into the apolitical celebration of formal innovation for its own sake.

If *Extremely Loud and Incredibly Close* merely reinforces existing sentiments associated with the 9/11 attacks, what would it look like for a work of literature to "render visible" feelings that "as far as Empire is concerned ... don't exist?"[23] The most thorough attempt to theorize the relationship between feelings that are widely recognized and those that escape recognition has been in the work of Brian Massumi, who finds that affect abuts both sensation and emotion in a chain of physiological experiences that leads from excitation by external stimuli to a conscious experience of feeling. If aesthetic encounters produce sensory excitement, he argues, our physical registration of that sensory change is affect, and our processing of that affect into recognizable psychological categories is emotion.[24] While the question as to whether or not the physiological dynamics of feeling follow these precise stages is still being debated in neuroscientific research, Massumi's vocabulary is useful in thinking about how feeling might function differently depending on its relative ease in finding a ready category for its apprehension.[25]

Massumi argues that affective provocation is often most intense in response to aesthetic works that refuse a project of representing clear emotions because affective changes are often counterintuitively dependent on a suspension of the very formal mechanisms through which aesthetic works often best produce clearly identifiable emotions: narrative succession and the linear fixing of significance. While recognizable feelings can intensify the bodily aspects of affect, forming a loop whereby conscious feeling provokes bodily reactions that in turn incite further feelings, this very process depends on a profound excitation of the body in the first place and thus cannot occur if an emotional cue is so readily available that it jumps the bodily circuit and remains purely mental. This is one way to understand the superficiality of the affective consequences of easy sentiment in narrative art: sadness that is too readily available, too easily recognizable, is likely to register mentally (as in the thought, "I understand that this is sad") and not physically (as in bodily reactions like stomach clenching and sweaty palms).

Affective experiences that do not translate easily onto an existing emotional map therefore indicate a possibility for change – insofar as they point to bodily changes taking place outside of sensory or emotional codification – even as they are also less recognizable. But this situation causes a problem for a literary analysis of affect. How to read for the production of bodily shifts that are defined in part by their existence prior to intellectual definition? One clue we might seek out is the presence of a different set of feelings – not those directly associated with stories of suspense, tragedy, comedy, or horror, but those that point to a suspension of these traditional literary feelings, a limiting of access to recognizable emotion. The inability to place aesthetically produced affects in an emotional vocabulary, in other words, inevitably generates its own feelings: feelings of dissonance, of uneasiness, of being unsettled and not knowing precisely why. Indeed, Sianne Ngai defines these senses of disconcertedness as "ugly feelings," or aesthetic affects that hold a mirror up to the limiting and restraining forces of modern society on the individual subject. Uneasiness is the epitome of an ugly feeling, insofar as it is "a meta-feeling in which one feels confused about *what* one is feeling … the dysphoric affect of affective disorientation – of being lost on one's own 'cognitive map' of available affects."[26] But if we take Badiou and Massumi seriously this uneasiness might index not only the "suspension of action," as Ngai suggests; it also might indicate that while clear emotional, definitional, and productive possibilities are suspended, something transformative might be taking place on a bodily level: changes in physical sensation, in corporeal orientation, that cannot be mapped precisely because they are unfamiliar and new.

Uneasy Metaphors: The Case of *The Exquisite*

Where can we find the production of such unsettling affects in relation to September 11? As we have seen, the attempt to represent (or even perform the horrifying unrepresentability) of trauma in the wake of the event often slips into discourses around trauma that at best obscure the continuity of neoliberal political, economic, and social policies in the period and at worst justify continued U.S. geopolitical exploitation. Representing September 11 as narrative content is therefore a highly problematic endeavor, as doing so tends to either exceptionalize U.S. deaths or testify to the rupturing force of the event, either of which simply reinforces dominant political positions. As Badiou and Massumi suggest, however, the relationship between art and change has as much to do with aesthetic form as it does content; in this case we might turn to formal gestures that disrupt expectations, that leave us emotionally unmoored and affectively stimulated, that excite without rigidly codifying.[27]

One such gesture appears in a strange use of metaphor in Hunt's novel *The Exquisite*. Set in the immediate aftermath of the World Trade Center collapse in Lower Manhattan, the novel's version of New York is both meticulously realized in perfect detail and undeniably strange. Henry, the novel's central character, is a thief who wanders the streets of the East Village and the Lower East Side. Homeless and desperate, he becomes friends with a beautiful young woman, Tulip, and her elderly companion, Aris Kindt. When he learns that Mr. Kindt is associated with an underground business that offers fake murders to the traumatized denizens of the city, Henry becomes one of the organization's most successful "murderers." He is paid to break into apartments at the residents' requests and, with as much verisimilitude as possible, strangle, hang, stab, and otherwise "kill" his customers and leave them streaked with cow's blood, covered in ash, or simply unconscious. These New Yorkers are themselves recognizable – materialistic, hungry for experience, and ready to try anything trendy – but the ease with which their heavily satirized reactions to the events of September 11 are pushed toward such crude approximations of trauma is, at the very least, suggestive of a less pious rendering of the vicarious victims of the event than we see in many of the other novels of the period.[28] Things get even stranger when the novel switches into a second, equally credible but incompatible reality. In this version of the story, Henry is in a hospital for the criminally insane where the drone of dump trucks as they move the rubble of the World Trade Center to Staten Island's Fresh Kills Landfill is hauntingly audible. He is attended by a beautiful young doctor, Dr. Tulp (who resembles in every way Tulip from the other narrative), and is visited by the ghost of his elderly friend, Mr. Kindt. The two realities switch back and forth, never resolving into a credible single plot.

The Exquisite, like *Falling Man* and *Extremely Loud and Incredibly Close*, uses a range of experimental strategies; it employs a variety of textual tricks that highlight the novel's artificiality, it wears its intertextual play on its sleeve, and it blends a degree of realism with injections of the absurd.[29] Yet unlike the other two novels, it refuses to use these strategies in order to represent or perform emotions like grief, sadness, and fear that we tend to associate with the aftermath of the September 11 attacks. As the novel is narrated by a possibly psychotic young man who appears only marginally aware of what he refers to numbly as "the recent events downtown," we are given no tonal guide as to what to feel about the event despite its geographic proximity. And even though the story begins before September 11, the event itself is never directly figured and so, in a sense, it strangely never takes place. Instead of providing the focal point for the action of the novel it therefore seems to bleed out into an indistinct nebula of metaphors, many of them ecological rather than geopolitical.[30]

In what could be considered the central vignette of the novel, given that it includes the only use of the title of the book, Henry is visited in his hospital room by the eccentric Mr. Kindt. Mr. Kindt takes advantage of his captive audience to hold forth at length on his many obsessions, most prominent of which is the common herring, a fish that he admires for its beauty and consumes with nauseating abandon. In this scene, Mr. Kindt meditates on the "exquisite" cyclical mass birth and death of the herring:

> The female of the species lays up to fifty thousand tiny eggs, which sink to the sea bottom and develop there, the young maturing in about three years.
> And then?
> And then they rise.
> So many.
> Yes. And other fish come to feed upon them.
> Eat them all?
> Most, and in dying, it's quite lovely, they luminesce ... they give off light as they die. As they drift off through the dark waters.
> Most of them, as you say, are killed by other fish.
> By other fish, yes, Henry, which is an utterly acceptable form....
> Form of what?

> Of undoing. Of annihilation… Think of the beauty of it, Henry, he
> said. It happens over and over, and will continue to happen long after we
> are gone, long after we have laid aside our skin and bones or whatever it is
> we have here and have shuffled off. (*TE*, 197–8)

This passage clearly presents a metaphor for the collapse of the World
Trade Center, not only because the fish are figured as victims of murder (they are "eaten by other fish") but also because in a novel about
post–September 11 New York, the image of spectacular mass death insis-
tently recalls the televised collapse of the World Trade Center. The col-
umn of blue light emitted by the rising fish as they die and luminesce is
also eerily reminiscent of the columns of blue light used to memorialize
the towers on the anniversary of their destruction. Putting the tragedy in
ecological terms in this passage is, on the one hand, comforting. The ecological metaphor allows for the event to be placed within a cycle of birth
and death, generation and extinction, that touches human beings and fish
alike. Yet on the other hand, there is a disturbing aestheticization of violence at work in the image that relies on its detachment and isolation, and
this dark underside to the beauty of the image will not allow the metaphor to sit comfortably: to suggest that this mass death is beautiful, not to
mention "utterly acceptable," is highly troubling, and to cast the victims
of the attack as fish is absolutely horrific. The comparison therefore offers
a measure of comfort but contains within it disturbing ethical valences
that fray the metaphor from within, producing as much unease as calm.[31]

But precisely how is this use of ecological metaphor particular to the
contemporary context? Throughout literary history, figurations of nature
have populated texts that take up violence, death, and catastrophe.
Consider, for instance, Ernest Hemingway's paradigmatic use of nature
as metaphor in the context of a traumatic event in his short story "The
Big Two-Hearted River," which follows World War I veteran Nick Adams
as he journeys back to his boyhood home through the woods and rivers in which he spent his childhood camping and fishing. Although the
story never mentions the horrors of the war directly, it has since its publication been read as an account of the shock and healing that follows
the end of the war for many combatants.[32] To achieve its allegorical force,
the story, like *The Exquisite*, relies on a set of ecological metaphors: the
scorched land of the riverbank stands in for the devastation of Europe as
a whole ("Even the surface had been burned off the ground"), the black
bodies of the once-green grasshoppers stand in for the altered physical and
emotional states of the soldiers ("they had all turned black from living in
the burned-over land"), and the difficult-to-fish swamp stands in for the

hopeless effort to engage with the trauma of the war ("in the fast deep water, in the half-light, the fishing would be tragic").[33] The story both narrates a healing process and offers the reader a general sense of calm – generated first through the functionality of these metaphors, which are not fundamentally undermined at any point in the story by tension between their tenor and vehicle, and then through a gradual resumption of a phenomenological here-and-now account of fishing that slowly detaches from a metaphorical project and stages a reattachment to the present tense of outdoor activities. This pleasurable return to sensory experience is epitomized when, for instance, "Nick climbed out onto the meadow and stood, water running down his trousers and out of his shoes, his shoes squelchy. He went over and sat on the logs. He did not want to rush his sensations any."[34] The need for metaphor-as-cure fades as Nick forms present reattachments to the land and his body. For the reader, the metaphorical reference gives way to pleasure in a phenomenological account of a human being's encounter with nature. The affective content and force of the story is therefore relatively even and stable, as the story moves from a working metaphor to a sense of the wholeness and immediacy of ecological connection.

But Mr. Kindt's herring image does not settle as easily as Nick's meditations on the charred bodies of his once-familiar grasshoppers, in part because the danger of the aestheticization and naturalization of mass death is foregrounded in Hunt's work much more than it is in Hemingway's. By the early twenty-first century, the dangers of aestheticizing violence are well established, and formal innovation – whether through the construction of allegory or through the undoing of allegory in favor of the pared-down immediacy of writing like Hemingway's descriptions of fishing – can no longer be imagined to reconnect the body of the reader to an untainted imminence of nature or recreation. Indeed, Hemingway's work has more in common with Foer's therapeutic formal interventions than it does with Hunt's despite the ecological content that it shares with *The Exquisite*.

Furthermore, the destabilizing affective work of the ecological metaphor in *The Exquisite* is not solely dependent on the looming sense of danger and discomfort that accompanies the aestheticization of the dying herring. The uneasiness produced by the image becomes even more acute immediately following Mr. Kindt's speech, when Henry interjects with further complications:

> What about the fishing industry?
> Of course, the fishing industry. Yes, that's true, the fishing industry complicates things, and has most certainly taken a hideous toll.

A hideous toll that puts that pickled herring into your mouth every day.

Mr. Kindt smiled. Oh, I'm simply full of contradictions, Henry, he said. Aren't you?

I shrugged. I wasn't sure what I was full of. A neat scalpel trench, some metal sutures, and a lot less morphine than usual, for starters. (*TE,* 198)

Henry's riff on the phrase "full of" foregrounds the bodily resonance of the expression – recovering from prefrontal cortex surgery, he is literally full of sutures and wounds. It therefore recasts Mr. Kindt's position in relation to the aestheticized image of the herring by making his assertion that he is "full of contradictions" material and bodily. Mr. Kindt is, indeed, "full of" these contradictions, as he is literally full of pickled herring, whose natural state he worships, but whose peril he continues to ensure with his support of damaging fishing practices. This passage interrupts both the perfect aestheticization of the death of the herring and the suggestion that such a mass death is part of the natural order of things by reinserting the human harvesting and processing of fish as commodities into the ecological system. The beauty and isolation of the image is, then, entirely disrupted. No longer do the dying herring compose a perfect tower of glowing blue and silver; now the scene is marred by the inevitable presence of fishing boats, sonar, drift nets, and, of course, Mr. Kindt himself, perhaps with his teeth violently sunk into the belly of a luminescent fish. This interruption of the spectacle of ecological catastrophe with a more banal, but much more crushing invocation of a socially produced ecological disaster brought by human consumption might leave us, like Henry, wondering exactly what we are "full of" these days.

Henry's response to Mr. Kindt drives what was already a tense metaphor, pregnant with the contradictions and risks of aestheticizing violence, toward a fracturing confrontation with the inexplicable complexity of human engagement with nature. For the reader of *The Exquisite,* the ecological contact invoked in Henry's rejoinder to Mr. Kindt involves as much implication, guilt, and confusion as it does peace, and this heightened sense of embeddedness in global systems of exploitation inevitably reflects back on the geopolitical tenor of the original metaphor. Henry's follow-up questions throw us into an affective soup by highlighting the perpetual presence of a web of global technologies around consumption and exploitation.[35] In this sense, the altered image offers a perspective that we might set in opposition to that of Foer's exceptionalism. Confronted with the inevitability of human participation in the death of the fish once Henry brings up the fishing industry, there is no easy way to imagine that the problem might be solved for any given "we" without touching on much larger ecological and economic systems.

Yet try as we might, it is impossible to read Henry's amendment to Mr. Kindt's original vision as either part of a consistent metaphor or a return to a less complicated physical engagement with the natural; there is no precise perspective upon the World Trade Center collapse that provides an analog to Henry's invocation of the fishing industry in relation to the lifecycle of the herring and no way to connect viscerally and immediately with the mind-boggling span of global commercial fishing practices. In other words, what starts out as a metaphor for the attacks (albeit a problematic one) is interrupted; it ends up producing no traceable argument but merely a feeling that resembles Henry's sensation of being "full of" something without quite knowing what one is full of. The image's ultimate indeterminacy continues to resonate with the September 11 context of the novel, but it does so in a way that registers the impossibility of fully feeling, let alone articulating, what it is that one's body experiences when confronted by the need to envision the embeddedness of the catastrophe in a broader context. *These deaths, too, are connected to a highly coordinated network of exploitation and consumption*, the image seems to whisper. But we as readers are left in a suspended state, unable to volunteer, as Henry does, a name for that missing element in the picture. The corresponding term for "the fishing industry" in the September 11 context remains indiscernibly shrouded despite the eerie sense that it might be just beyond our grasp.

The metaphorical contact initiated in the novel between the ecological and the geopolitical in relation to the September 11 events emphasizes that what cannot be comprehended in this instance is a result of the entanglement of the event in a network of global relationships, rather than the externality of the traumatic event. The undermining of any clear isolated view of a catastrophe that occurs in this passage and elsewhere in the novel suggests that what bursts forth in the events of September 11 cannot be imagined to be external, but must be conceived of, in its incomprehensibility, as part of a complex system of interactions. What is unrepresentable in September 11 fiction is therefore not the trauma itself, but the intricacy of the web from which it emerges and that it causes to vibrate in turn.[36] The affective consequences of this sense of entanglement do not match up with the emotions we have come to expect from representations of September 11 and its aftermath. Indeed, faced with the numb prose of *The Exquisite*, these metaphorical confrontations with September 11 are likely to produce merely a vague sense of uneasiness, of mild distress, of dissonance, affects that are at once weaker than traumatic shock and possibly more indicative of qualitative change. As Massumi points out, although "structure is the place where nothing ever happens ... in which all eventual permutations are prefigured in a self-consistent set of invariant generative rules," the suspension of those structures – even those that are necessary for feelings to register as conscious emotions with clear objects and causes – might lead to a situation where we could find "a tinge of the unexpected, the lateral, the unmotivated ... a change in the rules."[37]

Perhaps, then, what we are full of when faced with this interrupted metaphor is, at last, something closer to the "organic shrapnel" to which Keith in *Falling Man* is inexplicably immune. The suspicion that one is full of something contradictory that involves death, consumption, spectacle, and social entanglement might provide the smallest feeling of uneasiness that, like the bit of human tissue or bone that can be lodged in a survivor's skin, could slowly grow and make its presence known, not through argument or even a clearly defined emotion, but through a bodily disruption of expectations, a palpable insistence that we are more permeable to others than we might think, an unmistakable bump under the skin that could hold the promise of a different mode of interaction with the social and political circumstances of our contemporary moment.

3

Reading Like an Entrepreneur: Neoliberal Agency and Textual Systems

In his essay "Cognitive Mapping," Fredric Jameson establishes one of the most enduring theories of the political importance of art. He argues that we have reached a point in the historical development of capitalism where, because of the distance between the limited perspective of the individual on the one hand and the dispersed social and geographic sites of capital on the other, "there comes into being ... a situation in which we can say that if individual experience is authentic, then it cannot be true; and that if a scientific or cognitive model of the same content is true, then it escapes individual experience."[1] In this view, the totality of capital extends so far beyond the capacity of any individual to experience it directly that its registration requires some form of representation or figuration that will allow the individual to comprehend the totality to a useful enough degree to act productively within it. This is particularly crucial because "the incapacity to map socially is as crippling to political experience as the analogous incapacity to map spatially is for urban experience."[2] Without the capacity to thoroughly map the global social system, individuals have no way to gain agency in relation to those systems. They remain lost, powerless, and adrift in the disorienting morass of late capitalism.

Confronted with this dilemma, Jameson turns to aesthetics. Works of art, he suggests, can uniquely figure relationships and connections beyond the perceptive capacities of any individual. They can therefore provide opportunities for "cognitive mapping," or the means through which it might be possible to conceive of the stultifying complexity of the social relations that constitute global capitalism.[3] Cognitive mapping, in Jameson's view, allows individuals the opportunity to locate themselves in the capitalist system and reclaim agency in relation to it. This occurs through the process of critical engagement initiated when an artwork invites its audience to examine the contours of the social system it represents.

Many affective approaches in literary studies echo this aspiration by expanding the assumptions that underpin cognitive mapping to affective experience.[4] Most explicit of these is Jonathan Flatley's work, *Affective Mapping*. Whereas cognitive mapping occurs through formal innovations that allow readers to conceive of the complexity of capital flows and the despatialized world of finance, affective mapping contextualizes the affective experiences of the reader within a larger social framework. Flatley explains:

> Such a representation is accomplished by way of a self-estrangement that allows one to see oneself in relation to one's affective environment in its historicity, in relation to the relevant social-political anchors or landmarks in that environment, and to see the others who inhabit this landscape with one. [Texts] function as affective maps to the extent that they work as machines of *self-estrangement* ... making one's emotional life – one's range of moods, set of structures of feeling, and collection of affective attachments – appear weird, surprising, unusual, and thus capable of a new kind of recognition, interest, and analysis.[5]

Once a reader recognizes what appears to be her own private emotions as historical, the argument goes, she might not be as paralyzed by them and thus can "figure out how to negotiate the new affective terrain, to exert some agency in it."[6]

This model of how literature works both politically and affectively, however, comes under stress in the context of neoliberalism, where subjects are encouraged to act as rational agents in all spheres of life. There are disorienting aspects of neoliberalism, to be sure, but neoliberal subjects are also constantly provided with forms of location, transparency, and information, and are expected to use the agency these experiences offer in order to make smart entrepreneurial decisions. Neoliberalism therefore entails the cultivation of subjects who can locate themselves effectively within certain situations, who can take stock of the rules and operating functions of a given system, and who can productively claim agency in relation to that system.

The situation is further complicated by the fact that these situations of apparent free choice always exist within a limited terrain: we can choose among three different private insurers; six different charter schools; eighteen different espresso drinks; four different student loan providers; organic bananas or free trade; natural gas or oil; twelve blockbuster films. And it is often the thrall of emotional experience that allows these choices to appear free: the pleasure of a trip down the aisles of Whole Foods; the comfort of a latte; the satisfaction of making a smart life decision. As a result, works of art that make readers feel as if they are in a position of agency in relation to the textual systems they produce look less like opportunities for the cultivation of political action and more like reverberations of neoliberalism's tendency to mobilize feelings in order to cultivate a particular sense of the self as a free, rational agent.

In light of this tension between the need for forms of mapping to penetrate the obscurities of global capitalism and the possibility that some forms of mapping merely reproduce feelings that reinforce neoliberal norms and expectations, this chapter turns to two works of contemporary literature that self-consciously expose the structures of their own textual systems to readers, offering unusual access to their formal mechanisms. Dave Eggers's *A Heartbreaking Work of Staggering Genius* appears to offer a radical form of agency to its readers through its satirical encyclopedic disclaimers and meta-explanations. These devices seem to place readers on an equal footing with the writer, letting them in on the narrative choices driving the book and allowing them to see through its many sentimental layers down to its formal scaffolding. Yet Eggers's work is ultimately so emotionally absorptive that it limits the capacity of the reader to engage with it as a critical agent regardless of the degree to which its formal instruments are exposed. The work therefore mirrors the neoliberal dynamics of agency by appearing to offer freedom from the constraints of various systems on the one hand while regulating individual freedom by offering restricted means for its expression on the other.

Ben Marcus's *The Age of Wire and String*, however, demonstrates that not all gestures toward the unmasking of textual systems lead to the belief that readers are or should be in control of their textual experiences. Marcus's work, a self-proclaimed "catalog of a culture," has a highly schematic and seemingly transparent structure, but it also emphasizes the fact that readers will never fully understand its world because of the multiple and conflicting relationships it draws among language, objects, and other animate and inanimate things. Marcus's work suggests that the affective experience of readerly difficulty can disrupt a sense of easy agency without lulling readers away from rigorous engagement with the structure of a text. As I argue at the end of this chapter by turning to the work of Bruno Latour, this puts Marcus's work in line with contemporary efforts to imagine alternatives to practices of critique that decenter the agency of the critic while retaining a commitment to the careful representation of the many systems, organic and inorganic, that both restrain and enable human activity.

Neoliberal Agents

The belief that individuals are better off when they are able to thoroughly locate themselves within a system and subsequently assert themselves within that system stems from the liberal conception of agency, which has provided the basis for Western political concepts of autonomy and freedom since at least the seventeenth century.[7] Agency, in the liberal paradigm, tends to be valued as a good in and of itself, regardless of the intention or outcome of its expression. As Saba Mahmood explains in *Politics of Piety*, liberalism's innovation is not the notion of self-realization, as we might be inclined to think. Self-realization exists within a range of preliberal and antiliberal political and religious practices, many of which see the self as most thoroughly actualized through submission to extreme forms of ritual and constraint. Rather, liberalism's unique contribution is in its inexorable linking of "the notion of self-realization with individual autonomy."[8] In its liberal incarnation, what constitutes the actualization of the self is constrained to what the self is able to achieve independently. Mahmood argues that this emphasis on independent agency prevents liberal subjects from recognizing modes of self-transformation that do not see independent action as essential to liberation; her particular case study is the women's mosque movement in Cairo, where practices that look like forms of submission to domination, like gender-segregation and veiling, provide opportunities for women to deepen their religious experiences. In contrast to those traditions, within the liberal context, "in order for an individual to be free, her actions *must* be the consequence of her 'own will' rather than of custom, tradition, or social coercion."[9] This focus is so primary that it transcends even questions of content. Mahmood points out that, paradoxically, "freedom, in this formulation, consists in the ability to autonomously 'choose' one's desires no matter how illiberal they may be."[10] In the liberal model, servitude can be an expression of agency if the pursuit of servitude follows the form of autonomous expression, while forms of self-determination that rely on the abdication of autonomy are not counted as forms of agency and therefore look to the liberal subject to be unfree.

In John Locke's conception of innate human freedom, the formation of communities and political societies requires precisely this kind of elective giving over of some portion of individual autonomy. Locke writes:

> Men being, as has been said, by nature, all free, equal, and independent, no one can be put out of this estate, and subjected to the political power of

another, without his own consent. The only way whereby any one divests himself of his natural liberty, and puts on the bonds of civil society, is by agreeing with other men to join and unite into a community for their comfortable, safe, and peaceable living one amongst another, in a secure enjoyment of their properties, and a greater security against any, that are not of it.[11]

The restrictions of civil society, in this view, are not at odds with the notion of the essentially free subject; they are understood to be evidence of the free exercise of individual agency in the form of the social contract. Embedded within the liberal notion of agency and civil society is the belief that individual autonomy precedes association. Interconnection is a voluntary state of affairs that is understood to be the consequence of individually motivated action. Nevertheless, certain forms of association – religious, civil, and social – are stable enough that this prehistory of individual volition remains in the liberal age a mythical foundation for social institutions. In practical terms, individuals act as if these systems and the restrictions they entail are natural and inevitable. The lived experience of liberalism is therefore one of compromise between relative freedom and relative restriction.

The primary shift that occurs between liberalism and neoliberalism is the withering of these stable forms of association and the subsequent increased emphasis on the autonomous agency of the individual in producing a successful self. The notion of the priority of the individual remains from the liberal model, but forms of life that were not previously understood to function on the model of the market are organized through a market-based rationality. As a result of the dissolution of civil society and other forms of collective activity that were understood to arise out of a notion of public well-being and were therefore once seen as superseding the liberal good of individual agency, not only are subjects understood to be fundamentally free and secondarily associational but also stable forms of association are increasingly seen as unnecessary or even prohibitive to the achievement of individual freedom. Each individual is imagined to be fundamentally free of social constraint from the start of her own lifetime and, as a result, is responsible for her own safety, happiness, and well-being.

Paradoxically, one consequence of this shift is that the exercise of individual freedom becomes a requirement that the subject is compelled to fulfill. As Steven Shaviro explains, under neoliberalism "the objective function of the market is that it 'forces us to be free,' forces us to behave 'rationally' and 'efficiently,' forces us to act concertedly in our own individual interests."[12] In seeing freedom as the result of force, Shaviro echoes Marx's ironic use of the word "free" in his discussion of primitive accumulation in *Capital*. Marx argues that with the emergence of capitalism, serfs were freed from slavery only to be "freed" from their means of subsistence and therefore forced to sell their labor on the open market. Marx emphasizes the violence of this enforced freedom: "These newly freed men became sellers of themselves," he writes, "only after they had been robbed of all their own means of production, and all the guarantees of existence afforded by the old feudal arrangements. And this history, the history of their expropriation, is written in the annals of mankind in letters of blood and fire."[13]

Both of these accounts see privileging freedom as, paradoxically, a justification for violence, control, and domination. Yet Shaviro's observation that "no measure of surveillance, and no form of education or propaganda has been able to constrain human freedom as comprehensively – or as invisibly – as the neoliberal market has done" should cause us to ask how the tactical deployment of freedom as a form of control might differ from other forms of force and other forms of ideology.[14] What is it that makes this form of control so resilient? In David Harvey's view, the power of the concept of freedom is not, as Shaviro argues, primarily a result of the violence of the compulsion behind it but more generally a result of its ideological seductiveness, its use as a "conceptual apparatus ... that appeals to our intuitions and instincts."[15] The notion of freedom is particularly appealing, Harvey claims, because it has personal significance "to anyone who values the ability to make decisions for themselves," which, given the cultural value of agency with which most Western subjects were raised, describes most U.S. citizens.[16] But Harvey's argument belies another reason for the force with which neoliberal concepts of freedom have managed to push through competing forms of ideology and power. His implication that the notion of freedom attaches to activities that are not explicitly political or social – "decisions for [oneself]" could mean anything from choosing what to wear on a given morning to choosing which pasta dish one will order at a restaurant – demonstrates how the force of the concept of freedom rests not only on forms of economic compulsion or the concept's ideological power but also on its intimate relationship to the way we interpret the causes of our everyday actions. Most of us are accustomed to believing that when we decide to sit down or stand up, we are willing ourselves to do so freely. The concept of freedom is so compelling, then, in part because of its attachment to a range of everyday bodily attitudes that are seen as expressions of agency.[17] Nearly any action that appears to be the result of individual motivation – such as getting out of bed in the morning, going to the gym, or deciding what to do in the evening – can be seen as an expression of freedom and therefore an intensification of a commitment to freedom in a kind of affective-ideological feedback loop. The more we act "freely," in other words, the more we see freedom as the very foundation of our actions. Pursuing individual freedom therefore does not merely appeal to our instincts; it has itself become an instinct, one that has been cultivated by the cultural prevalence of liberal concepts of the self and is therefore easily appropriated into the mechanisms of neoliberalization.[18]

Of course, the neoliberal paradigm does not, in fact, allow for absolute individual freedom. Neoliberal society, even in its ideal form, is not the Lockean state of nature, no matter how much its proponents would like to portray it as such. It is a system characterized by rigorous regulation and governmental intervention on the level of monetary policy and highly restricted fields of choice on the level of daily experience. Wendy Brown reminds us that, far from being the achievement of laissez-faire capitalism, neoliberalism requires strong state intervention at all times:

> Neoliberalism does not conceive of either the market itself or rational economic behavior as purely natural. Both are constructed – organized by law and political institutions, and requiring political intervention and orchestration. Far from flourishing when left alone, the economy must be directed, buttressed, and protected by law and policy as well as by the dissemination of social norms designed to facilitate competition, free trade, and rational economic action on the part of every member and institution of society.[19]

In order to function, neoliberalism requires subjects prepared to make individual choices. And this requires the dissemination of certain kinds of strategic transparency. In order to make choices, neoliberal subjects are accustomed to having easy access to prices of goods across a wide range of vendors, ratings of service providers, and data on different careers and relative earning capacities. This emphasis on transparency and choice is not limited to economic matters. Neoliberal subjects also expect to be able to make educational choices based on data on different careers and their earning potential, health choices based on the latest scientific studies, and lifestyle choices based on easily accessible demographic information.

Yet alongside these transparencies, neoliberalism relies on key forms of opacity when it comes to the systems that produce such limited choices. We may be able to choose very effectively among a range of smartphones, for instance, based on information about their features and design, but it is extremely difficult to get information on the manufacturers of the smartphones or what happens to the products after we discard them. The same goes for financial products generally; it is possible for consumers to have a strong sense of choice and transparency in their selections of mutual funds without having the ability to trace the vast number of complex transactions that underpin these products. And we see this perhaps most radically in the meat industry, where despite labeling efforts and the increased presence of organic and free-range meats, so-called ag-gag laws prohibit photographing feed lots and other agricultural facilities in many states. We are therefore in a peculiar situation, in our neoliberal moment. We are animated toward free activity in a field that appears to be transparent, reliable, and mappable while, at the same time, that mappable field is surrounded by unknowns, barriers, and obscurity. Thus the choices we are encouraged to make exist within a restricted set of options, all of which fundamentally run in accord with the foundations of the neoliberal state.

Choose Your Own Adventure: The Case of *A Heartbreaking Work of Staggering Genius*

In this context, a work like Dave Eggers's *A Heartbreaking Work of Staggering Genius* can be read as a fascinating and troubling response to neoliberal concepts of agency. Eggers's book is a hybrid work of autobiography and fiction, written and published after the memoir boom of the 1980s and 1990s, which explicitly addresses the problems with memoir and associated forms of "real life" culture that, by the time of the work's publication, had become central to popular culture with the proliferation of reality television shows. The book is highly self-referential and self-problematizing, and it seems to do the work of demystification for its imagined critic, offering tens of pages of paratextual information before the narrative starts. It also features a series of interventions within the text where characters suddenly serve as fictional interlocutors, criticizing the author for his omissions, simplifications, and ethical missteps.[20] Yet despite the cynicism that seems to motivate these devices, the book is also a very sad, direct account of Eggers's loss of his parents within five weeks of one another and his struggle to care for his seven-year-old younger brother, Toph, while only in his early twenties himself. Indeed, the surprise of the book is that, in spite of its irony, it turns out to be a genuinely heartbreaking work. The novel therefore formally mirrors the neoliberal model of agency, making gestures toward readerly choice in the form of self-awareness and paratextual devices, while reserving for itself an opaque and propulsive force of necessity that overrides those apparent transparencies. Eggers's work puts readers in an odd emotional position, one in which they are invited to take a stance of reasoned distance, of awareness of the structure of things, and yet at the same time are emotionally encouraged to choose absorption and selective blindness. The inevitability with which this structure unfolds, along with its apparent naturalness, offers an affective and aesthetic analog to the neoliberal tendency to value apparent choice and consent that mask systemic forms of absorption of subjects who feel themselves to be free.

A Heartbreaking Work of Staggering Genius begins with more than forty pages of disclaimers, summaries, caveats, and metadiscourse on the memoir. Sidonie Smith and Julia Watson describe these sections as "elaborate foreplay" but they could just as easily be read as the primary intervention of the book.[21] The book begins with a page titled "RULES AND SUGGESTIONS FOR ENJOYMENT OF THIS BOOK," which lists six pieces of advice for the prospective reader of the text. These include the suggestions that "many of you might want to skip much of the middle, namely pages 342–481"; "you can also skip the table of contents, if you're short on time"; and "the first three or four chapters are all some of you might want to bother with."[22] There are no actual "rules" on the page, and the phrasing of the suggestions often parodies the language of neoliberal transparency and individual choice.[23] For instance:

1. There is no overwhelming need to read the preface. Really. It exists mostly for the author, and those who, after finishing the rest of the book, have for some reason found themselves stuck with nothing else to read. If you have already read the preface, and wish you had not, we apologize. We should have told you sooner.

2. There is also no overarching need to read the acknowledgments section. Many early readers of this book suggested its curtailment or removal, but they were defied. Still, it is not necessary to the plot in any major way, so, as with the preface, if you have already read the acknowledgments section, and wish you had not, again, we apologize. (*HW*, "Rules and Suggestions")

"We should have told you sooner" is, of course, a joke, given that the list is posted on the very first page of the book, but it is a joke that, albeit satirically, registers the social expectation that it is the author's responsibility to ensure the happiness and enjoyment of the reader. This and other apologies reflect an ethos of "the customer is always right," where the role of the customer is seamlessly integrated into the role of the reader. And while the page is a satire of this tendency to serve the reader, it is also accurate. It is true, for instance, that the acknowledgments are not necessary to the plot in any way, that the first three or four chapters could work as a set piece of a "nice novella sort of length," and that "pages 342–481 … concern the lives of people in their early twenties" (*HW*, "Rules and Suggestions"). One enters the book laughing but also genuinely oriented toward the form of the book to follow. As with much of the rest of the work, jokes, satire, and distance do not act as obstructions to the communication of real information or emotional authenticity; indeed, the performed failure of these modes seems to emphasize the authentic content of the narrative, which appears to push through in spite of all odds.[24]

This paradoxical pairing of distanced satire with sincere gestures toward narrative orientation exists in much of the remaining prefatory material. This includes the preface, which makes it clear from the start that "many parts" of the work "have been fictionalized in varying degrees, for varying purposes" (*HW*, "Preface") and then outlines each of those parts, degrees, and purposes in detail; and also a section of the acknowledgments, where the author lists "the major themes of this book" including, of course, "c) THE PAINFULLY, ENDLESSLY SELF-CONSCIOUS BOOK ASPECT," which, paradoxically, is explained not as a form of layered distancing but as a symptom of emotional immediacy. Eggers explains:

> The author doesn't have the energy or, more important, skill, to fib about this being anything other than him telling you things, and is not a good enough liar to do it in any competently sublimated narrative way. At the same time, he will be clear and up-front about this being a self-conscious memoir, which you may come to appreciate, and which is the next theme: C.2) THE KNOWINGNESS ABOUT THE BOOK'S SELF CONSCIOUS-NESS ASPECT." (*HW*, "Acknowledgments")

While the first explanation of self-consciousness diagnoses it as a natural condition of the author's inability to be dishonest and uses it as an occasion to make a promise of clarity and honesty, the explanation of this next theme is precisely the opposite. Eggers writes that

> the gimmickry is simply a device, a defense, to obscure the black, blinding, murderous rage and sorrow at the core of this whole story, which is both too black and blinding to look at – avert … your … eyes! – but nevertheless useful, at least to the author, even in caricatured or condensed form, because telling as many people as possible about it helps. (*HW*, "Acknowledgments")

In a circular way, the self-consciousness of the work is used as evidence for the guilelessness of the author and the authenticity of the author's pain.

This leads to a counterintuitive reversal from the typical reading of such techniques that sees them as evidence of coldness and the priority of style over authentic substance. Here techniques associated with postmodernism are used against postmodernist goals – to encourage readerly identification, to build an alliance with the reader, and to suggest that the author is a recognizable, locatable, trustworthy individual.[25]

This pairing of self-referential distance with promises of emotional sincerity leads to a situation where a reader is likely to feel as if they are in a transparent field in which they have a choice of what to read, what to believe, and how to respond. This sense is augmented by moments in the text when characters themselves talk back to Eggers. This happens for the first time in the book during an early chronicle of Eggers's life with Toph after the loss of their parents. As he puts his brother to bed after a long day, what seems like a standard tucking-into-bed scene turns strange as Toph weighs in on the lack of plausibility of the chapter that precedes the scene:

> "The half day at school, then the basketball, and then dinner, and the open house, and then ice cream, and a movie – I mean, it was almost as if … a number of days had been spliced together to quickly paint a picture of an entire period of time, to create a whole-seeming idea of how we are living, without having to stoop (or rise) to actually pacing the story out."
> "What are you getting at?"
> "No, I think it's good, it's fine. Not entirely believable, but it works fine, in general. It's fine."
> "Listen, you, we've had plenty of days like this, and many that were much more complicated.... Really, if anything, this is a much more pedestrian day than most. This is just a caricature, this, the skeleton of experience – I mean, you know this is just one slivery, wafer-thin slice. To adequately relate even five minutes of internal thought-making would take forever – It's maddening, actually, when you sit down, as I will once I put you to bed, to try to render something like this, a time or place, and ending up with only this kind of feebleness – one, two dimensions of twenty."
> (*HW*, 193–4)

The conversation that follows sees Toph interrogating Eggers's reasons for telling the story the way he does and his psychological and creative limitations. It resolves with the brothers making an uneasy truce and returning to the project of getting ready for bed. This vehicle functions similarly to the paratextual material, distancing the reader insofar as it exposes the formal choices and manipulations that provide the basic structure of the narrative. Yet these scenes do not ultimately disrupt the sense of authentic emotional connection and confession that the narrative overwhelmingly relies on, as they act as occasions for Eggers to reveal the even more complex emotional state his compositional practices reflect.

The device also serves potentially skeptical readers, who, represented by Eggers's characters, are able to see their concerns voiced and have them addressed. While characters are usually thought of as inert puppets animated by their author, in *A Heartbreaking Work of Staggering Genius*, they confront their author and dispute his methods. The result is a radically open, highly democratic textual field, which elides the age-old problem of authorial power and readerly passivity by allowing everyone to enter into the story armed with information, aware of the ways they are to be manipulated, and able to hear their objections sounded. In other words, *A Heartbreaking Work of Staggering Genius* appears to offer readers a degree of agency in relation to itself that is unprecedented except among more obvious departures from traditional narrative form like the Choose Your Own Adventure series of gamebooks or hypertext narratives.[26] But while this is true on an epistemological level – readers enter the text with almost total knowledge of what they will encounter and how – it is not necessarily true on an affective level. Despite all of the warnings, caveats, disputes, and navel-gazing jokes, *A Heartbreaking Work* remains emotionally captivating. While readers are invited to skip entire sections, or to agree with characters who see the form of the work as overly precious, in all likelihood most do not. This is because readers are likely to attach to the sentiments that lie beneath these devices – feelings of loss, concern, hope, and frustration – all the more so because they feel as if they have a choice in the matter. As Dan Savage describes it:

> What's most amazing about Mr. Eggers' very fine new book … is how thoroughly Mr. Eggers' self-deprecating tone and narrative tricks suck the reader in. Mr. Eggers allows us to remain as wary of cheap sentiment as he himself clearly is, paying us the compliment of not presuming we'll weep on cue, like Oprah's studio audience. Mr. Eggers doesn't rely on the facts of his family tragedy or on his readers' too-often-taken-for-granted empathy. He dares to entertain us, and then, once we've let our guard down, his very fine new book breaks our motherfucking hearts.[27]

This makes for an extraordinary reading experience, which generates feelings all the more genuine because they seem voluntary. But this only works because the audience for this book prefers not to "weep on cue," demands to be entertained, and is more able to feel given the sense that they do so by choice.

It is as if *A Heartbreaking Work of Staggering Genius* was written specifically for an audience affectively shaped under a neoliberal dominant, and indeed it was. Eggers uses terms to describe his generation that defy common interpretations of "Generation X" and instead emphasize their interest in marrying social consciousness with an entrepreneurial spirit:

> We find strength in people doing things we find worthwhile, heroic, and who are getting great press for doing such things.... We love people like this, who are starting massive organizations, trying new approaches to age-old problems, and getting the word out about it, with great PR, terrific publicity photos, available in black and white or color transparency. (*HW*, 267)

This notion that an easy compromise can be achieved between entrepreneurialism and service to one's community follows a similar logic as the neoliberal notion that a compromise can be achieved between individual freedom and obedience to the mechanisms of global capitalism. Books such as *A Heartbreaking Work* are able to function as they do because they are so sensitively aimed at the affective needs of a new generation of young adults who were largely raised under neoliberal assumptions. This does not mean that *A Heartbreaking Work* is a bad book, but that the pleasure it produces is symptomatic of how comfortably it sits with neoliberal emotional norms, providing a strong sense of readerly orientation that allows the experience of sentimental feelings to seem as if they easily coincide with the individual pursuit of autonomy.

Making the Familiar Strange: The Case of *The Age of Wire and String*

The apparent agency produced by the paratextual material of *A Heartbreaking Work of Staggering Genius* reflects the neoliberal celebration of choice, giving readers a sense of freedom while constraining that freedom through the production of sentimental attachment. But not all attempts to expose the structures of textual systems lead to this feeling. Ben Marcus's first book-length work of fiction, *The Age of Wire and String*, performs the capacity of narratives to trace social and ecological relationships while at the same time intensifying a sense of embeddedness within those relationships. The book fashions itself as a catalog of a fictional time and place (called "The Age of Wire and String"), with section headings indicating the book's explication of fundamental cultural categories that include "God," "Food," "Animal," "Persons," and "The Society." "There is no larger task than that of cataloging a culture," the book states in its first section, "Argument," appearing to suggest that the collection will offer a clear mapping of its place and age.[28] Yet this assertion is immediately followed by a caveat:

> A catalog of poses and motions produced from within a culture may read … like a form of special pleading, or, at the very least, like a product that must be ravaged of bias by scholars prepared to act as objective witnesses. It has, however, been demonstrated … that the outer gaze alters the inner thing, that by looking at an object we destroy it with our desire, that for accurate vision to occur the thing must be trained to see itself, or otherwise perish in blindness, flawed.…
>
> Let this rather be the first of many forays into the mysteries, as here disclosed but not destroyed. For it is in these things that we are most lost, as it is in these things alone that we must better be hidden. (*AWS*, 3–4)

From the start, the work calls into question the notion that the task of "cataloging a culture" means to clarify, present an objective map, or orient readers definitively. Indeed, the production of such an effect is seen as an act of "ravaging" that can only be accomplished by "scholars prepared to act as objective witnesses," not those who produce the catalog itself. Instead, the catalog is understood to enact an attitude, "a form of special pleading"; a practice of training a culture "to see itself"; and an act of disclosure as opposed to destruction, committed to the ambivalent need for mysteries to both remain hidden and become self-conscious. From the start, the catalog is presented not as a form of direct access to agency vis-à-vis a thorough understanding of society but rather as a form of tense reckoning with the degree to which societies tend to be invisible to themselves. *The Age of Wire and String* suggests that there is reason to hover within that tension rather than attempting to resolve it toward action, in part because training a thing to see itself thoroughly cannot be accomplished merely by turning that thing into an object of reasoned study; it involves the thoroughgoing transformation of the thing itself.

The sections that follow "Argument" each consist of a series of stories followed by a brief glossary of terms. The defined terms range from the familiar ("Sadness," "Salt," "Jennifer," "Rain") to the unusual ("Bird Seven," "God-Burning System," "Beef Seeds," "Drowning Method"). Yet the definitions of "familiar" and "unfamiliar" terms both undermine common meanings of familiar words and remain uncannily attached to those meanings. For instance, the entry on "Eating" reads:

> 1. Activity of archaic devotion in which objects such as the father's garment are placed inside the body and worshiped. 2. The act or technique of rescuing items from under the light and placing them within. Once inside the cavity, the item is permanently inscribed with the resolutions of that body

and can therefore be considered an ally of the person. 3. Dying. Since the first act of the body is to produce its own demise, eating can be considered an acceleration of this process. Morsels and small golden breads enter the mouth from without to enhance the motions and stillnesses, boost the tones and silences. These are items which bring forth instructions from the larger society to the place of darkness and unknowing: the sticky core, the area within, the bone. 4. Chewing or imbibing elements that have escaped from the member or person into various arenas and fields. (*AWS*, 41–2)

Each of these definitions is consistent in some way with what we understand eating to be: a ceremonial act, a form of consumption and self-expansion, an aid to life processes that will ultimately result in death, and the incorporation of materials that can be understood to be both organically of the same material as the eater and separate from him. Yet in no way does the definition seem consistent with the operative definitions of the word "eating" in contemporary U.S. culture. A similar paradox occurs with "Sadness," which is defined as "the first powder to be abided upon waking. It may reside in tools or garments and can be eradicated with more of itself, in which case the face results as a placid system coursing with water, heaving" (*AWS*, 13). Clearly a description of the familiar notion of crying as a cure for sadness, this definition nevertheless is undeniably strange. In both cases, it is as if elemental human experiences are at the same time illuminated and obscured, explained and therefore brought closer and made strange – and therefore taken farther away.[29] The words are not entirely redefined to the point where a reader can merely replace her existing understanding of a word with a different meaning, nor are the words consistent with their familiar definitions in such a way that would allow a reader to read as she normally would.

This definitional tension results in a complex reading experience, where encountering familiar words within the forty-one vignettes that comprise *The Age of Wire and String* constantly seems to stretch language beyond itself. As the definitions of terms often appear after their use in the stories, there is always a question as to whether a given word means what a reader believes it to mean or whether it will later be revealed to mean something else. The stories themselves often exert this kind of pressure on common understandings of objects and processes, as in an early story, "Sky Destroys Dog," which outlines the history of "air days." These are "days of foodless observance to sanctify the season of Charles, which was notable for its storms of airlessness and heavy frontals near the north that caused all but the dogs to retreat to the air hostels" (*AWS*, 9). In a single page of text, the story describes how these "air days" commemorate a time in which "difficulties with dog populations" generated a series of "mass suffocation[s]" as a result of the people "breaking their fasts before the season of Charles had restored air to their homes, when the storm dogs still stalked the houses, breathing up the airless wind and eating the air and rain, praying to Charles that the people would not return" (ibid.). The basic plot of the story is comprehensible, even with common understandings of the words that comprise it intact: it is basically clear that the story outlines a holiday that commemorates a mass death from suffocation that had something to do with dogs taking up too much air and people quitting a fast too soon. But even this crude understanding of the story begins to push against typical ways of understanding the relationships among weather, eating, animals, and humans. Why does quitting a fast leave one vulnerable to suffocation? How is it that an animal could literally eat up all of the air in an environment? How is an "airless wind" possible? An easy recourse might be to chalk it all up to the quirkiness of Marcus's universe, a speculative version of our reality where such things happen. But this reading is complicated by the fact that in the story we are told that these events took place in recognizable places during actual historical time, in "Ohio (1973)" and "Buffalo and Schenectady (1980–1982)" (ibid.). The world described is therefore both our world and not our world, and the laws of that world are both within the realm of legibility for us and impossibly outside of our basic understandings of how our world works.

It only makes things more complicated when we learn later in the text that "Ohio" is defined as follows:

> The house, be it built or crushed. It is a wooden composition affixed with stones and glass, locks, cavities, the person. There will be food in it, rugs will warm the floor. There will never be a clear idea of Ohio, although its wood will be stripped and shined, its glass polished with light, its holes properly cleared, in order that the member inside might view what is without – the empty field, the road, the person moving forward or standing still, wishing the Ohio was near. (*AWS*, 61)

This definition casts a different reading back on the earlier story, suggesting that the airlessness experienced in Ohio could be understood not as a statewide epidemic but as a plague on a single house. Around the same point in the text, we also get the definition of "eating," which gives a more layered understanding of how the dogs could be understood to eat air and rain. Even "rain" itself is defined in a subsequent section, not as water but as a "hard, shiny silver object, divided into knives and used for cutting procedures" (*AWS*, 95).

The task of tracing each and every redefined term in each and every story in *The Age of Wire and String* is next to impossible, and even if one embarked on such a project, the results would not give much clarity. In the most fundamental sense, it does not change the overarching effect of "Sky Destroys Dog" to know the text's definitions of Ohio, eating, or rain. These definitions would not make more sense of the story; they are not necessary to its general plot. But the existence of these definitions does heighten the general sense that one never quite knows entirely what is going on in any of these stories. As D. W. Daniels argues in his review of *The Age of Wire and String*, this disorientation is central to the work's power. "It is this inability to control, to have power over, to be master of the text," he writes, "that creates the longing to enter and re-enter this particular universe of worlds."[30]

This sense of disorientation paired with an extremely vivid visual and elemental palette of images produces the collection's pronounced sense of specificity of place, time, and general environment. Whereas mere disorientation would cause the work to seem like an empty experiment or a clever trick, when that sense accompanies the development of an enclosed world comprised of simple materials – weather, cloth, electricity, wire, shelters, animals, fields, and leather – the feeling of being to some extent lost seems fundamental to the process of coming to a basic understanding of an ecology. The feeling of relative inhibition of agency in relation to the text is therefore scripted by the text as being what it feels to truly learn about how the things in a world connect to one another. In this sense, the book is, as Peter Vernon argues, "pedagogical."[31] Yet the pedagogy the book offers does not offer a sense of easy agency in relation to the world it describes. The attempt to catalog a society in *The Age of Wire and String* leads first and foremost to an awareness of how tracing associations among a system's elements, no matter how simple, is likely to produce a sense of relative inhibition of autonomous action and not a sense of mastery.

In *The Age of Wire and String*, the development of this formal sense coincides with a thematic recasting of human agency in relation to nonhuman things. For instance, in the first story of the collection, "Intercourse with Resuscitated Wife," the demands of electricity lead to the vignette's disturbing central image:

> Electricity mourns the absence of the energy form (wife) within the household's walls by stalling its flow to the outlets. As such, an improvised friction needs to take the place of electricity, to goad the natural currents back to their proper levels. This is achieved with the dead wife. She must be

found, revived, and then penetrated until heat fills the room, until the toaster is shooting bread onto the floor. (*AWS*, 7)

The relationship between a husband and wife, which tends to be seen as the governing logic of a household, is here subordinated to the needs of the house's many electrical appliances. This is typical of the central vision of *The Age of Wire and String*. Throughout the work, elements including forces of physics, weather, and geological features take precedence over human activity, necessitating what seem to be extreme forms of human restriction. But here, the result is more ambivalent. While the central image of the story is horrifying, the final sentence of the story suggests that there is still room for the feeling of specific human attachment within this world: "It is always there, that moving into a static-ridden corpse that once spoke familiar messages in the morning when the sun was new" (ibid.). There is still room for sentiment, but that sentiment is nested within many other forms of relation and demand, both human and nonhuman.

The Age of Wire and String fashions itself as a text of orientation, of cataloging, of mapping a society and its environment. It is rigorously organized in such a way that gestures to the possibility of readerly control – the focus of each section is mapped in advance, and important terms are defined in glossaries. Yet the consequence of these gestures is not mastery but the awareness that such mastery is impossible. And this awareness is created not for its own sake – not to make readers feel powerless or passive – but as an attempt to create the specific feeling of what it feels like to think outside of one's forms of daily awareness. This feeling is not offered up as an affect to be mapped, reflected upon, or understood; it is rather a by-product of the formal innovations of the text.[32] In this way, *The Age of Wire and String* itself acts as the many forces and objects it describes, making demands on humans and shaping human modes of living and thought.

The Limits of Critique

There is no doubt that *The Age of Wire and String* sees feelings as central to a project of cataloguing a culture. But it is also clear that the feelings generated by the work do not provide opportunities for an affective mapping of a particular social system. Instead, the book highlights feelings of difficulty, tension, and senses of disorientation in the face of the pronounced effort involved in reconciling oneself to one's environment. This sense of tension, which seems so strange in Marcus's work, is, for John Dewey in his *Art and Experience*, the surprising core of emotional experience in general. He argues that emotion is the primary means by which human participation in environmental systems is registered:[33]

> Life itself consists of phases in which the organism falls out of step with the march of surrounding things and then recovers unison with it – either by effort or by some happy chance. And, in a growing life, the recovery is never a mere return to a prior state, for it is enriched by the state of disparity and resistance through which it has successfully passed.... Life grows when a temporary falling out is a transition to a more extensive balance of the energies of the organism with those of the conditions under which it lives.[34]

For Dewey, these phases in which organisms fall out of line with an environment and then adapt in order to regain a connection to that environment exist for both human and nonhuman beings. But, he goes on to say, humans have a unique capacity to become aware of this condition:

> The rhythm of loss of integration with environment and recovery of union not only persists in man but becomes conscious with him; its conditions are the material out of which he forms purposes. *Emotion is the conscious sign of a break, actual or impending.* The discord is the occasion that induces reflection. Desire for restoration of the union converts mere emotion into interest in objects as conditions of realization of harmony.[35]

Emotions are envisioned here as the immediate material results of the relationship between individuals and their environment. Reflection therefore is not driven toward the achievement of agency in relation to emotions. Instead, it directs the person feeling the emotion to engage with the environment with "interest." This is particularly true, Dewey argues, of the artist, who "does not shun moments of resistance and tension" but "cultivates them, not for their own sake but because of their potentialities."[36]

Dewey's understanding of the function of emotion, in both art and life, calls for a different critical posture than those approaches to feelings that seek to grant agency to the subject. Rather than developing critical distance from emotions, Dewey suggests that critics should more thoroughly inhabit them in order to better understand the relationships humans have with their environments. He recognizes that this argument runs against the tendency for critics to see art as existing outside the messiness of other environmental conditions, but he insists that if we wish to "grasp the sources of esthetic experience it is ... necessary to have recourse to animal life below the human scale" in order to recognize that human activity takes place in a world where "environing objects avail and counteravail."[37] Human sensory experience, and the art that stems from it, is, for Dewey, "heightened vitality. Instead of signifying being shut up within one's own private feelings and sensations, it signifies active and alert commerce with the world; at its height it signifies complete interpenetration of self and the world of objects and events."[38] And this interpenetration, while blocking anything resembling total autonomy or perfect human agency, is nevertheless enabling. Insofar as its rhythms of disruption and unification are catalysts for growth – not to mention art – the environment of matter, of which humans are a part, is a field of potential that ultimately exceeds the managed terrain of the individual and personal.

Affects, then, are essentially the conscious registration of ecological situatedness – if, by "ecological," we mean the interconnection of living and nonliving things. This definition reflects Dewey's argument that emotions are the awareness of productive tensions between self and environment. It also has sympathies with Spinoza's claim that affects are changes that occur in the body as a result of its interactions with other bodies paired with the idea of those changes.[39] In these and other formulations, affects are the primary means by which humans become conscious of contact with human and nonhuman elements of our environments. Affects, understood in this model, are also evidence of what Jane Bennett calls "*distributive* agency" as opposed to agency imagined as the consequence of the specific liberal form of human subjectivity that is generally seen as its prerequisite.[40] For Bennett, the notion of distributive agency means that there are "active powers issuing from nonsubjects" and "material agency" that stems from "nonhuman or not-quite human things."[41] This capacity for nonsubjects to exert agency, however, is often elided in contemporary criticism precisely as a result of the tendency to privilege the notion of the autonomous individual. If affects are the consciousness of the impact of human and nonhuman factors on individuals, then they can also be understood to be evidence of the presence of distributive agency. Put another way, affects are signals that we are not the only agents in the ecologies in and through which we live.

This suggests that works of literature that, like *The Age of Wire and String*, assert the peculiarity and plurality of those agents – by emphasizing the presence of feelings of difficulty, disorientation, and tension – make conscious that bodily registration of ecological situatedness that might otherwise be backgrounded. This minimizing of environmental factors is especially likely in the social context of neoliberalism, where even liberal structures of human interdependence tend to be dissolved or pathologized and where self-sufficiency, autonomy, and individual freedom are held up as primary moral goods. In this context, works like *The Age of Wire and String* challenge this social presumption – not through a head-on critique, but by scripting feelings as more than mere symptoms of structural changes, and registering what it feels like to come into contact with the alterity that is nothing but one's own environment. The world of Marcus's collection is peculiar not because it differs from the one we recognize but because it seems like it could be our own, just understood through different rules. The sense of disorientation this uncanny positioning creates is crucially at odds with the myriad forms of locatability and manufactured senses of orientation and choice that prevail in neoliberal culture.

So does this mean that literature only allows us to capitulate to the systems of which we are a part, passively registering the effects of our embeddedness? As Bruno Latour reminds us, the work of tracing the associations that exist among people and things is far from finished. Indeed, without efforts to rigorously trace these associations, "we don't know what we have in common, we don't know through which connections we are associated together, and we would have no way to detect how we can live in the same common world."[42] While there are endless accounts of how the world functions, he explains, "the fact is that *no one* has the answers – this is why they have to be collectively staged, stabilized, and revised."[43] The best response to the contemporary tendency toward certain forms of mapping and locatability is, for Latour, the proliferation of less obvious, or less commonly accepted, tracings of relationships.

The difference between Jameson's interest in cognitive mapping and Latour's tracing of associations lies within the relationship between the production of maps and the possibility for those maps to grant greater freedom of movement to the individual who receives them. For Jameson, cognitive mapping is primarily driven toward bestowing agency upon the individual who maps or reads the map, a project he sees as necessary because of his belief that late capitalism functions first and foremost through disorientation and the resultant pacifying of potential agents within it. He writes of the "new political art" that its central function would be to allow us "to grasp our positioning as individual and collective subjects and regain a capacity to act and struggle which is at present neutralized by our spatial as well as social confusion."[44] Latour, on the other hand, argues that tracing associational networks will lead to precisely the opposite conclusion. A well-traced network, he explains, reveals that any given actor will be unable to function in a unidirectional or fully intentional manner. Beyond merely seeing human agents as subject to the power of ideological constructs and mystifications, as Jameson does, Latour argues that

> it's crucial *not* to conflate all the agencies overtaking the action into some kind of agency – "society," "culture," "structure," "fields," "individuals," or whatever name they are given … Action should remain a surprise, a mediation, an event. It is for this reason that we should begin, here again, not from the "determination of action by society," the "calculative abilities of individuals," or the "power of the unconscious" as we would ordinarily do, but rather from the *under-determination of action,* from the uncertainties and controversies about who and what is acting when "we" act.[45]

Latour sees the urgency behind this correction as stemming from what he perceives as a disciplinary catastrophe within the social sciences, where attempts to offer a unilateral and predetermined "social explanation" of worldly phenomena often reduce the complexity of those phenomena and expose an operative assumption that some actions can still occur outside of that social force. Indeed, he argues, critique itself often assumes this imagined posture of autonomy from larger systems of mutual determination.

As a result, the traditional critical posture, wherein intellectuals see themselves as vehicles for the exposure of "ideological arguments posing as matters of fact," no longer addresses the major dangers of the present.[46] Latour's most compelling example of this change is the way climate change deniers have used the protocols of ideology critique to question climate research. Just as academics in the humanities and social sciences have been trained to question the ideological assumptions that underpin so-called objective research, climate deniers argue that climate science is merely a vehicle for politics. Given this situation where the tools of leftist intellectuals are more and more commonly used against their political interests, Latour argues that the fundamental methods of critical work are in need of revision:

> Critique did a wonderful job of debunking prejudices, enlightening nations, and prodding minds, but, as I have argued elsewhere, it "ran out of steam" because it was predicated on the discovery of a true world of realities lying behind a veil of appearances…. It had the immense drawback of creating a massive gap between what was felt and what was real.[47]

The presumption that there is a choice to be made between critique and capitulation is itself a symptom of the dominance of critique as an intellectual mode: if we are to be at all times looking for something beyond what we see and feel, then what we see and feel is always assumed to be a mystification. Moving away from this posture, in Latour's view, can mean merely embracing the notion that before a world can be recognized, assessed, called into question, or acted within, it first needs to be carefully composed by tracing the associations that exist within it. Composing that world can take place in a range of disciplines and through a range of scholarly practices, from dense ethnographies to works of deep description in the humanities.[48]

But alongside efforts in the academic disciplines to take stock of the relationships that exist among a range of human and nonhuman actors, literature and other works of art also compose worlds, trace associations, and forge unlikely connections, and they do so where our most stubborn assumptions will otherwise not budge. Even Latour concedes that after sociological methods have been tried, and "when everything else has failed, the resource of fiction can bring – through the use of counterfactual history, thought experiments, and 'scientification' – the solid objects of today into the fluid states where their connections with humans may make sense."[49] Fiction, in this view, is useful in its capacity to speculate on worlds and realities beyond those recognized by the sciences. But there is another important difference between sociology and literature in this regard. Not only can literature fictionalize, and therefore posit different worldviews other than those that we assume to be permanent, it can also provide glimmers of consciousness that precede the capacity to fully describe. Those senses of a different way of putting together the elements that compose our world are often felt as much as understood, registered as moments of discomfort, disorientation, or strangeness that might catalyze new approaches to tracing and composing the ecologies of which we are a part.

4

Ecology, Feeling, and Form in Neoliberal Literature

In a recent poem by Billy Collins, "The Sandhill Cranes of Nebraska," the speaker recounts a series of missed opportunities to witness noteworthy environmental phenomena. As he travels around the country, he finds that he always seems to arrive at the wrong time. He manages to miss wonders everywhere he goes: the annual migration of sandhill cranes to the Platte River in Nebraska, the blooming of azaleas in Georgia, and the peak of autumn foliage in Vermont.[1] "The Sandhill Cranes of Nebraska" has a conventional rhetorical structure, but because of the speaker's persistent bad timing, its perspective is oddly displaced. The result is a strange version of a nature poem, where spectacular events are narrated from a position of remove. The poem begins:

> Too bad you weren't here six months ago,
> was a lament I heard on my visit to Nebraska.
> You could have seen the astonishing spectacle
> of the sandhill cranes, thousands of them
> feeding and even dancing on the shores of the Platte River.
>
> There was no point in pointing out
> the impossibility of my being there then
> because I happened to be somewhere else,
> so I nodded and put on a look of mild disappointment
> if only to be part of the commiseration.

The remaining stanzas follow a form similar to the first: the speaker visits a place, someone who lives there tells him that he has just missed an event, and the event is described in a line or two of verse. Each time, the speaker notes but does not mourn the inevitable result of temporal and spatial displacement: "the impossibility of my being there then / because I happened to be somewhere else."

Yet the irony of "Sandhill Cranes" is that the speaker appears to have not missed the events at all, evidenced by their vivid presence in the poem.

The cranes are "feeding and even dancing on the shores of the Platte River," the "spectacular annual outburst of azaleas" is "brilliant against the green backdrop of spring," and "Mother Nature, as she is called" has "touched the hills with her many-colored brush" in the poem, if not in reality. These images appear with all of the lyrical beauty and drama that one would expect from a traditional nature poem where the speaker is witness to natural occurrences, despite the fact that these phenomena occur, as the final stanza describes,

> around the same time every year when I am apparently off
> in another state, stuck in a motel lobby
> with the local paper and a styrofoam cup of coffee,
> busily missing God knows what.

The speaker's personal environment is entirely artificial; his access to the world of events is entirely mediated. Nevertheless, because natural occurrences are registered in the poem regardless of this displacement, the speaker is only "apparently off," as the first enjambed line of the stanza suggests. Despite the fact that he is "stuck in a motel lobby / with the local paper and a styrofoam cup of coffee," he has not, in fact, missed anything. His putting on "a look of mild disappointment" therefore does not signal resignation to the limitations of his perspective as much as it suggests a false front for those who do not understand that the poet might capture images such as these regardless of his material location. What appears to be a work about the limits of the individual human to take in the richness of natural events instead turns out to be a poem that performs the free movement of human perception – perception so flexible that it need not even be constrained to a particular place in order to register what is important about that which is perceived.

The speaker in Collins's poem, in other words, demonstrates how human aesthetic activity can be understood to constitute total liberation from spatial and temporal limitations, so that the wonders of the natural world might be experienced by anyone anywhere.[2] This flexible lyric seems to do the impossible: to embrace the perspective of a contemporary jet-setter, whose concerns are too pressing to be subject to the temporality of seasonal events, and still perform an expansive appreciation for the wonders of the natural world. This have-it-all aesthetic is deeply consonant with neoliberalism. The poem celebrates the man who will do what he has to do for his own economic advancement – the undistinguished motel lobby and styrofoam cup of coffee suggest that his travel is for some form of professional purpose, whether corporate, artistic, or academic.

But the poem also suggests that these activities do not limit his ability to imagine in broad but sufficient strokes the seasonal events that this kind of schedule forces him to miss.[3] In other words, the subject sketched by the poem is liberated to cultivate himself in an entrepreneurial fashion and also to avoid missing anything too important in the meantime, and aesthetic activity is posited as the means by which this liberation is achieved. The poem therefore reinforces the belief that the individual can float freely and easily above the complexity of the systems he inhabits, drawing the poetic form into the same logic of flexibility that characterizes the information work of the neoliberal subject.

This compatibility of Collins' mode of nature writing with neoliberal values makes sense in the context of the larger tendency for neoliberalism to appropriate ecological concepts and environmental concerns. We see this occur in activities ranging from the most base exercises in corporate greenwashing to the more noble attempts of environmental economists who, often with the best of intentions, attempt to quantify in monetary terms everything from clean air and water to biodiversity.[4] These latter efforts, while often intended to support the goals of environmentalists, also perpetuate the belief that the nonhuman environment is understandable in capitalist terms. As Vandana Shiva argues of "sustainable development," a term coined initially to address the need for development policies to recognize the environmental impact of efforts at global industrialization, it "protects the primacy of capital. It is still assumed that capital is the basis of all activity."[5] As a result, it draws attention away from aspects of ecology that contradict that assumption, even as it emphasizes the need for forms of environmental awareness that can coexist with the imposition of neoliberal reforms. This is just one example of a growing tendency to see ecological needs and neoliberal mechanisms as mutually beneficial in contemporary society, despite the critical consensus among climate scientists and others that maintaining planetary ecological health is impossible at current growth rates.

The ease with which neoliberalism has appropriated the vocabulary of environmentalism has led some to read contemporary interest in ecology as yet another ideological distraction from the analysis of labor, production, and class. But the argument can just as easily be made that the concept of ecology offers perhaps the greatest threat to the central neoliberal tenet that the market is the system that structures and underlies all other systems.[6] This is because while environmental rhetoric, given its lifestyle dimensions, is easily appropriated into discourses of consumerism, the affective dimensions of ecology are more stubbornly resistant to economic codification than those cultivated in relation to other systems of circulation. It is common enough to see the appropriation of ecological terms to capitalist ends, from the figuring of the market itself as an "ecology" to media "webs," and customer "networks." Engaging in actual ecosystems, however, exposes how complex systems tend to undermine the kinds of attempts at calculation and intervention that lie behind neoliberal market practices. More than merely "interconnected," ecosystems are unpredictable and difficult to manage.

This chapter examines a central paradox of environmental writing: the desire to represent ecological thinking as an alternative to neoliberal thinking on the one hand, and the danger that exists in making ecosystems the subjects of human narratives, and therefore domesticating them, on the other. As Collins's poem shows, if it is the wildness of ecology that makes it challenging to neoliberalism, there is always the danger that, in attempting to represent the nonhuman world, literature will unwittingly appear to tame it, making it seem as if it were readily available for human consumption, administration, and exchange. In Lydia Millet's *How the Dead Dream*, this tension is reflected in the form of the novel. The book begins as a bildungsroman that chronicles the coming of age of a successful real estate developer. The foundations of the bildungsroman form, however, slowly dissolve as the central character's concerns turn to envisioning the world from the perspectives of endangered animals. By the end of the novel, the impulse to produce stories is itself indicted as privileging human concerns over the needs of nonhumans. As a result, the novel ends up positing immediate physical contact with the nonhuman world as the only alternative to the bodily investment of neoliberal subjects in the circulation of capital.

In contrast to the skepticism toward storytelling in *How the Dead Dream*, Richard Powers's novel *The Echo Maker* suggests that a literary form that envisions itself as an ecological force and, at the same time, acknowledges the potential pitfalls of that form, might provide a corrective to prevailing tendencies in environmental writing. Powers's novel allows for a sprawling perception of human, animal, plant, and mineral life. It brings together the story of the evolution of the sandhill cranes, a species that dates back to the Pleistocene; detailed descriptions of the water cycle of the Platte; entire sections told exclusively from the perspective of migrating birds; and a display of encyclopedic neurological knowledge that appears to make the material basis of human cognition fully visible and understandable. One might think that Powers, marshaling all the encyclopedic resources of the novel form, would aspire to an accurate and thorough representation of the complexity of the natural world. But *The Echo Maker*, like *How the Dead Dream*, ultimately stresses the limitations of human cognition by performing the failure of aesthetic activity to allow humans to make sense of both human and nonhuman behavior. Unlike *How the Dead Dream*, however, *The Echo Maker* persists in challenging this limitation. In the place of an attempt to thoroughly map ecological systems, the novel shows how the circulation of literary texts catalyze affective responses in relation to human and nonhuman systems in such a way that they might be accepted in their incomprehensibility. Powers's work therefore suggests that the ecological role of aesthetics could better be understood as formal rather than representational – as a training ground for more expansive forms of cognition that might better register the many ways humans are entangled in ecological systems.[7]

The Paradox of the Environmental Bildungsroman: The Case of *How the Dead Dream*

How the Dead Dream begins as a satirical bildungsroman, tracing the childhood and education of T., an avid real estate developer, who in mid-life becomes so obsessed with endangered animals that he breaks into zoos to sleep with them in their cages. But the chronicle of T.'s life confronts a contradiction as it describes his turn away from market-based forms of valuation and toward attachment to nonhuman creatures. The end of the novel sees narrative form floundering in the face of a Copernican revolution in species supremacy. The implication is that the form of the novel itself, and indeed perhaps the form of stories in general, is so firmly ensconced in the legacy of capitalism and, more radically, in human exceptionalism that it cannot articulate challenges to these foundational beliefs without ceasing, in some fundamental sense, to tell a story. Story and ecological consciousness, the novel suggests, are, at root, incompatible, and the only ecological role remaining for the novel is to tell the story of this incompatibility. In a startling final image T., starving and shelterless, lies on his back in a Belizean jungle while an orphaned and endangered baby tapir sleeps on his chest. Thus *How the Dead Dream* ultimately offers up direct physical communion as the only way to thoroughly engage with the alterity of the natural world. This renunciation of the aesthetic logic that characterizes the lyric perspective of poems like Collins's, however, ends up falling into another trap: rather than suggesting that literature can master the complexity of ecology through its powers of representation, *How the Dead Dream* sees literature as entirely incapable of representing humans as ecologically decentered, a perspective it nonetheless sees as urgent to the prevention of ecological crises. As a result of this tension, the novel turns to physical immediacy as an ecologically transformative force but in doing so recalls an older tradition of wilderness worship, a tradition marred by a history of Eurocentrism, sexism, classism, and racism.[8]

The novel begins with T.'s childhood, during which he has an unusually pronounced physical connection with money. In addition to sleeping with his bills under his pillow, he develops "a habit of secreting coins on his person, a thick and powerful quarter lodged under his tongue or discreet dimes tucked into the cheek pouches."[9] From this bodily obsession with currency, he moves on to more advanced forms of capitalist involvement. He goes on to sell goods on the black market in grade school and to speculate on developments for Superfund sites by the age of twenty-two. By the time he becomes an adult, T. forges connections exclusively through market transactions, convinced that "currency infused all things" (*HDD*, 14). When the second chapter of the novel begins, T. is wealthy and fully free from any social or familial commitments, desiring only to "have a hand in the revolutions of the market itself, in the ebb and the flow" (*HDD*, 31). Through this language of organic circulation, T. is envisioned as experiencing the market not only through his own bodily rhythms but also as an ecology into and of itself, as he is soothed by the market's "infinite, open potential" (*HDD*, 13).

T. is figured in his youth as a rare master of this capitalist ecology. Through his investment efforts in college, he is "gratified to see how effort and control could yield steady returns" (*HDD*, 22). It looks as though his life will progress according to this measured temporality despite occasional foreshadowing to the contrary; for instance, when he begins development work in California, he notes that "speculators tended to ignore the foreshortened future of the hills, their promise of imminent collapse by mudslide, quake or fire" but his awareness of such possible threats does not deter or interrupt the seamlessness with which he perceives his own life narrative (*HDD*, 28).

Both T.'s demeanor and the pacing of the novel reflect "a confident nonchalance, an air of serene neutrality" that T. sees as the attitudinal basis for successful capital accumulation (*HDD*, 37). For that reason, when the second chapter opens with the phrase "He killed her driving to Las Vegas," the effect is to suggest not only the violence of murder but also a traumatic interruption of an otherwise temporally and thematically continuous biography. This impression is weakened but nevertheless remains even after it is revealed that the "her" that T. kills is a coyote, not a human being. Driving contentedly down the Interstate in his S-Class Mercedes, which is figured, like the circulation of capital itself, as his bodily extension, massaging him with "the smoothness of his buttery seat leather against the backs of his thighs" (*HDD*, 35), T. suddenly hits something that darts into the road. He stops and sees that the coyote is still alive despite the fact that "its back legs were pulp" (*HDD*, 36). He drags the animal to the side of the road and holds her as she slowly dies. The scene is wrenching, gruesome, and unforgiving. Uncharacteristically, T. falls into a moment of profound empathy:

> He imagined the shock from the ruined legs coursing through her body, what must be the blind surge of pain as the end closed in. A loud end – the rush of cars still distant punctuated by the searing noise and glare of those approaching, bearing down viciously and then fading again. She was dying in the smells of asphalt, exhaust, and gasoline, no doubt also the smell of her own blood, and him, and other smells he could not know himself.
> The fullness, the terrible sympathy!
> Had he felt this before, he wondered? Maybe when he was a boy? Animals died by the road and you saw that all the time, everyone did.... You thought: that is the difference between them and me. My insides are firmly contained. (*HDD*, 37)

T.'s awareness of the alterity of the coyote's experience is unique in the narrative up to this point. His recognition of the effects of his own violence, a recognition countless teachers and even his own mother have tried to construct during his early years of extortion, bribery, and fraud, occurs seemingly without effort in the face of the dying animal. Yet despite the brutality of this scene, T.'s absorption is interrupted by, rather than cleanly incorporated into, the narrative. The presence of the single line "The fullness, the terrible sympathy!" set off, as it is, by itself in its own paragraph, reads as an interruption at an extradiegetic level, so that the heretofore transparent third-person narrator might be read as commenting on the circumstances of the scene.[10] The friction that results between epiphany and distanced reporting creates affective distance from the scene at hand, emphasizing the role of interpretation in defining T.'s actions as performing acts that signify the codified emotional states of "fullness" and "terrible sympathy." The line therefore performs a kind of affective irony, as its emotional commentary pulls the reader away from the consuming scene under way at the diegetic level.

Add to this the much-discussed parallels between the plot of *How the Dead Dream* and Joseph Conrad's *Heart of Darkness*,[11] and "The fullness, the terrible sympathy!" is further separated from a sense of authentic emotional immediacy by its syntactical recollection of Kurtz's famous last words, "The horror! The horror!"[12] The intertextual reference stresses the discursive construction of such epiphanies and their political, ecological, and social failings. Indeed, just as Kurtz's exposure to "horror" does nothing to stop his, or others', participation in the crimes of colonial conquest, T.'s exposure to "sympathy" too fails to substantively alter the course of even his own participation in violence toward nonhumans. Whereas the novel describes T.'s experience as one of profound physical connection to a nonhuman being, the intra- and intertextual complexity of the moment detracts from the possibility of identification with the character during the scene. The result is a prevailing sense of unease, alienation, and distress, as the need for communion with the nonhuman is urgently declared and the opportunity for interspecies relation through emotional codification is denied. This tension is worked out on the level of plot as well. In the weeks that follow the incident, T. is altered, but not transformed. He trades in his S-Class for "a modest 190" and adopts an abused dog from a local animal shelter, but he not only continues his environmentally questionable work as a developer, building a subdivision over the habitat of one of the last colonies of nearly extinct kangaroo rats, he amplifies the extent of his destructiveness, turning next to a massive and wasteful eco-tourism development in the mangrove forests of Belize. The result is a narrative that is tonally, thematically, and formally in flux. It is, in turns, affectively brutal, cold, and heartbreakingly desperate.

The novel ultimately sees the representation of deep emotional connections to nonhumans as impossible. Yet despite this failure of emotional representation, the novel figures affective responses as comprising the ground for the battle between capitalist and ecological forms of engagement. The thematic struggle that characterizes the bulk of the novel takes place between two systems of circulation of value, both having a strong physiological as well as ideological pull: capitalism on the one hand and ecology on the other. Throughout the novel T. continues to participate in the former to the detriment of the latter, while feeling shocks of terror for the human species as a whole in moments when he recognizes that the ecological resilience of the planet is crumbling in response to exploitative and ill-considered human activities like his own. The moment of clearest contradiction between the needs of capitalist accumulation and those of the biosphere comes when he learns that his attempts to resettle the displaced, endangered kangaroo rats from his subdivision have failed, the population of captive rats has crashed, and extinction is the likely result. It is at this moment when T. begins to insert himself bodily among threatened animals and habitats, beginning with habitual walks in the area of land set aside for the rats and now barren with the exception of anthills. In a reversal of the incorporation of money into his body that we see in the coin-sucking scenes at the beginning of the novel, walking in the set-aside land T. feels "permeable ... oddly inseparate from the dirt and the dry golden grass" (*HDD*, 130). This feeling, for him, is a traditionally sublime combination of terror and wonder. He reflects that the wild land

> was trying to invade him and he should be alarmed. He was in danger. What you needed more than anything, for the purposes of ambition, was certainty, was a belief that the rest of being, the entirety of the cosmos, should not be allowed to penetrate and divert you from the cause – the chief and primary cause, which was, clearly, yourself.
>
> Yet he was laid out to receive it. He was laid out by the force of gravity itself, by elemental physics. Sediment accumulated on him, buried him gradually, and more and more he was silted in. (Ibid.)

The difference between the system of capitalism and the system of ecology for T. is that the former is understood to be controllable, consumable, and absorbable, even on the level of the body, into the cohesive self of the willful capitalist. The latter, oppositely, requires that one be incorporated, buried, and thoroughly penetrated by the system at large. To recognize oneself as existing within an ecosystem in this sense requires both seeing oneself from a decentered position and feeling the consequences of that decentering on the level of the body itself.

This requirement for ecological vision turns out to be incompatible with the formal requirements of the bildungsroman. Despite T.'s existential revelations, the novel stubbornly continues to put him at the center of the action, seemingly more in accord with the novel's form than in any way consistent with the beliefs and motivations of T. as a coherent character. About halfway through the novel, the structure turns increasingly surreal, as T. takes radical actions to put himself in a vulnerable physical position vis-à-vis nonhuman nature under threat, sneaking into zoos to sleep in the cages of a Mexican gray wolf, a Sumatran rhinoceros, a Morelet's crocodile, and other species on the brink of extinction that he calls piously "last animals" (*HDD*, 164, 199, 242). The coming-of-age narrative only frays further when, looking for even more immediate connection with animals under threat, T. takes a *Heart of Darkness*–style trip down a river in Belize in search of jaguars and other "last animals." In the final pages of the novel, the narrative seems to give way to clownish pastiche on the one hand (complete with a local who is named "Marlo" but otherwise bears no discernible resemblance to Marlow in Conrad's novel) and aphoristic existential reflections on the other, as the action plot, wherein T.'s guide dies and he is left wandering the river with few provisions in search of the sea, becomes less and less plausible, the social satire all but disappears, and T.'s existential meditations take center stage.[13] In one of these, he considers the relationship between stories and human exceptionalism:

> He had left the settlements now, all the old geographies. For so many years they had been the one thing: you did what you did and whatever it was consumed you, as though your actions were the heart of experience. As though without a series of actions there would be no story of your life.
>
> Those who loved stories also loved the human, to live in cities where there was nothing but men and their actions as far as the eye could see. Once it had been believed that the sun revolved around the earth; now this was ridiculed as myopic, yet almost the same belief persisted. The sun might be the center of the planets and then the sun might be only one star among galaxies of them: but when it came to meaning, when it came to being, in fact, all the constellations still revolved around men. (*HDD*, 234)

In this passage, stories are understood to be narcissistic on the personal level and chauvinistic on the species level, privileging individual actions as the basis for valuing a life and human actions as the basis for understanding the universe. Of course the paradox articulated here – the notion that "without a series of actions there would be no story of your life" – is the very paradox reflected in the novel's form. At the beginning of the novel, T. values his actions and the bildungsroman form reflects that self-interest. Yet when T. begins to question his own centrality to the plot of his life, the form of the life-narrative persists despite its growing inappropriateness to the central character's belief system. The result is a narrative that plunges into an odd combination of silliness, incoherence, existential insight, and surrealism, a novel that cannot fulfill its bildungsroman promise, even as social satire, because of its thematic drift toward seeing the representation of *bildung* itself as nothing but human-centric distraction from the complexity and significance of nonhuman events.

The novel suggests that only physical bodily contact with nonhumans can adequately challenge the seductions of capitalism and the human exceptionalism that is both its cause and its consequence. This radical merging with the nonhuman is figured in the final scene of the novel when T. allows a motherless baby tapir to crawl onto his chest and fall asleep. The novel ends with an odd incorporation of T.'s and the tapir's perspectives, suggesting a narrative as well as a phenomenological point of contact that hinges on their body-to-body contact.[14] In a rare shedding of irony, the narrative comments on the comfort with which this merging takes place:

> The tough skin, the coarse hair. The animal breathed thickly. For a time he did not know what he felt. In out, in out, they breathed and breathed. They both had lungs, they loved to sleep, they liked to be alongside each other in the comfort of their rhythm. He slept, or thought he slept; he dreamed, or thought he dreamed. Did it matter? If the animal was speaking to him, fine: if it was only what he believed was the animal, that was fine too. To know was to be. (*HDD*, 243)

T. therefore sheds questions of narrative centrality altogether, privileging the feeling of breath, of sleep, of shared bodily rhythms. Yet the novel cannot sustain engagement with this level of experience, and it ends abruptly, precisely when meaningful contact with the nonhuman begins.[15]

Wonder and the Wild

In the final pages of his foundational work *The End of Nature,* Bill McKibben advocates a similar state of wordless exposure to nonhuman aspects of existence as an antidote to the thoroughness with which nature is, for the most part, contaminated by the effects of human culture.[16] Describing a night under the stars, where "the vast nature above our atmosphere still holds mystery and wonder," he writes: "The ancients, surrounded by wild and even hostile nature, took comfort in seeing the familiar above them – spoons and swords and nets. *But we need to train ourselves not to see those patterns. The comfort we need is inhuman.*"[17] Taken to its logical extension, McKibben's argument, like that of *How the Dead Dream,* seems to indict writing about the environment from the start as inevitably imposing human patterns on nonhuman nature, stripping it of its difference. Yet this emphasis on unmediated bodily experience suggests that the only way for humans to register ecological connection is through direct encounters that, as the ambiguous outcome of T.'s hubristic journey at the end of *How the Dead Dream* suggests, may not even hold the kind of authenticity humans, desperate for some form of ecological connection, attribute to them.

The work of environmental historian William Cronon offers one possible alternative to this belief that the shedding of language and other forms of codification allows for a more thorough recognition of the nonhuman. While he, too, sees the cultivation of wonder as central to contemporary environmentalism, arguing that "the striking power of the wild is that wonder in the face of it requires no act of will, but forces itself upon us – as an expression of the nonhuman world experienced through the lens of our cultural history – as proof that ours is not the only presence in the universe," a large measure of the ecological importance of wonder for Cronon is that it runs contrary to our capacities to control our environment.[18] It does not emerge out of conscious contemplation, nor is it the consequence of finding rare and exceptional points of physical contact with uncontaminated nature; rather it "forces itself upon us," whether we like it or not, positioning the human species as one earthly form of existence among many. In an explicit departure from McKibben's view, Cronon identifies this feeling of wonder as only circumstantially attached to aspects of nature entirely untouched by humans. Wonder, in his view, is a result of "the autonomy and otherness of the things and creatures around us – an autonomy our culture has taught us to label with the word 'wild.' "[19] Unlike the concept of wilderness, which, as Cronon chronicles, is largely a Western fiction with a destructive legacy, "wildness (as opposed to wilderness) can be found anywhere: in the seemingly tame fields and woodlots of Massachusetts, in the cracks of a Manhattan sidewalk, even in the cells of our own bodies."[20] Cronon therefore sees McKibben's focus on the unnamed and untouched as overly restricting the terrain of the potentially wild. "To think ourselves capable of causing 'the end of nature' is an act of great hubris," he writes, "for it means forgetting the wildness that dwells everywhere within and around us."[21] For Cronon, the necessary human response to ecological threat is not the preservation of a notion of untouched nature, but rather the discovery of otherness in that which is most familiar, by learning to both "recognize and honor nonhuman nature as a world we did not create, a world with its own independent, nonhuman reasons for being as it is," and accept the fact that humans are part of, not outside of, natural ecosystems.[22]

The challenge for literature is to inspire this recognition without codifying it to the point where the nonhuman no longer possesses wildness.[23] Brian Massumi addresses this need for thinking at large:

> Social constructivism easily leads to a cultural solipsism analogous to subjectivist interpretations of quantum mechanics. In this worst-case scenario, nature appears as immanent to culture (as its construct). At best, when the status of nature is deemed unworthy of attention, it is simply shunted aside. In that case it appears, by default, as transcendent to culture (as its inert and meaningless remainder).... In either case, nature as naturing, nature as having its own dynamism, is erased.... It is meaningless to interrogate the relation of the human to the nonhuman if the nonhuman is only a construct of human culture, or inertness. The concepts of nature

and culture need serious reworking, in a way that expresses the irreducible *alterity* of the nonhuman in and through its active *connection* to the human and vice versa.[24]

It is not enough, according to Massumi, to say that the concept of nature is socially and historically contingent; we are by now well aware that notions of nature as perfectly untouched by humans tend to be contaminated by cultural assumptions, just as Thoreau's view across Walden Pond was marred by the train that ran on the pond's opposite shore. Yet nature, if we understand the word to mean that which is not merely the consequence of human design, undoubtedly exists, as Cronon suggests, even in the places closest to human activities.[25] Given this paradox, can literature produce a sense of that alterity, the feeling Cronon and McKibben call "wonder"?[26] Can a work of literature negotiate between the tendency to ignore and the tendency to overcodify? If works of literature proceed by patterning, can they assist in training us against the patterns that obscure the strangeness of the nonhuman? In other words, is there a literary mode that sufficiently addresses the profound influence that ecological systems have on humans without descending into an uncritical celebration of the immediate?

Narrative Patterns and Ecological Form: The Case of *The Echo Maker*

If we read literature's ecological significance as primarily descriptive and representational, we tend to see it as either performing an expansion of the perceptive capacities of the individual beyond all limits or as gesturing toward the limitation of humans to meaningfully interact with the wildness of the natural world. As we have seen, the former impulse is in danger of mirroring the logic of neoliberal flexibility, while the latter seems to lead to the conclusion that literature itself is a form of human domination. There is, however, a third option: we can read literature as acting ecologically insofar as it is itself one of many nonhuman actors that addresses, affects, and circulates among human participants in ecological systems. This entails, as Karl Kroeber argues, the difficult task of "realizing that anything cultural must be understood as part of a natural ecosystem," a realization that he believed "should radically reorient *all* critical theorizing of the past 50 years."[27] While Kroeber was confident that this insight would be "commonplace within a decade," two decades later it is still the case that the nature/culture divide, while recognized as a social construct, has not been called into question to the point where many scholars of environmental literature have discussed seriously what it means to think of literature as itself having an ecological function.[28] Even fewer works of literature themselves have engaged explicitly with this possibility and its ramifications.

One key exception is *The Echo Maker*. The novel addresses two distinct systems: the delicate and highly connective cognitive system of the human brain on the one hand and the vulnerable and interwoven ecosystems of Nebraska's Platte River on the other.[29] In positioning these two systems next to one another, the novel envisions the relationship between cognition and ecology in several related ways. In integrating aspects of the brain that carry evolutionary traces of other species into the neurological plot, Powers's novel explores the human cognitive capacities that are shared with nonhuman species and what the consequences might be of those shared capacities. In turning to these structures, the novel also positions humans in a kinship role with other species, most notably the threatened sandhill cranes whose annual migration temporally structures the novel. Finally, and perhaps most provocatively, it lines up the cognitive effects of reading with an ecological hope for literature, a hope that the novel suggests relies on the affective powers of literature. This last affective/ecological possibility, I will argue, offers a way of envisioning the ecological role of literature in such a way that eludes the two dangers I articulated earlier: the danger of easy mastery on the one hand, and the retreat from all forms of literary engagement on behalf of a crude commitment to unmediated experience on the other.

The novel begins with a car accident that causes one of the novel's central characters, Mark Schluter, to become unable to recognize his sister, Karin. He is diagnosed with Capgras syndrome, a rare disorder characterized by the belief that loved ones are doubles, robots, or other imposters. Karin, hurt and confused by Mark's unwillingness to accept that she is who she says she is, writes to famous neurologist and nonfiction writer Gerald Weber, a composite character who appears to be equal parts V. S. Ramachandran, Oliver Sacks, and Daniel Dennett.[30] Curious about the unusual case, Weber agrees to examine Mark. In explaining the condition to Karin, he suggests that Capgras is, at root, an affective disorder: "The loved one's face elicits memory, but no feeling. Lack of emotional ratification overrides the rational assembly of memory. Or put this way: reason invents elaborately unreasonable explanations to explain a deficit in emotion. Logic depends upon feeling."[31] The estrangement that Mark feels toward Karin and that he exemplifies in relation to his former self is envisioned throughout *The Echo Maker* as stemming from a lack of affective response rather than either a lack of reason or a traceable emotional or psychological narrative. His belief that Karin is not his sister is not reflective of any larger psychosis nor does it correspond to a psychoanalytically identifiable neurosis; it is merely reflective of the primacy of affective impulse. Mark's capacity for rationality is entirely intact; if anything, his disorder is evidence of the capacity for narrative run amok. Faced with an affective situation that does not make sense, Mark produces a mad narrative to force it into the realm of reason.[32]

The ecological extension of the Capgras metaphor occurs primarily within a parallel plot to Mark and Karin's unfolding drama that concerns the annual migration of sandhill cranes to the area around Kearney, Nebraska, where Mark lives. A section of the Platte River that provides a resting ground to 500,000 cranes every year is under threat of being damaged by the development of a vast ecotourism resort, which will ironically destroy the very spectacle it is built to showcase by draining much of the river's remaining water. This is particularly dangerous for the Platte, a river that is already said to be "a mile wide and an inch deep" (*EM*, 55). In efforts to find a distraction from Mark's illness, Karin joins a preservationist group's effort to stop the development. At the hearings that will decide the fate of the river and its birds, she falls into a reverie:

> For an instant, as the hearing turned into instinctive ritual, it hit her: the whole race suffered from Capgras. Those birds danced like our next of kin, looked like our next of kin, called and willed and parented and taught and navigated all just like our blood relations. Half their parts were still ours. Yet humans waved them off: *imposters.* . . . But before Karin could fix the thought taking shape in her, it turned unrecognizable. (*EM*, 347–8)

Human threats to biodiversity are here diagnosed as stemming from an affective disorder analogous to Capgras, which prevents humans from recognizing other species as their kin. That humans might possess some buried knowledge that they are more closely linked to animals than they recognize is revealed in this passage through an ironic use of diction: describing the hearing's banalities as "instinctive ritual" even before the revelatory moment in the passage in which Karin recognizes that the "whole race suffered from Capgras" suggests that she already possesses an awareness of the animal properties of human social behavior on some level. When the realization "hits her," then, what we see is only the seeming suddenness with which this fundamental knowledge leaks into consciousness, even though we witness the continuity between Karin's bored observation of the scene and her epiphany. The narrative in this sense mirrors the model of cognition that underpins the very notion of Capgras: the belief that affect precedes narrative recognition. But once that epiphany occurs, Capgras syndrome strikes even Karin's own attempt to face her realization, estranging her from her own thought at the very moment of its conscious registration. The feeling of recognition, fleeting and sudden, escapes full actualization for Karin, but not for the reader, for whom it is actualized on the page. What this passage records, then, is not the moment of epiphany itself but the substrate of knowledge that is always present and provides material for the moment of conscious recognition and that, even when that moment happens too quickly to fix it in consciousness, continues to exist.[33] Read in this light, what appear to be revelations of the internal lives of humans in the novel are, in fact, always understood to be superficial narratives that cover the deep continuities and deindividualizing affective forces that bind humans to one another and to other species.[34]

The Echo Maker addresses the results, interpersonal and ecological, of affective deficiencies thematically through the metaphor of Capgras. The metaphor also indicts narrative itself, because the delusions characteristic of Capgras syndrome are the results of the brain's tendency to create narratives that make feelings, or in this case, their absence, make sense. The narratives that result, in the case of Capgras, are crazy, but the brain insists on them because they *feel* right: Karin doesn't *feel* like Mark's sister, so she must be a robot. Stories, according to the Capgras metaphor, are therefore likely to be covers for affective deficiencies. This suspicion is extended in *The Echo Maker* to call into question the realist mode that seemingly dominates the novel. Late in the book, we find out that Mark's beloved nurse's aide Barbara was once an investigative journalist who suffered from burnout after covering serial human catastrophes: the destruction of the Branch Davidian compound in Waco, the death of infants and children in the Oklahoma City bombing, the Heaven's Gate suicides, and finally the collapse of the World Trade Center. Thoroughly traumatized by these examples of human self-destruction, Barbara is sent to Nebraska on what is intended to be a fluff piece: a "human interest" story about the sandhill crane migration (*EM*, 435). Instead, she learns of the development plans for the banks of the Platte and the water policy that would drain the shallow river for good. She explains to Weber, "They wanted Disney. I tried to make it bigger. So I dug a little. It didn't take much to find the water. I dug a little more. I learned that we were going to waste that river, no matter what I wrote. I could tell a story that broke people down and made them ache to change their lives, and it would make no difference. That water is already gone" (ibid.). The insufficiency of the sentimental power of narrative, the only power that Barbara sees herself as able to wield, ultimately leads her to total despair. This is metafictionally damning: it suggests that the novel's critique of narrative extends to the conventional role of the novel form itself, as a mode of entertainment that focuses on "human interest."[35] What can narratives do, *The Echo Maker* seems to ask, other than cover over our various affective deficiencies?

One answer appears in the scene of the novel that describes Barbara's suicide attempt. The scene appears late in the novel, in flashback, after it is revealed that the cause of Mark's accident was his swerving to avoid her in the road. Driving aimlessly one night, having just finished filming the dazzling display of the cranes dancing by the river, Barbara listens to the radio:

> Some woman's satin voice crawls up intimate into her ear. For a moment, it sounds like Christian revival. No believer left behind. But these words are worse than religion. Facts. The woman's voice recites a litany, somewhere between a shopping list and a poem. *It took the human race two and a half million years to reach a billion people. It took 123 years to add a second billion. We hit three billion, thirty-three years later. Then in fourteen years, then thirteen, then twelve....*
>
> Shaking, she pulls over onto the shoulder. Alone in this nowhere with these numbers. A storm breaks somewhere in her head. Signals surge, triggering one another. Nothing in evolution prepares her for this. Sheets of electricity cascade through her, fact-induced seizures, and when the headlights appear in her rearview mirror, the most rational thing in the world is to open the door and step out into them. (*EM*, 437–8)

This episode suggests that, contrary to Barbara's belief, narratives do have the power to touch humans affectively, as the signals that surge, the "sheets of electricity" that cascade, course through her body, pushing it toward action. Read one way, Barbara's suicide attempt is the direct consequence of this affective mobilization. But the novel's critique of rationality as a thin cover for the primacy of affectivity suggests that the use of the word "rational" in the passage should be read with a measure of irony. Indeed, if "rationality" here means the same thing as the rationality that propels Mark's Capgras delusions, "the most rational thing in the world" is likely to be anything but. Read according to the theory of cognition that the novel establishes, Barbara's action might be understood as having two parts: a preconscious bodily aspect (the response to the radio broadcast) and the way Barbara puts that bodily response into a narrative frame (stepping out in front of the truck). In this scenario, the headlights provide an opportunity for narrative direction of the impulse, which is otherwise distributed throughout Barbara's body and lacks direction. Until the headlights arrive, Barbara is merely a container of affective potential. Once the headlights appear, that potential is directed, in this case toward the action of stepping out in front of what turns out to be Mark's truck.

The passage therefore recapitulates what we already know from the novel's work with Capgras – that affect precedes and informs what we take to be rationality – but it adds a narrative dimension. If we understand Barbara's response to the radio broadcast as a metafictional comment on the power of stories, we get a model for how such stories might be understood to produce changes in individuals. Whereas affect is associated with potential, rationality is associated with ends-oriented action. The particulars of the action that results are figured as arbitrary. The signal of the headlights in this example could have been replaced by any number of triggers that might have actualized the affective potential in Barbara's body differently. This split between affect and action is emphasized in this particular example because the broadcast that catalyzes the changes in Barbara's body is not a sentimental narrative, nor is it, as she thinks it might be at first, a religious call to action. These narrative forms might provide clearer links between the incitement of affective potential and the direction of that potential. Sentimental narratives not only make changes in the body, they tell the individual how to understand and direct those changes. Barbara's mistake in thinking that the list of population numbers is a religious broadcast is telling in this regard: a religious sermon is perhaps one of the most effective narrative forms in both inciting affective energy and interpreting that energy as attached to a specific source with specific aims.[36] In this case, however, the arbitrariness of the action that results from the incitement of affective energy is accentuated because Barbara undergoes "fact-induced seizures" from a narrative that points only to its own components and does not signal a goal beyond itself.

In other words, human interest narratives might be understood to be ineffective not because they are emotionally inadequate but because they too easily package the volatility of affective potential. While such stories might make people "ache to change their lives," as Barbara suggests, this very direction – the immediate coding of that ache toward action – preempts the kind of cascade of impulses that Barbara experiences in the face of a simple list of facts, facts that, in their vast scale and complex implications, cannot be easily contained within either a sentimental or an instrumental narrative. The combination in the radio broadcast of sensory stimulation and a lack of emotional codification is figured as much more powerful than a story crafted to be emotionally provocative.

Insofar as novels are literally "human interest stories," *The Echo Maker*'s privileging of raw affective potential and criticism of narrative containment of that potential would seem damning to the form itself. On the level of the plot the novel does seem to flirt with this diagnosis, but on the level of form it offers an alternative. In a recent interview, Powers argues against reading the novel's relationship to cognition as one primarily based on representation despite its neurological content. Instead, he suggests that the novel's

> most powerful "representation of consciousness" is not a fixed, motionless, captive lying trapped in the plane of the page, but turbulent processes unleashed in the cubic space between the page and the reader. We grow aware, we re-enter these processes, conscious of the glimpse of consciousness, neither through identification alone nor through recursive interruption of identification, but through the edge induced on moving from one state to another.[37]

These "turbulent processes" are, for Powers, initiated by a hybrid form that invites readers to enter the story and identify with its characters while also interrupting that identification in such a way that allows for a retrospective analysis of the form of consciousness initiated by the experience of narrative absorption. Neither offering the suspense of disbelief that characterizes psychological realism nor producing the self-reflexive cerebral distance of metafiction, the structure of the novel Powers envisions absorbs and distances, giving readers the experience of identification but also making them aware of the mechanics behind that experience. He explains:

> If mimetic fiction, on one hand, inviting an act of unbroken identification that willfully takes the symbol for the symbolized, trades in what John Gardner called the "vivid and continuous" fictional dream, and if postmodernism, on the other hand, calling attention to itself as an artifice through all sorts of anti-narrational devices, employs willful interruption of this unbroken dream, the novel I'm after functions as a kind of bastard hybrid, like consciousness itself, generating new terrain by passing "realism" and "metafiction" through relational processes, inviting identification at one gauge while complicating it at others, refracting the private through the public, story through form, forcing the reading self into constant reciprocal renegotiations by always insisting that no level of human existence means anything without all the others.[38]

Powers argues that this positioning of the reader into oscillating forms, relational processes, and "reciprocal renegotiations" allows the novel to reflect the dynamics of emergent complexity. Complex systems require, as Powers points out, "rich, evocative models" that can "explore the systemic effects of small changes."[39] No longer able to explore variables in isolation, systems scientists involved in exploring complex systems dynamics require simulations that reflect the massive interdependence of variables in a given system. Powers finds the novel particularly apt in this context, because it "has the potential to be the most complex set of experimental networks ever built, one that can model feedback passed along all other gauges of speculation and inhabitation, fact and concern, idea and feeling."[40] In this view, the novel does not simplify complexity, nor does it have the duty to withdraw from the project of codification. Instead, it performs a simulation of complexity in such a way that makes the reader aware that, in experiencing what she experiences through fiction, she is registering what being a working part of a complex system feels like. The novel is therefore envisioned as a therapeutic remedy to the affective deficiencies associated with ecological damage. In placing readers in a situation where they can feel what it is like to be part of a system, the novel can be understood to affectively train those readers to feel those systemic relations outside of the simulation as well.

The Echo Maker performs this incorporation and simulation through its narrative patterning. While the bulk of the novel is written in a relatively straightforward realist style, each of its five parts is framed by two devices that undermine the kinds of attachment and identification that characterize most forms of psychological realism. The first of these is the opening vignette of each section, which is told from the point of view of the migrating sandhill cranes. Each of these sections describes a part of the seasonal cycle of the cranes, and the novel begins and ends when they land at the Platte. The human plot is therefore subordinated to the temporality of the cranes' migration, which literally structures the way that the novel chronicles human activities. Furthermore, there is no human action that is not framed by the action of the cranes, which puts the human plot literally second to the plot of the migration. This migration plot includes its own priorities: births, deaths, and the many challenges and historical valences of the trip south and back north again.

Strangely, it is also in one of these passages that we get the only real-time account of Mark's accident:

> A squeal of brakes, the crunch of metal on asphalt, one broken scream and then another rouse the flock. The truck arcs through the air, corkscrewing into the field. A plume shoots through the birds. They lurch off the ground, wings beating. The panicked carpet lifts, circles and then falls again. Calls that seem to come from creatures twice their size carry miles before fading.

> By morning, that sound never happened. Again there is only here, now, the river's braid, a feast of waste grain that will carry these flocks north, beyond the arctic circle. As first light breaks, the fossils return to life, testing their legs, tasting the frozen air, leaping free, bills skyward and throats open. And then, as if the night took nothing, forgetting everything but this moment, the dawn sandhills start to dance. Dance as they have since before this river started. (*EM*, 4)

The central human event of the novel is narrated in this passage from a position of inhuman remove. Told from the perspective of the cranes, the event is erased from paragraph to paragraph rather than invested with any depth of personal meaning. The telling of the event seems to be an aesthetic gesture for its own sake, much like the dance of the cranes, which is figured as both eternal and nonspecific, distanced from the individual plight of any single bird. Aesthetic activity is figured as a species-specific behavior that, crucially, is not representational but performative. It incites physical response precisely as a result of its detachment from any project that involves conscious cause and effect or attention to any single person, crane, or event. The self-conscious aestheticization of Mark's accident in this section therefore distances the reader from the psychological narrative that follows, placing the human emotional response to the accident – the story of Mark and Karin – within a larger system of events, one that is affected, although not profoundly so, by the event. Yet in doing so, the novel does not diminish the force of the tragedy for Mark and Karin. The dynamics of identification are still firmly in operation in the realist portion of the narrative. The tension that results underscores the relative smallness of any single human event within the Earth's systems while nevertheless producing, through identification, an affective connection between the reader and the human terrain on which the effects of such systems are registered.

The second framing device of each part stems from one of the central mysteries of *The Echo Maker*: an anonymous note that Mark finds on his bedside table after awaking from his coma. The note reads:

> I am No One
> but Tonight on North Line Road
> GOD led me to you
> so You could Live
> and bring back someone else. (*EM*, 146)

Mark spends a full year trying to figure out who wrote the note, convinced that it was written by the person who saved him from his wreck. He sees the note as a mandate to do something – to bring back someone – as repayment for the anonymous act of generosity he received. But in the end, he discovers that he himself wrote the note to Barbara during a few moments of lucidity after the accident before falling into a deep coma. The note was therefore issuing a mandate to Barbara to "bring back someone" in response to Mark's act of selflessness in swerving and wrecking to avoid hitting her. But because his act of sacrifice in wrecking his truck in order to avoid Barbara is understood to have happened too fast for him to make a conscious decision whether or not to swerve, or even to see clearly what was in front of him, the command, "bring back someone else" seems to issue an impossible instruction that compels someone to do something similarly instinctive. Regardless, Mark insists that the note be followed. Confronting Barbara at the end of the novel, he argues:

> *This is yours. Your curse, not mine.*
>
> Her mouth works, asking, *How? Who?* But no sound emerges.
>
> His rage bursts. *You're the one who's supposed to do this. Go bring back someone.*
>
> Someone stands mute in the doorway, brought back by a note that will forever circulate. *So you might live.* And now that curse is his. (*EM*, 439–40)

Despite Barbara's panic and conviction that she cannot possibly follow the note's instructions, she has already, without knowing it, brought back someone. Weber, the neuroscientist interested in Mark's case, has returned to Nebraska against his better judgment in order to see Barbara, with whom he has fallen in love. Having been trapped in a narcissistic haze as a result of his fame, his attraction to Barbara jars him out of his self-interested patterns and reawakens him to the presence of human and ecological difference. Weber, who stands in the doorway, by the end of the novel carries the burden of the note that will "forever circulate," catalyzing acts that by their very nature cannot be the result of instructions as they occur too quickly to be subject to conscious control.

This notion of "bringing back someone" to a given place and an eternal form of circulation, of course, also recalls the migration patterns of the cranes, suggesting that human activity can mimic the repetition and evolution that characterize crane existence. Given that the five lines from this note provide the five chapter titles for the novel and therefore act as structuring devices for the work as a whole, the novel, too, seems to imagine for itself this power of impulse excitation through its movement from reader to reader. The novel is therefore envisioned as existing within and perpetuating a system of migration-like circulation, effecting small changes on readers that either will or will not have bearing on larger system dynamics.

Each chapter of the novel is framed by these two devices: the chapter title drawn from the note and a section told from the perspective of the birds. As the bulk of each chapter is taken up with the remaining realist narrative, it is easy enough to see the framing devices as mere accessories to the main event: the story of Mark and Karin. But if we read the novel as a performance of patterning, of sequential gestures of provocation, codification, and performative antirealism, these framing devices suddenly take on enormous power. They provide an alternative to the very form of narration that the novel calls into question through its thematization of Capgras: psychological realism that assumes the position of mimesis by suggesting that the concerns of individual humans should naturally provide the focal core of all stories. The alternative, *The Echo Maker* suggests, is a novel that provides a human-centered narrative but places it in relation to other narratives with other centers, other temporalities, and other forms of motivation. The result is a form that produces enough identification to pull readers in and enough recognition to unmoor those readers' expectations, placing readerly emotions and nonhuman affects in relation to one another, articulating their connections, and, the novel seems to hope, instigating a sense of affective connection that reaches beyond the concerns of the narrowly human in the process.

Neoliberalism, Affect, Ecology

This book has argued that capitalism functions affectively, instigating patterns of behavior that perpetuate the circulation of goods, services, and capital. With the advent of neoliberalism comes an intensification of this tendency as a result of its gathering of aspects of life not explicitly tied to the market under the logic of capitalism. Consequentially, other possibly competing systems of circulation have become invested with a capitalist logic and are understood to perpetuate economic goals. Subjects are, in turn, trained affectively to recognize their forms of engagement with a range of systems as obeying a market logic. This occurs in part through the development of what Lawrence Grossberg calls "affective epidemics": the cultivation of physiological impulses that pull subjects along affective vectors toward certain forms of action.[41] One of these affective epidemics is certainly the tendency to see one's participation in a system of circulation – whether social, environmental, or textual – as best realized through postures and attitudes expected in the practice of market circulation. As a result, subjects tend to insert themselves into a range of diverse systems attitudinally in ways that echo the typical postures of the market: as entrepreneurs, competitors, and consumers.

How the Dead Dream demonstrates that there is a fundamental tension between the necessary physiological orientation one is expected to take toward the capitalist market and the one cultivated by engagement with one's role in an ecosystem. For T., the distinction is dramatic: when participating in the capitalist system, he seeks control at all costs. His activities – bulldozing, eating, driving fast, golfing, paving, building, deforesting – all involve mastering the land to some degree or another, whether through the instrumentalization of space, through practices of consumption, or through practices of destruction. When engaging with the nonhuman world, he seeks the opposite. He longs to be penetrated by the environment around him and subordinated to its whims. When, at last, he finds comfort literally pinned on his back by a sleeping tapir on his chest, this desire for domination by nonhumans is literalized.

As environmental writers from Thoreau to Wendell Berry have argued, seeing oneself as part of an ecosystem leads away from a tendency toward valuing productivity and toward valuing limitation.[42] At the same time, this tendency to value limitation can, in turn, lead environmental thinkers away from attempts to engage with larger systemic dynamics that are central to thinking about ecology in any meaningful and truly interdisciplinary fashion.[43] These two ecological attitudes – the embracing of limitation on the one hand and the pursuit of an understanding of complex systems on the other – are not as opposed as it might seem. Indeed, it is through the recognition of complexity that we lose a sense of our own exceptionalism and begin to suspect that we might not be as able to conduct the orchestra of the natural world with as much finesse as we think. Anyone who has tried to create or manage a functioning ecosystem, even a fish tank, terrarium, or vegetable garden, learns very quickly that taking steps to intervene in one part of the system often has unpredictable results for other parts of that system. We might try to play God in our gardens, but we are often disabused of our grand ambitions. It is for this reason that genetic modification of crops might be understood to be a particularly neoliberal phenomenon: not only because it privatizes a common resource but also because it attempts to render the unpredictability of a life form predictable, masterable, and efficient for humans wanting to assess nature in economic terms.[44] While one need only to look to Margaret Atwood's *Oryx and Crake* for a startlingly reasonable projection of what the total neoliberalization of politics and nature through genetic manipulation of plants and animals could look like,[45] for the time being the attitudinal requirements of close engagement with ecological systems continues to challenge the kind of systemic manipulation seen as central to neoliberal models of capitalism.[46]

As the dissolution of narrative form at the end of *How the Dead Dream* suggests, it is easy to see literary activity as detracting from such ecological attitudes. If literature codes experience, placing it into easily digestible narratives, the loss of mastery that seems to come with a physical confrontation with the nonhuman looks as if it would be weakened by the performance of mastery involved in narrative description. Yet as *The Echo Maker* demonstrates, such a view rests on the belief that the affective operations of literature occur primarily through the dynamics of representation – through the narration of emotionally stimulating stories and a resulting emotional response that matches those that exist within that narrative. The novel's suspicion toward sentimental forms like the human interest story and its suggestion that narratives often mask or even underpin affective deficiencies like those seen in Capgras syndrome reinforces the notion that on the level of representation, novels are more likely to strengthen than to challenge the affective unresponsiveness *The Echo Maker* diagnoses as lying at the core of ecological irresponsibility. But in response to this dilemma the novel suggests that the circulation of texts might intervene not through the representation of emotional narratives but through the provocation of affective responses. Read this way, literature can be understood to intensify the challenge that identification with ecological systems poses to prevailing assumptions that all systems follow the model of the market.

Powers's novel demonstrates how reading literature as provoking affective responses might allow us to see literature as functioning ecologically. By using Mark's note as its primary structuring device, *The Echo Maker* offers a model of literary circulation that sees it as following the logic of ecosystems rather than markets, catalyzing unlikely changes in readers, and provoking physical responses with unpredictable results. This ecological understanding of literary circulation puts distance between our conceptual model of literary circulation and that of the market, an intervention meaningful not only in the context of neoliberalism but also in relation to the historical intimacy between capitalism and print culture. In his work on textual publics, Michael Warner outlines similar indeterminacies in terms of the social effects of textual circulation. For Warner, the circulation of texts produces specific self-organized publics, each understood as "a space of discourse organized by nothing other than discourse itself."[47] Warner argues that these publics are always the result of a textual "orientation to strangers" and therefore construct "stranger-relationality."[48] The result is an address that is "*both personal and impersonal*" insofar as "public speech must be taken in two ways: as addressed to us and as addressed to strangers ... we might recognize ourselves as addressees, but it is equally important that we remember that the speech was addressed to indefinite others."[49] The agency behind textual circulation is therefore distributed: neither authors nor readers have full control over membership in a textual public, and for the most part both are aware of their participation in something indeterminate.

This is particularly true of those situations in which, as Warner puts it, "the trace of our strangerhood remains present in our understanding of ourselves as the addressee" – situations where the contingency of our participation is foregrounded, where we as readers are made to understand ourselves as only circumstantially attached to a text.[50] In these situations, the reader understands herself as one of many potential strangers who might circumstantially come into contact with the text. Its circulation is therefore exposed as not exactly autonomous because its survival rests on the presence of those who are invested in its circulation, but as not exactly subordinate to any individual reader either. Textual circulation is both social and impersonal; in other words, it functions like any complex system, in which any individual participant might or might not have a dramatic effect on its function and in which participants are linked through their varying relationships to a circulating object, element, or force. This understanding of textual circulation deviates substantially from conventional concepts of the literary market, where texts are seen as commodities and readers as buyers who consume those commodities.

Moreover, this ecological understanding of literary circulation is underpinned by the fact that "the literary" is not a stable object – indeed, literary-ness can be attributable to a seemingly infinite range of things. A thing is defined as "literary" by its being read as having formal qualities that exist to some degree autonomously from its literal meaning. As we know from the New Critics, reading a work as literary involves judging it to be reducible to neither intention nor reception. And as this book has argued, one of the ways literature can be understood to function outside the prescriptions of writers and against the personal investments of readers is through its formal production of affective states. The circulation of literature and its provocation of affectivity in a range of unpredictable ways to indeterminate readers is therefore ecological in a literal sense. Literature affects human readers and, in doing so, it can change the orientations of those readers toward their environments – built or natural, human or nonhuman. Encounters with texts therefore do not merely represent non-human others, nor does the system by which we encounter literary works simply mimic an ecological system. Literature is part of our ecosystem. It interacts with us, it changes us, and sometimes it might even do so for the better. If it does, it is in its capacity to intensify affective connections to strangers, both human and nonhuman, that it can be understood to be socially and ecologically relevant – not by instruction nor by the cultivation of empathy or any other recognizable sentiment, but by alerting us to the possibility that there are forms of knowledge that we do not yet know and forms of feeling that we cannot yet feel.

Epilogue

> It is not the office of art to spotlight alternatives, but to resist by its form alone the course of the world, which permanently puts a pistol to men's heads.
>
> – Theodor Adorno

Writing about contemporary literature is an odd endeavor. Why study a cultural medium that by all evidence appears to be in decline?[1] If we are unsure as to what the social relevance of literature is today, then how much more unsure must we be as to the social relevance of literary scholarship, particularly when that scholarship is concerned with the relationship between aesthetics and politics? Surely there must be a better way to engage with the impact that art has on contemporary life.

This book responds to this problem with two linked arguments. First, in bringing together a set of contemporary texts that do the largely unrecognized work of shifting prevailing perceptions as to what constitutes a feeling, it has offered up an eclectic group of literary examples that demonstrate the continued vigor of contemporary literature. These works do not form anything like a coherent movement: some appeared on independent presses; others were published by major New York houses. Nor do they look like a traditional avant-garde: some are radically innovative; others are stylistically typical of today's mainstream. Nor are they generationally unified: some are late works of writers born in the immediate postwar years; others are early works of writers who could easily be their children. What unites this body of work is a shared interest in pushing the perceived limits of the dynamics of feeling and form. These works all perform formal-affective experiments, even if they are not clearly what we would call "experimental" in a colloquial sense. They test the structural limits of literature's capacity to register forms of experience that are not easily put into words. They therefore gesture toward an unlikely counter-tradition in contemporary literature, one based not on a coherent rejection of the mainstream, but rather on the formal rejection of our existing emotional vocabulary.

In drawing out some signal works of this counter-tradition, this book also stages a second intervention, this one oriented toward contemporary critical practice. The ways these works are challenging have been largely overlooked because of how we tend to read contemporary literature. Recognizing the work that these texts do requires attention to their formal disruptions at a moment when prevailing narratives see the very notion of radical form as increasingly outdated. While much debate still exists as to how to define the aesthetic movement that follows postmodernism, there is broad consensus that this period has seen the overturning of twentieth-century distinctions between the mainstream and the avant-garde.[2] There is a tendency to see the move away from this version of aesthetic polarization as signaling that a potentially permanent compromise has been reached that nullifies the need for radicalism in contemporary and future art movements. When techniques associated with experimentalism have proven useful in widely marketable works, and when strategies associated with the mainstream appear in the work of writers once associated with the avant-garde, it is easy enough to think that the very notion of formal opposition to mainstream aesthetics is no longer useful or realistic. Instead, we might be tempted to think, individual works will continue to innovate, but without allying themselves against the status quo in any meaningful way.

But there is reason to be suspicious of this conclusion, as the logic of successful aesthetic compromise has pronounced echoes of the logic of political compromise espoused by neoliberal utopianisms ranging from the putatively center-left claims of Thomas Friedman to the neoconservative arguments of Francis Fukuyama.[3] In both cases, a kind of end-of-history argument is advanced that imagines the possibility for endless innovation within a structure rendered stable by a large-scale consensus as to what the boundaries of that innovation will be: in the first case, mainstream aesthetic legibility and in the second case, global capitalism. Imagining the literary field as both plural and unified; multiple and peaceful; diverse and noncombative means believing that a formal logic that has as of yet been unachievable geopolitically – the thoroughgoing institution of a global capitalist utopia – is at least achievable aesthetically.

Against this assumption, this study has argued that the seemingly tranquil landscape of contemporary literature is more turbulent than it might seem, and that we are in need of critical approaches that make us attentive to that fact. While it may be true that writers are increasingly seeing techniques that were once the domain of the avant-garde as useful to projects that are ultimately aimed at larger audiences, there are still significant distinctions to be drawn among the various ways these strategies are employed. But these distinctions will not be drawn unless we complicate our narrative of what the contemporary cultural landscape looks like, and doing so demands new ways of parsing what is formally challenging and what is not. If we are looking for the avant-garde impulse on a twentieth-century model, we are going to see it on the wane. If we revise what it means to be formally challenging, on the other hand, we might be surprised at what kinds of aesthetic unruliness we find.

One of the major contentions of this book has been that works of literature are often challenging in ways we don't always entirely register consciously and that they do things to us that we often find difficult to pin down precisely because we don't have names for what they do. This is necessarily the case, I have argued, because if we did have that vocabulary at the ready, the experience that they produce would not be unsettling in the first place. We could say "this book makes me feel x," and that would be the end of it. So the argument is not that we need a better vocabulary for literary effects, but rather that we need ways of attending to those effects for which we do not have words. This is not to say that we will never be able to name what these works do, but that once we are able to do so, that will signal that their force has been, at least in part, diminished, and there will once more be a need to identify and engage with what we cannot effectively describe.

I find a particular trajectory of affect theory concerned with what I have been calling "impersonal feelings" useful in attending to these unmooring literary effects because it is in theories of affect that we get a recognition that sometimes there is a gap between what we feel and what we say we feel; what a work of literature does and what it says it does. And in the theories of affect that I turn to here, the result of this observation does not demand a turn to demystification, as if to say, you think you feel x, but really you feel y. Rather, the presence of these strange states demands attention to these forms of experience as sites from which to trace their causes and effects, where they are intentionally directed and where they go astray of that intention, what we can know that they do and what we can't.

The resulting critical practice is something closer to what Bruno Latour means by tracing networks: not exposing forms of connection that are understood to preexist the act of discovering them, but rather constructing one of many possible pictures of how elements in a system interrelate.[4]

Latour does this with scientific concepts, social assumptions, and technological changes. Working with textual affects as I do suggests that this practice can also work with literature, both internally (tracing associations among formal elements in a text) and externally (tracing associations between those forms, the text as a whole, readers, publishers, authors, and the social, political, and ecological concepts and controversies that the texts address).[5]

But doing so requires a change, not only in the methodologies we employ, but in our fundamental critical attitudes. It involves looking at literary texts not as examples of a set of concerns we already know exist, but as strange interlocutors that we assume we do not yet understand.[6] We might find ourselves asking what seem like obvious questions: *What do you do? Where do you come from? What do you have to say for yourself?* It might turn out that often the answers to these questions run very much in accord with the dominant assumptions of our time. These texts might best be read symptomatically, according to the protocols of ideology critique. But occasionally the answers are likely to run askew of our expectations, and when they do, it is worth charting precisely how this happens. Because, among other things, it suggests that humans are still capable of producing works of art that gesture to modes of thinking and feeling that go beyond the confines of how we are now inclined to think and feel. Which, in simplest terms, means that all is not lost: the way the world works is not yet resolved. And as long as art continues to reach beyond what is now imaginable, tracing, noting, and taking stock of those gestures remains a valuable endeavor.

Notes

Introduction: The Affective Hypothesis

1 The affective hypothesis is the corresponding aesthetic judgment to the ontological assumption that Rei Terada defines as "the expressive hypothesis" or "the claim that emotion requires a subject – thus we can see we're subjects, since we have emotions." *Feeling in Theory* (Cambridge, MA: Harvard University Press, 2003), 11. In both formulations, emotions are invoked to give value and substance to a cultural force, and in both cases that value and substance hinges on the notion that emotions are indexes of an essential quality of humanness. In addition, the belief that subjectivity and emotion are intrinsically linked underpins the affective hypothesis insofar as readers are prone to seeing the presence of a depth model of subjectivity as a definitive sign of the presence of emotion in a work of literature. Many of the formal characteristics that I see as vehicles for what I will call "impersonal feelings" destabilize the depth model of the subject. Features like flat characterization, metafiction, pastiche, and linguistic play all act as modes of estrangement from the illusion that characters in novels are fully realized subjects. Yet, as I discuss at greater length in Chapter 1, the prevalence of hybrid forms of experimentalism and mainstream accessibility in contemporary literature means that the affective hypothesis often continues to function even once familiar indexes of subjectivity are destabilized. As a result, my interest in this study is less in undermining the depth model of the subject and more in probing our fundamental assumptions about what constitutes a literary feeling, whether those assumptions rest on the presence of recognizable subjects or not.

2 In its emphasis on the relationship between literary experience and interpersonal connection, the affective hypothesis spans enormous critical divides, from traditional humanist accounts of literature's ethical value (see my discussion of the work of Martha Nussbaum later in this chapter) to cognitive science approaches that see reading as a mental practice of intersubjective "mind reading." See Lisa Zunshine, *Why We Read Fiction: Theory of Mind and the Novel* (Columbus: Ohio State University Press, 2006).

3 As Dierdra Reber argues, "In the years immediately following the fall of the Soviet Union ... affect began to come into view as the driver and protagonist of cutting-edge research and innovation in academic and public cultural

discourse alike," signaling "an epistemic shift from reason to affect." This shift in literary studies is most clearly manifest in the ubiquity of the affective hypothesis. See "Headless Capitalism: Affect as Free Market Episteme," *differences: A Journal of Feminist Cultural Studies* 23, no. 1 (2012): 63.

4 While there is wide consensus that the general advent of neoliberalism in political and economic policy dates back to the late 1970s, there is no clearly identifiable moment when neoliberal assumptions could be said to have firmly taken root in the daily lives of U.S. citizens. Geopolitically speaking, there is good reason to see the fall of the Berlin Wall in 1989 as the moment when capitalism began to be understood as potentially hegemonic in the world system. For work on the pivotal nature of 1989, see of course Francis Fukuyama, *The End of History and the Last Man* (New York: Free Press, 1992). See also Joshua Clover, *1989: Bob Dylan Didn't Have This to Sing About* (Berkeley and Los Angeles: University of California Press, 2009); and Christian Moraru, *Cosmodernism: American Narrative, Late Globalization, and the New Cultural Imaginary* (Ann Arbor: University of Michigan Press, 2010). Yet there is reason to believe that there would be a lag between the thorough instantiation of neoliberalism in political and global policy and the emergence of neoliberalism as a subjective dominant. In my reading of Dave Eggers's *A Heartbreaking Work of Staggering Genius* in Chapter 3 of this volume, I suggest that Eggers's description of his "non-slacker" Generation X friends might be seen as an alternative reading of those who came of age in their twenties in the 1990s as the first thoroughly neoliberal generation.

5 My definition of personal feelings is therefore distinct from efforts to describe how literature invokes certain forms of legal or political personhood. For one of the most compelling of these accounts, see Oren Izenberg, *Being Numerous: Poetry and the Ground of Social Life* (Princeton, NJ and Oxford: Princeton University Press, 2011).

6 Martha Nussbaum, *Poetic Justice: The Literary Imagination and Public Life* (Boston, MA: Beacon Press, 1997), 32.

7 Ibid., 53. Nussbaum's claim here is not new, dating back at least to George Eliot's contention that "the greatest benefit we owe to the artist, whether painter, poet, or novelist, is the extension of our sympathies. Appeals founded on generalizations and statistics require a sympathy ready-made, a moral sentiment already in activity; but a picture of human life such as a great artist can give, surprises even the trivial and the selfish into that attention to what is apart from themselves, which may be called the raw material of moral sentiment." Much gratitude to Megan Ward for this insight. See George Eliot, "The Natural History of German Life," *Westminster Review* 66 (July 1856): n.p.

8 Ibid.

9 Or, as Mark McGurl puts it, "It would be absurd to deny the large payoff to individuals living in the inherently pluralistic conditions of reflexive modernity, who are vested with a thrilling panoply of choices about how they will live their lives. But it would be equally wrong to deny the extent to which, as [Ulrich] Beck puts it, modern people 'are condemned to individualization.'"

The Program Era: Postwar Fiction and the Rise of Creative Writing (Cambridge, MA: Harvard University Press, 2009), 12. Qtd Ulrich Beck, Anthony Giddens, and Scott Lash, *Reflexive Modernization: Politics, Tradition and Aesthetics in the Modern Social Order* (Stanford, CA: Stanford University Press, 1994), 114. As I argue in the latter part of this study, a greater awareness of our embeddedness and participation in larger systems often has a destabilizing effect on the neoliberal assumption that market logics can be applied to nonmarket activities, as it highlights the contradictory forms of our participation in the many systems we inhabit. We may become aware, for instance, that our best efforts to succeed both emotionally and rationally in a capitalist system might conflict with our ability to survive in ecological systems.

10 As this book will argue, however, a more thoroughgoing interest in ontology should take us precisely in the opposite direction: toward texts that understand themselves as constructing literary experience in a way that runs counter to our expectations. These works often continue to use some of the formal mechanisms of postmodernism – those that have primarily been understood as deconstructive – in order to emphasize forms of affective experience that are not expressively anchored. On the relationship between the retention of postmodernist aesthetics and non-expressive affect in contemporary fiction, see my essay, "Postmodernism and the Affective Turn," *Twentieth-Century Literature* 57, nos. 3–4 (Fall/Winter 2011): 423–46.

11 My use of the term "dominant" draws from Brian McHale's understanding of Roman Jakobson's invocation of the term. McHale sees the concept of the dominant as a form of provisional and tactical totalization that is nevertheless aware of its own circumstantiality. Like McHale, I find the concept useful insofar as it allows critics to address not only the heterogeneous elements of a period or a text but also "the question of what *system* might underlie the catalogue." *Postmodernist Fiction* (London and New York: Routledge, 1987), 7. Italics in original.

12 David Harvey, *A Brief History of Neoliberalism* (New York: Oxford University Press, 2005), 2.

13 Ibid.

14 The economic crisis of the past few years has put the most radical neoliberal thinking under strain, but this has done little to change neoliberal policies. This has been particularly striking in Europe, where state-imposed austerity measures have been defended on the basis of a moral mandate for each individual to make sacrifices in the face of a crisis that was largely perpetrated by an elite few. Reactions to these measures in the European left, and the analogous response to the economic crisis in the United States in the form of the Occupy movements, have begun to provide language for a much-needed critique not only of individual neoliberal policies but also of basic neoliberal assumptions.

15 Harvey, *Brief History of Neoliberalism*, 3.

16 Jason Read, "A Geneaology of Homo-Economicus: Neoliberalism and the Production of Subjectivity," *Foucault Studies* 6(2009): 32. Emphasis in original.

17 While I find much to admire in the work of those interested in the effects of specific financial practices and instruments on society and culture at large, I follow Read and Brown in seeing neoliberalism as precisely defined by the ways in which it precludes efforts to understand it from the perspective of economics alone. Or, as Brown puts it, "neo-liberalism is not an inevitable historical development of capital and instrumental rationality." Marxian and other forms of economic analysis, for Brown, cannot account for "the shift neo-liberalism heralds from relatively *differentiated* moral, economic, and political rationalities and venues in liberal democratic orders to their discursive and practical integration." "Neo-liberalism and the End of Liberal Democracy," *Theory & Event* 7, no. 1 (2003), http://muse.jhu.edu.ezp.slu .edu/journals/theory_and_event/v007/7.1brown.html, accessed May 13, 2013. For one of the touchstone works on finance and contemporary social life, see Randy Martin, *The Financialization of Daily Life* (Pennsylvania: Temple University Press, 2002).

18 Wendy Brown, "American Nightmare: Neoliberalism, Neoconservatism, and De-Democratization," *Political Theory* 34, no. 6 (2006): 693.

19 Wendy Brown, "Neo-liberalism and the End of Liberal Democracy."

20 Jonathan Franzen, *The Corrections* (New York: Farrar, Straus & Giroux, 2001), 137.

21 As James Annesley points out, Gary's emotional accounting and other similar moments of the text represent "relationships between individual psychology and economics in terms that suggest that even these areas of personal experience are increasingly finding themselves coordinated and controlled." "Market Corrections: Jonathan Franzen and the 'Novel of Globalization,'" *Journal of Modern Literature* 29, no. 2 (2006): 115.

22 Brown, "Neo-liberalism and the End of Liberal Democracy."

23 The past few years have seen extensive work on the imperative to be happy and its relationship to capitalism, as well as the possibility that sad affects might be claimed productively for left politics. On the former, see Sara Ahmed, *The Promise of Happiness* (Durham, NC: Duke University Press, 2010) and Lauren Berlant, *Cruel Optimism* (Durham, NC: Duke University Press, 2011). On the latter, see Heather Love, *Feeling Backward: Loss and the Politics of Queer History* (Cambridge, MA: Harvard University Press, 2009) and Jonathan Flatley, *Affective Mapping: Melancholia and the Politics of Modernism* (Cambridge, MA: Harvard University Press, 2008).

24 The FDA approved the use of Magnetic Resonance Imaging (MRI) scans for diagnostic procedures in 1985, while Functional Magnetic Resonance Imaging (fMRI) appeared in the early 1990s. The latter particularly contributed to the 1990s becoming the "Decade of the Brain," as it allowed not only for the localization of certain cognitive processes but also for observation of the movement of functions across different localizations. On the relationship between the turn to neuroscience in the 1990s and literature of the period, see Stephen J. Burn, "Don DeLillo's *Great Jones Street* and the Science of the Mind," *MFS: Modern Fiction Studies* 55, no. 2 (2009): 349–68.

25 Prozac, the first of the Selective Serotonin Reuptake Inhibitors (SSRIs), was approved by the FDA in 1987, followed by Zoloft and Paxil. By 2008 antidepressants were the third most commonly prescribed drugs in the United States. See Siddhartha Mukherjee, "Post-Prozac Nation," *New York Times Magazine*, April 19, 2012, http://www.nytimes.com/2012/04/22/magazine/the-science-and-history-of-treating-depression.html?pagewanted=all&_r=0, accessed May 13, 2013.

26 While the self-help industry has a lengthy history, its major period of growth occurred during the 1990s, with self-help book sales rising by nearly 100 percent between 1991 and 1996. See Micki McGee, *Self-Help, Inc.: Makeover Culture in American Life* (Oxford and New York: Oxford University Press, 2005), 6.

27 For a history of the deregulation of DTC advertising, see Julie M. Donohue et al., "A Decade of Direct-to-Consumer Advertising of Prescription Drugs," *New England Journal of Medicine* 357, no. 7 (2007): 673–81. For a study on the relationship between DTC and the prescription of antidepressants, see Richard L. Kravitz et al., "Influence of Patient's Requests for Direct-to-Consumer Advertised Antidepressants: A Randomized Controlled Trial," *Journal of the American Medical Association* 293, no. 16 (2005): 1995–2002.

28 The notion that endless economic growth is possible is not exclusively a neoliberal belief, but neoliberal economists are vocally opposed to any attempt to limit growth or move toward a stable state economy. As Harvey argues, neoliberalism entails the belief in "endless capital accumulation and economic growth no matter what the social, ecological, or political consequences" (*Brief History of Neoliberalism*, 181).

29 Sam Tanenhaus, "Peace and War," *New York Times*, August 19, 2010, http://www.nytimes.com/2010/08/29/books/review/Tanenhaus-t.html?pagewanted=all, accessed May 13, 2013. Tanenhaus quotes James Wood, "Tell Me How Does It Feel?," *The Guardian*, October 6, 2001, http://www.theguardian.com/books/2001/oct/06/fiction, accessed May 13, 2013.

30 See James Wood's contention that the novel vacillates between emotional warmth and "an easy journalism of style." "What the Dickens," *The Guardian*, November 9, 2001, http://www.guardian.co.uk/books/2001/nov/09/fiction.reviews, accessed May 13, 2013.

31 Annesley, "Market Corrections: Jonathan Franzen and the 'Novel of Globalization,'" 124.

32 Colin Hutchinson, "Jonathan Franzen and the Politics of Disengagement," *Critique: Studies in Contemporary Fiction* 50, no. 2 (2009): 205.

33 In this way, I am indebted to Michael Clune's innovation in giving a formal definition to the way literature engages economic structures in his *Literature and the Free Market: 1945–2000* (New York: Cambridge University Press, 2010).

34 Wood, "Tell Me How Does It Feel?"

35 James Wood, "Human, All Too Inhuman," *New Republic* 223, no. 4 (2000), http://www.newrepublic.com/article/books-and-arts/human-all-too-inhuman#, accessed May 13, 2013.

36 E. M. Forster, *Aspects of the Novel*, electronic ed. (New York: RosettaBooks, 2002), 51.

37 Ibid.

38 Forster offers the following definition of character: "The novelist ... makes up a number of word-masses ... , gives them names and sex, assigns them plausible gestures, and causes them to speak by the use of inverted commas, and perhaps to behave consistently. These word-masses are his characters." This definition is, from the start, impersonal. Characters are not representations of human beings, they are "word-masses," animated by particular formal traits like the use of quotation marks to establish dialogue and the use of proper names to indicate specificity. While they may reflect an author's idea of what constitutes a human, characters need not be human. Indeed, in a lengthy aside Forster speculates that the superficiality of nonhuman characters could merely be a function of his time, and that in the future nonhuman characters might emerge that are every bit as complex as those intended to reflect human forms of consciousness and activity. It is perhaps this emphasis on the aesthetic composition of character out of the material of language that leads Forster to argue against his contemporaries who see flat characterization categorically as a formal flaw.

39 I. A. Richards, *Principles of Literary Criticism* (London and New York: Routledge, 2002), 109–10.

40 Thus Richards's engagement with developments in science in general and neuropsychology in particular. See also I. A. Richards, *Science and Poetry* (New York: W. W. Norton, 1926). For one of the few works of scholarship on this understudied work, see Vincent B. Sherry, *The Great War and the Language of Modernism* (New York: Oxford University Press, 2004).

41 Richards, *Principles of Literary Criticism*, 121.

42 See Henri Bergson, *Matter and Memory* (Cambridge, MA: Zone Books, 1990).

43 See Martin Heidegger, *Being and Time*, trans. Joan Stambaugh (Albany: State University of New York Press, 1996); and Jacob von Uexküll, *A Foray into the Worlds of Animals and Humans* (Minneapolis: University of Minnesota Press, 2010).

44 Walter Benjamin, *The Work of Art in the Age of Its Technological Reproducibility, and Other Writings on Media* (Cambridge, MA: Harvard University Press, 2008); and Sergei Eisenstein, *Film Form*, trans. Jay Leyda (New York: Harcourt, 1977).

45 William James, *The Principles of Psychology*, vol. 2 (New York: Dover, 1918), 450.

46 Ibid., 448.

47 Along with Baruch Spinoza, James has been adopted as a kind of conceptual grandfather figure by neuroscientists interested in the cognitive primacy of affective response.

48 W. K. Wimsatt and Monroe C. Beardsley, *The Verbal Icon: Studies in the Meaning of Poetry* (Lexington: University Press of Kentucky, 1954).

49 For a detailed chronicle of the turn from materialist approaches to psychology to psychoanalysis in the early twentieth century and its effect on literary work and criticism, see Jane F. Thrailkill, *Affecting Fictions: Mind, Body, and Emotion in American Literary Realism* (Cambridge, MA: Harvard University Press, 2009).

50 See, for instance, Jacques Derrida, "Signature, Event, Context," *Limited, Inc.* (Chicago, IL: Northwestern University Press, 1988): 1–23.

51 See Raymond Williams, *Marxism and Literature* (Oxford: Oxford University Press, 1978).

52 Patricia Ticineto Clough, *The Affective Turn: Theorizing the Social* (Durham, NC: Duke University Press, 2007).

53 Gilles Deleuze and Félix Guattari, *What Is Philosophy?* (New York: Columbia University Press, 1994), 164.

54 Wimsatt and Beardsley, *Verbal Icon*, 21.

55 Deleuze and Guattari, *What Is Philosophy?* 174.

56 Indeed, it was Deleuze who in one sense constructed this tradition by tracing it in his single-author studies of these thinkers. See *Spinoza: Practical Philosophy*, trans. Robert Hurley (San Francisco, CA: City Lights Books, 1988); *Nietzsche and Philosophy*, trans. Hugh Tomlinson (New York: Columbia University Press, 2006); *Expressionism in Philosophy: Spinoza*, trans. Martin Joughin (Cambridge, MA: Zone Books, 1992); and *Bergsonism*, trans. Hugh Tomlinson and Barbara Habberjam (Cambridge, MA: Zone Books, 1990).

57 Baruch Spinoza, *Ethics* (Indianapolis, IN: Hackett, 1992), 103.

58 Spinoza's term *affectus* is generally translated as "emotion," though as Samuel Shirley admits in his translator's preface to his edition of *The Ethics*, "it certainly seems odd to speak of 'the emotion of desire,' and this is a sufficient indication that 'affectus' is not quite the equivalent of our 'emotion'" (Spinoza, *Ethics*, 28). Equally problematic, however, is the tendency for some commentators to collapse the distinction between *affectus* and *affectio* in the text, the latter of which, while often translated as "affection," "*never* means love, liking regard, and so forth. It is the form 'taken on' by some thing, a state of that thing, and therefore logically posterior to that of which it is an affection" (23–4).

59 Spinoza, *Ethics*, 106.

60 See among others Lauren Berlant, *The Female Complaint: The Unfinished Business of Sentimentality in American Culture* (Durham, NC: Duke University Press, 2008); Love, *Feeling Backward* and Ann Cvetkovich, *An Archive of Feelings: Trauma, Sexuality, and Lesbian Public Cultures* (Durham, NC: Duke University Press, 2003).

61 Sianne Ngai, *Ugly Feelings* (Cambridge, MA: Harvard University Press, 2004), 28.

62 Ibid.

63 Ngai, *Ugly Feelings*, 28–9.

64 Ibid., 30.

65 Sianne Ngai, *Our Aesthetic Categories: Zany, Cute, Interesting* (Cambridge, MA: Harvard University Press, 2012), 57.

66 Brian Massumi, *Parables for the Virtual: Movement, Affect, Sensation* (Durham, NC: Duke University Press, 2002), 27–8.

67 Ibid.

68 Brecht's term, *verfremdungseffekt* is translated in the original 1961 publication of Brecht's "On Chinese Acting" as "alienation effect." My use of "estrangement" is consistent with Jameson's insistence that the word should be distinguished from the Marxist implications of alienation, although Jameson ultimately prefers the use of "V-effect" in order to preserve reference to the original German. See Fredric Jameson, *Brecht and Method* (London and New York: Verson, 1998).

69 Bertolt Brecht, "On Chinese Acting," *The Tulane Drama Review*, vol. 6, no. 1 (1961): 130.

70 Ibid.

71 See Richard Powers, *Galatea 2.2* Richard Powers, *Galatea 2.2* (New York: Harper Perennial, 1996) and "The Brain Is the Ultimate Storytelling Machine, and Consciousness Is the Ultimate Story," Interview with Alec Michod, *The Believer* (February 2007), http://www.believermag .com/issues/200702/?read=interview_powers.

72 Stacey Levine, "An Inter(e)view with Ben Marcus," *electronic book review* (December 15, 1998). http://www.electronicbookreview.com/thread/wuc/ disruptive.

73 "The Brain is the Ultimate Storytelling Machine"; Levine, "An Inter(e)view."

74 While I find his distinction between more and less recognizable feelings useful, I am less interested in following Massumi in seeing an absolute cognitive split between emotions and affects. For work in the tradition that does put more emphasis on this divide, see John Protevi, *Political Affect: Connecting the Social and the Somatic* (Minneapolis: University of Minnesota Press, 2009) and William Connolly, *Neuropolitics: Thinking, Culture, Speed* (Minneapolis: University of Minnesota Press, 2002). For a critique of the neuroscientific work underpinning the emotion/affect divide, see Ruth Leys, "The Turn to Affect: A Critique," *Critical Inquiry* 37, no. 3 (2011): 434–72.

75 Karen Tei Yamashita, *Tropic of Orange* (Minneapolis, MN: Coffee House Press, 1997).

76 I focus on the impersonality of characterization in *Tropic of Orange* here, but it is worth noting that Yamashita is generally interested in not only impersonal but also nonhuman interventions in apparently human-driven narratives. While the central plot of *Tropic of Orange* is put into motion as a result of the movements of an orange, the narrative center of her earlier work, *Through the Arc of the Rain Forest*, is not a human but a small black ball. See Karen Tei Yamashita, *Through the Arc of the Rainforest* (Minneapolis, MN: Coffee House Press, 1990). On the importance of the nonhuman in Yamashita's work, see Caroline Rody, "The Transnational Imagination: Karen Tei Yamashita's *Tropic of Orange*," in *Asian North American Identities: Beyond*

the Hyphen, ed. Eleanor Ty and Donald C. Goellnicht (Bloomington: Indiana University Press, 2004).

77 Alissa Quart calls this narrative structure in film "hyperlink cinema," in which "information, character, and action co-exist without hierarchy." "Networked: Don Roos and 'Happy Endings,'" *Film Comment* (July/August 2005): 51.

78 Wood, "Human, All Too Inhuman," 43.

79 Rody, "Transnational Imagination: Karen Tei Yamashita's *Tropic of Orange*," 139.

80 Sue-Im Lee argues that *Tropic of Orange* "postulates another model of global collectivity" that differs from those posited by the rhetoric of globalization in "'We Are Not the World': Global Village, Universalism, and Karen Tei Yamashita's *Tropic of Orange*," *MFS Modern Fiction Studies* 52, no. 3 (2007): 503.

81 Yamashita, *Tropic of Orange*, 207.

82 See Rachel Adams's argument that while Franzen, in his reflections on his own process of turning away from the social novel, sees social critique in the novel as no longer possible, Yamashita finds ways of engaging contemporary economic developments that remain critically oriented. She writes, "While Franzen was decrying the numbing effects of global consumer culture, contemporary fiction in the U.S. was being transformed by an infusion of new writers whose distinctive responses to the conditions of globalization were hardly in danger of 'making the same point over and over.'" "The Ends of America, The Ends of Postmodernism," *Twentieth-Century Literature* 53, no. 3 (2007): 43.

83 I therefore ally myself with the diverse tradition of critics including William Cronon, Timothy Morton, Karl Kroeber, Bruno Latour, and Elizabeth Grosz who see distinctions between nature and culture as not only artificial but also detracting from attempts to understand both domains.

84 Timothy Morton, *The Ecological Thought* (Cambridge, MA: Harvard University Press, 2010), 7.

85 For this reason, while I am not interested in insulating the term "ecology" from application to non "natural" things, I am suspicious of the tendency to call any network an ecology. As I employ the term, while human management can enter into ecological systems, ecologies are more self-organizing and less intentionally shaped than, say, Facebook networks or corporate team structures.

86 Morton, *Ecological Thought*, 11.

87 Bennett's definition, like the one that underpins this study, is based on "a Spinozist notion of affect, which refers broadly to the capacity of any body for activity and responsiveness." *Vibrant Matter: A Political Ecology of Things* (Durham, NC: Duke University Press, 2010), xii.

88 Works associated with the philosophical school known as Object Oriented Ontology also emphasize the social effects of nonhuman things, but my interest in relationality and systems behavior leads me to find more use in work

like Bennett's than in most of the work associated more directly with OOO itself. In addition, while Bennett, Morton, and Latour see nonhuman things as having influence in human and nonhuman systems dynamics, they all also acknowledge distinctions among human and nonhuman forms of agency that can often get lost in the more radical OOO pronouncements. For key works on OOO, see Ian Bogost, *Alien Phenomenology, or What It's Like to Be a Thing* (Minneapolis: University of Minnesota Press, 2012), Levi Bryant, *The Democracy of Objects* (London: Open Humanities Press, 2011), and Graham Harman, *Guerilla Metaphysics: Phenomenology and the Carpentry of Things* (Chicago, IL: Open Court, 2005).

89 See Bruno Latour, "The Promises of Constructivism," in *Latour, Reassembling the Social: An Introduction to Actor-Network Theory* (Oxford and New York: Oxford University Press, 2005); and Bruno Latour, "Why Has Critique Run Out of Steam? From Matters of Fact to Matters of Concern," *Critical Inquiry* 30 (Winter 2004): 225–48.

90 On the neoliberalization of creative work, see Sara Brouillette, *Literature and the Creative Economy* (Palo Alto, CA: Stanford University Press, 2014).

91 Ngai, *Ugly Feelings*, 14.

92 In its interest in works of art that withdraw from a project of transmitting recognizable sentiments, this project is largely in agreement with the work of Walter Benn Michaels and others that the personalization of aesthetic experience reinforces the assumptions underlying neoliberalism. I part ways with this argument, however, when it comes to the precise definition of how specific forms of aesthetic and affective experience conform to or depart from an emphasis on the personal. In *The Shape of the Signifier*, Michaels argues for the importance of a focus on authorial intention in the context of the contemporary social tendency to see politics through the lens of individual and cultural identity. "If you think the intention of the author is what counts," he argues, "then you don't think the subject position of the reader matters, but if you don't think the intention of the author is what counts, then the subject position of the reader will be the only thing that matters." See Walter Benn Michaels, *The Shape of the Signifier* (Princeton, NJ, and Oxford: Princeton University Press, 2004), 11. For Michaels, because of the tendency for neoliberal art to value identity over a focus on political and economic structures, any focus on the relationship between works of art and feelings tends to lead to a celebration of subjective idiosyncrasy. This argument is expanded in his recent work on neoliberal aesthetics, where he argues that there is a direct relationship between "the rise in economic inequality" characteristic of neoliberalism and "the emergence of a theory of the work of art which, imagining the escape from the artist's intention, insists on the primacy of the beholder." Walter Benn Michaels, "Neoliberal Aesthetics: Fried, Ranciere and the Form of the Photograph," *nonsite.org*, issue 1 (2011). But in arguing for a more nuanced parsing of what kinds of literary feelings are personalizing and which are not, I am in agreement with Michael Clune's response to Michaels's essay, in which he argues that its reading of Michael

Fried's concept of absorption "seems right only insofar as absorption is under-stood as subjective experience." In Clune's reading of Fried, "the experience of art is precisely not the submission of the object to the subject, but a mode of experience in which both are subsumed in the work." Michael Clune, from "Responses to *Neoliberal Aesthetics*," *nonsite.org*, issue 2 (2011). Also see Michael Fried, *Absorption and Theatricality: Painting and Beholder in the Age of Dierot* (Chicago, IL: University of Chicago Press, 1988).

1 Personal and Impersonal: Two Forms of the Neoliberal Novel

1 Henry James, "The Art of Fiction," in *The Norton Anthology of Theory and Criticism*, ed. Vincent B. Leitch (New York and London: W. W. Norton, 2010), 747.

2 Henry James, *The Portrait of a Lady* (New York: Random House, 1966), xxxi.

3 James, "Art of Fiction," 754.

4 Of course, the twentieth century has seen a range of literary modes that have been said to escape the relatively rarefied debates between conser-vative "approachable" fiction and avant-garde or "difficult" fiction. In par-ticular, the middlebrow literary tradition of the twentieth century brought modernist invention to a mainstream audience in a relatively digestible form. Middlebrow writers share with the contemporary writers I examine here the ability to be, as Nicola Humble points out, "very good at co-opting and commercializing the highbrow" (quoted in D'hoker, "Theorizing the Middlebrow," 261). Yet most historians of middlebrow culture agree that in reception and motivation, "the middlebrow is all about class" insofar as mid-dlebrow works are particularly aimed at a nonacademic, nonelite market of readers (ibid., 260). The very designation "middlebrow" is dependent on a class-based identification of a specific readership; it is not a stable or auton-omous aesthetic category. Consequentially, no matter how much the recent works I discuss here might seem to echo the middlebrow mode formally, their celebration in high literary culture is specific to the contemporary moment. Unlike the middlebrow compromises between accessibility and innovation of the past, today's compromises are not restricted to the needs of a specific class position, defined by either monetary or cultural capital. Instead, they perme-ate the highest echelons of academic and literary institutions and are mar-keted to readers traditionally associated with the literary highbrow. See Elke D'hoker, "Theorizing the Middlebrow: An Interview with Nicola Humble," *Interférences littéraires/Literaire interferenties* 7 (November 2011): 259–65. Many thanks to Mark McGurl, whose comments on an earlier version of this chapter helped me clarify this distinction.

5 The formal problems created by this effort to compromise, however, have largely been ignored. As the history of work in politics and aesthetics sug-gests, maintaining a project of aesthetic novelty while catering to the reading

tastes of a general public is not as easy as it might seem, and thinking of the solution as mere compromise involves seeing contemporary literature as existing at the end of literary history, as a satisfactory conclusion to a centuries-old aesthetic dilemma. For one of the most enduring workings through of this problem, see Walter Benjamin, "The Author as Producer," *New Left Review* 62 (July–August 1970): 83–96.

6　Robert L. McLaughlin, "Post-Postmodern Discontent: Contemporary Fiction and the Social World," *Symplokē* 12, nos. 1–2 (2004): 55.

7　Stephen Burt, "Review of *Smokes*, by Susan Wheeler," *Boston Review* (Summer 1998), http://www.bostonreview.net/BR23.3/burt.html, accessed May 23, 2013.

8　In suggesting that the formal innovations of ellipticism are intended to confront the entertainment powers of television, Burt's analysis recalls one of the earliest assertions of a compromise aesthetic, David Foster Wallace's essay "E Unibus Pluram: Television and U.S. Fiction," in which the author speculates that the "next real literary 'rebels' in this country" might respond to the hijacking of narrative entertainment by television by returning to a project of emotional sincerity. This next generation, he imagines, would treat "old untrendy human troubles and emotions in U.S. life with reverence and conviction" rather than the ironic distance practiced by their postmodernist predecessors. "E Unibus Pluram: Television and U.S. Fiction," *Review of Contemporary Fiction* 13, no. 2 (1993): 193.

9　In fiction, this leads to a renewed focus on forms of characterization driven to reflect as realistically as possible the emotional life of the individual. In poetry, this manifests in a return to the lyric subject, albeit with an awareness of the ways that subject has been destabilized by the avant-garde experiments of the twentieth century.

10　Jonathan Franzen, "Mr. Difficult," *New Yorker*, September 30, 2002, 100. Further references will be cited parenthetically as *MD*.

11　See Ben Marcus, "Why Experimental Fiction Threatens to Destroy Publishing, Jonathan Franzen, and Life as We Know It: A Correction," *Harper's Magazine*, October 2005: 39–52.

12　In his work in progress, *After Critique: Twenty-First Century Fiction in a Neoliberal Age*, Mitchum Huehls defines this kind of paradox, in which leftist critique is either subsumed into the model of neoliberalism or finds itself defending unlikely conservative positions as "the neoliberal circle."

13　Wendy Brown, "Neo-liberalism and the End of Liberal Democracy," *Theory & Event* 7, no. 1 (2003), http://muse.jhu.edu.ezp.slu.edu/journals/theory_and_event/v007/7.1brown.html, accessed May 23, 2013.

14　Michel Foucault, *The Birth of Biopolitics*, trans. Graham Burchell, ed. Michel Senellart, Francois Ewald, and Alessandro Fontana, *Lectures at the College de France* (New York: Palgrave Macmillan, 2008), 226.

15　Ibid.

16　Ian Watt, *The Rise of the Novel: Studies in Defoe, Richardson and Fielding* (Berkeley and Los Angeles: University of California Press, 1957), 70.

17　Ibid., 64.

18　Ibid., 14.

19　This observation is the affective extension of Alex Woloch's contention that the character system of the realist novel formally recalls the asymmetry of the capitalist economy, with round protagonists commanding a disproportional amount of readerly attention compared to flat minor characters. *The One and the Many: Minor Characters and the Space of the Protagonist in the Novel* (Princeton, NJ: Princeton University Press, 2003).

20　E. M. Forster, *Aspects of the Novel*, electronic ed. (New York: RosettaBooks, 2002), 35.

21　Ibid., 55.

22　Foucault, *Birth of Biopolitics*, 229.

23　This argument is consistent with much of the work on affective labor in the neoliberal era. See in particular Paulo Virno, A Grammar of the Multitude, trans. Isabella Bertoletti, James Cascaito, and Andrea Casson (Los Angeles: Semiotext[e], 2004) and Michael Hardt and Antonio Negri, Empire (Cambridge, MA: Harvard University Press, 2000).

24　While Foucault argues that biopower evolves alongside capitalism in *The History of Sexuality*, the material on neoliberalism in his lectures on biopolitics makes clear that for him neoliberalism ushers in an era of a more overt and totalizing biopolitical form of control. *The History of Sexuality, Volume One: An Introduction* (New York: Random House, 1978).

25　Lauren Berlant chronicles the political ambivalence of intimacy in *The Female Complaint: The Unfinished Business of Sentimentality in American Culture* (Durham, NC: Duke University Press, 2008).

26　The neoliberal novel therefore involves a transformation in how the character system reflects prevailing concepts of the economy. For Woloch, in the nineteenth-century realist novel, "a dialectical literary form is generated out of the relationship between inequality and democracy ... On the one hand, the asymmetric structure of realist characterization – which rounds out one or several characters while flattening, and distorting, a manifold assortment of characters – reflects actual structures of inequitable distribution. On the other hand, the *claims* of minor characters on the reader's attention – and the resultant tension between characters and their functions – are generated by the democratic impulse that forms a horizon of nineteenth-century politics" (31). The realist novel therefore puts pressure on the asymmetry of the capitalist economy through the constant suggestion that minor characters are always potentially protagonists, and are simply prevented from being so by the economy of scarcity that the character system of the novel produces. In the neoliberal novel, however, the multiplicity of protagonists looks like the triumph of the democratic impulse behind realism over inequality, just as the attribution of entrepreneurial subjectivity to workers and managers alike under neoliberalism appears to abolish the class system. Instead of a form that highlights the presence of inequality, in other words, the form of the neoliberal novel reinforces the belief that inequality no longer exists. See Woloch, *The One and the Many*.

27 The argument that the minimal nature of McCarthy's prose signals interest in developing an ahistorical, elemental system of values in *The Road* has been called into question by Andrew Hoberek, who finds that just as Hemingwayesque minimalism dominates the novel's style, forms of unusual specific reference also make an appearance, linking the action of the story to a particular regional history, ecology, and literary tradition and offering moments when aesthetic activity is posited as a way out of the otherwise nihilistic world of the novel. While I agree that these moments exist on the level of the sentence, my emphasis here is on the overwhelming tone achieved not only by syntactical minimalism but also by minimalisms of chromatic palette, plot, and character, all of which I argue serve to encourage a restricted focus on the two central characters of the novel. "Cormac McCarthy and the Aesthetics of Exhaustion," *American Literary History* 23, no. 3 (2011): 483–99.

28 See Ashley Kunsa's contention that "the style of The Road … is pared down, elemental, a triumph over the dead echoes of the abyss and, alternately, over relentless ironic gesturing" (58). In "Maps of the World in Its Becoming: Post-Apocalyptic Naming in Cormac McCarthy's *The Road*," *Journal of Modern Literature* 33, no. 1 (2009): 57–74.

29 Cormac McCarthy, *The Road* (New York: Random House, 2006), 6.

30 Hoberek sees these *Crusoe*-ian valences of *The Road* as evidence of its interest in the possibility of world making out of disaster, noting, "what novel that contains as one of its central episodes a man swimming out to a ship to salvage supplies could fail to resonate with *Robinson Crusoe*'s narrative of isolation as an opportunity for remaking the social order?" "Cormac McCarthy and the Aesthetics of Exhaustion," 490.

31 McCarthy, *The Road*, 49–50.

32 For a longer examination of color in *The Road*, see Chris Danta, "'The Cold Illucid World': The Poetics of Gray in Cormac McCarthy's *The Road*," in *Styles of Extinction: Cormac McCarthy's The Road*, ed. Julian Murphet and Mark Steven (London and New York: Continuum Books, 2012).

33 This description of the burnt-looking man echoes Ernest Hemingway's description of the grasshoppers who had become black in order to camouflage themselves in their "burned-over land" in his short story "The Big Two-Hearted River" in *In Our Time* (New York: Scribner, 1958). I discuss this image in greater depth in Chapter 2.

34 Michael Chabon, "After the Apocalypse," *New York Review of Books* (February 15, 2007), http://www.nybooks.com/articles/archives/2007/feb/15/after-the-apocalypse/?pagination=false, accessed May 23, 2013.

35 Annie Dillard, "The Wreck of Time: Taking the Century's Measure," *Harper's Magazine* (January 1998): 56.

36 Margaret Thatcher, "Press Conference for American Correspondents in London," *Thatcher Archive: COI Transcript* (June 25, 1980), http://www.margaretthatcher.org/document/104389, accessed May 23, 2013.

37 For this reason, while I agree with George Monbiot's observation about *The Road* that it "exposes the one terrible fact to which our technological hubris blinds us: our dependence on biological production remains absolute," I do

not agree with his overarching assessment that the novel is "the most important environmental book ever written." George Monbiot, "The Road Well
Travelled," *The Guardian* October 30, 2007.

38 Brooke Allen, "Review of *The Book of Illusions* by Paul Auster," *Atlantic
Monthly* 290, no. 2 (September 2002): 154. See also Maggie Gee's description
of the novel as "cool, cerebral writing, characterized by indirection, full of
references to art." The rhetorical question that ends the review clearly reveals
a bias toward psychological realism: "If there is no human life or truth in a
work of art, how can the living be expected to believe in it, no matter how
artful it is?" "Review: Fiction: The Book of Illusions by Paul Auster," *Sunday
Times* (October 20, 2002), http://www.thesundaytimes.co.uk/sto/culture/
books/article55211.ece, accessed May 23, 2013.

39 For a defense of Auster's metafictional strategies on political grounds, see
Martin Butler and Jens Martin Gurr's argument that readings such as Allen's
neglect the degree to which "it is precisely when [fiction] is most con-
fined and seemingly self-reflexive and hermetic that it seems to be most
engaged with extratextual reality" (209). In "The Poetics and Politics of
Metafiction: Reading Paul Auster's *Travels in the Scriptorium*," *English Studies*
89, no. 2 (2008): 195–209.

40 James Wood, "Shallow Graves: The Novels of Paul Auster," *New Yorker*
(November 30, 2009), http://www.newyorker.com/arts/critics/books/2009/
11/30/091130crbo_books_wood, accessed May 23, 2013.

41 Ibid.

42 Ibid.

43 Paul Auster, *The Book of Illusions* (New York: Picador, 2002), 8. Further references will be cited parenthetically as *TBI*.

44 Charles Cullum sees this scene as evidence of David's attempts to "deny his
own selfhood" in the wake of grief (a condition that he reads as remedied
later in the novel), while I read it as resonant with various modes of gestural
and performative identity that exist throughout the novel. "The Blue Stone,
Heidegger, and 'I': The Issue of Identity in Paul Auster's *The Book of Illusions*,"
EAPSU Online: A Journal of Critical and Creative Work 5 (2008): 36–44.

45 Jim Peacock reads the metafictional work of *The Book of Illusions* in more
conventional terms as offering "a profoundly bleak postmodern portrait of
human subjectivity as fractured, contingent, powerless, forever within the
frame and informed by the inevitability of death," which leaves the reader
"with the aesthetic artefact declared to be *The Book of Illusions* – a collection of textual frames-within-frames which, despite its inception in virtual
nihilism, is a compelling work" (69). My reading is more optimistic, suggesting that the contingency of human subjectivity in the work does not index
a nihilistic worldview but rather points to a performative ethic of affective
engagement with the world. In "Carrying the Burden of Representation: Paul
Auster's *The Book of Illusions*," *Journal of American Studies* 40 (2006): 53–69.

46 Timothy Bewes, "Against the Ontology of the Present: Paul Auster's
Cinematic Fictions," *Twentieth Century Literature* 53, no. 3 (2007): 282. Bewes
argues that by representing the cinematic image as the formal unit capable of

generating an alternative to traditional understandings of aesthetic representation and consumption, Auster "looks longingly toward cinema as a symbol
of everything that writing is unable to achieve" (296). Yet, as I argue here,
there are traces of cinematic form in Auster's prose, particularly in its atten-
tiveness to the thinness of narrative explanation of emotional states.

47 Ibid., 284.
48 Daniel Heller-Roazen, *The Inner Touch: Archaeology of a Sensation* (Brooklyn,
NY: Zone Books, 2007).
49 Ibid., 92–3.
50 Gilles Deleuze, *Cinema 1: The Movement-Image* (Minneapolis: University
of Minnesota Press, 1986), 96. Deleuze draws heavily from Henri Bergson's
definition of affect, which sees affect as occurring cognitively in a temporal
hesitation between stimulus and response. As a result, spatiotemporal decon-
textualization heightens and extends the durational force of the affective stage
in cognition. See Henri Bergson, *Matter and Memory* (Cambridge, MA: Zone
Books, 1990); and Gilles Deleuze, *Bergsonism*, trans. Hugh Tomlinson and
Barbara Habberjam (Cambridge, MA: Zone Books, 1990).
51 Deleuze, *Cinema 1: The Movement-Image*, 97.
52 Ibid., 99.
53 For a more optimistic reading of the scene in *The Road* in which the man and
the boy share the last remaining bottle of Coca-Cola, see Raymond Malewitz,
"Regeneration through Misuse: Rugged Consumerism in Contemporary
American Culture," *PMLA* 127, no. 3 (2012): 526–41.
54 For a particularly smart and ambitious version of this argument, see Jeffrey
Nealon, *Post-Postmodernism: or, The Cultural Logic of Just-In-Time Capitalism*
(Stanford, CA: Stanford University Press, 2012).
55 This comfort with existing emotional definitions even extends to Eve Kosofsky
Sedgwick's work, despite its commitment to seeing feeling as something that
exists prior to discursive shaping. In their foundational essay, "Shame in the
Cybernetic Fold," Sedgwick and Adam Frank write, "ask yourself this: how
long does it take you after being awakened in the night by (a) a sudden noise
or (b) sexual arousal, to cognitively 'analy[ze]' and 'apprais[e] ... the current
state of affairs' well enough to assign the appropriate '*quale*' to your emotion? That is, what is the temporal lag from the moment of sleep interruption to the 'subsequent' moment when you can judge whether what you're
experiencing is luxuriation or terror? No, it doesn't take either of us very long
either." Eve Kosofsky Sedgwick and Adam Frank, "Shame in the Cybernetic
Fold: Reading Silvan Tomkins," *Critical Inquiry* 21, no. 2 (1995): 516.

2 Affect and Aesthetics in 9/11 Fiction

1 Don DeLillo, *Falling Man* (New York: Simon & Schuster, 2007), 3.
2 Ibid.
3 Ibid., 16.
4 Ibid.

5 Richard Gray, "Open Doors, Closed Minds: American Prose Writing at a Time of Crisis," *American Literary History* 21, no. 1 (2009): 7.

6 See Michiko Kakutani's contention that the novel's diction is "tired and brittle"; Kakutani, "A Man, a Woman and a Day of Terror," *New York Times* (May 9, 2007), http://www.nytimes.com/2007/05/09/books/09kaku .html?pagewanted=all, accessed August 13, 2013. See also Andrew O'Hagan's insistence that the novel is marked by DeLillo's "inability to conjure his usual exciting prose" in "Racing against Reality," *New York Review of Books* (June 28, 2007), http://www.nybooks.com/articles/archives/2007/jun/28/racing -against-reality/?pagination=false, accessed August 13, 2013.

7 Linda S. Kauffman gives DeLillo considerable political credit, arguing that the novel "asks the questions America needs to ask in order to see itself" (372). Yet I, like Gray and others, disagree with her contention that the book does so by attesting to "our howling grief" about the event (ibid.). To the contrary, if the book makes a strong political statement it seems to do so by pointing to its own insufficiency in the face of such an emotional task. "The Wake of Terror: Don DeLillo's 'In The Ruins of The Future,' 'Baader-Meinhof,' and *Falling Man*," *MFS: Modern Fiction Studies* 54, no. 2 (2008): 353–77.

8 Gray, "Open Doors, Closed Minds," 7. Gray quotes Kirby Farrell, *Post-Traumatic Culture: Injury and Interpretation in the Nineties* (Baltimore, MD: Johns Hopkins University Press, 1998), 19.

9 Some have also suggested that better novels will simply emerge with time. This position is articulated by Paul Auster and Salman Rushdie in a 2002 NPR interview. Both authors insist upon the decades that often pass between a historical event and the best fictional works about that event, invoking examples ranging from *The Red Badge of Courage* to *War and Peace*. Yet Auster also suggests that post–September 11 novels are likely to register the event "obliquely" in ways that demonstrate the transformative effect of the events. It could be argued that the novel I will turn to by Laird Hunt (who has received a great deal of praise from Auster) offers this kind of slant address. See Linda Wertheimer, "Paul Auster and Salman Rushdie Discuss Reimagining the Shape of the World since September 11th," *All Things Considered*, National Public Radio, September 8, 2002.

10 For one of the most powerful of these critiques, see Elizabeth S. Anker, "Allegories of Falling and the 9/11 Novel," *American Literary History*, vol. 23, no. 3: 463–82.

11 Shoshana Felman and Dori Laub, *Testimony: Crises of Witnessing in Literature, Psychoanalysis and History* (New York: Routledge, 1991), 25.

12 Cathy Caruth, *Unclaimed Experience* (Baltimore, MD: Johns Hopkins University Press, 1996), 8, 11.

13 Ruth Leys, *Trauma* (Chicago, IL: University of Chicago Press, 2000), 299.

14 For a particularly noteworthy instance of trauma theory providing a justification for a political assessment of September 11 that privileges U.S. unity over a more complex geopolitical critique, see E. Ann Kaplan's contention that the event demands to be dealt with "in its specificity" rather than in

the context of a more thorough consideration of global history and politics. *Trauma Culture* (New Brunswick, NJ: Rutgers University Press, 2005), 15.

15 Jonathan Safran Foer, *Extremely Loud and Incredibly Close: A Novel* (New York: Mariner Books, 2006), 326.

16 Ibid.

17 The danger of such limits to "grievability" is the topic of Judith Butler's essay "Violence, Mourning, Politics," in *Precarious Life: The Powers of Mourning and Violence* (New York: Verso, 2004) and *Frames of War: When Is Life Grievable?* (New York: Verso, 2009). Butler shows how the tactical uses and prohibitions of public mourning participate in the expansion of militarism and the limiting of possibilities for other, possibly more fertile, relationships to collective suffering.

18 David Harvey, *A Brief History of Neoliberalism* (New York: Oxford University Press, 2005).

19 Milton Friedman, *Capitalism and Freedom* (Chicago, IL: University of Chicago Press, 2002), xiv. Naomi Klein seizes upon this argument of Friedman's as evidence of the foundational role of crises in the institution of a range of corporatist policies in *The Shock Doctrine: The Rise of Disaster Capitalism* (New York: Continuum, 2007).

20 Klein, *Shock Doctrine*, 299.

21 Ibid., 289.

22 Alain Badiou, "15 Theses on Contemporary Art," *Lacanian Ink* 23 (2004): n.p. All references are to the online version of this article (no page number citations): http://www.lacan.com/issue22.php, accessed August 13, 2013. Further references to "15 Theses on Contemporary Art" will be cited parenthetically as *CA*.

23 Indeed, much of the work on affect and 9/11 serves to obscure the geopolitical situation of the event by focusing on ethics instead of politics. Viewed from such positions, 9/11 literature's emphasis on the emotional vulnerability of the U.S. populace looks like an ethical, pro-social, empathetic gesture. Such readings neglect to engage with the ways the very notion of the 9/11 victim as apolitical served as a justification for the militarism of the war on terror. For examples of this trend within affect studies and ethics, see Laura Savu, "Souls Shifted Sideways": The Ethics and Aesthetics of Affect in Post-9/11 Narrative," *Studies in American Culture* 35, no. 1 (2012): 31–58 and Kristiaan Verslys, *Out of the Blue: September 11 and the Novel* (New York: Columbia University Press, 2009). For a more nuanced articulation of the relationship between ethics and politics in the 9/11 novel, see Georgiana Banita, *Plotting Justice: Narrative Ethics and Literary Culture After 9/11* (Lincoln and London: University of Nebraska Press, 2012).

24 As neuroscientist Antonio Damasio points out, feeling relies on high cognitive functions on both ends of the sensory chain, but a large measure of the process is still experienced bodily: the initial instigation of feeling often depends on the rational or pattern-based assessment and judgment of external stimuli, but the triggering and execution of feeling within the body

primarily involves more primitive neural structures (the amygdala and brain stem) as well as dispersed disruptions throughout the body (in the viscera and musculoskeletal and circulatory systems). The mapping of these disruptions back into consciousness once again requires higher cognitive functions. It is this recognition of the body's movement, change, and disruption that we call feelings or emotion. Damasio's conceptual vocabulary relies on translating Spinoza's references to *affectio* in his *Ethics* as "emotion," while most others, including Massumi whose distinction between emotion and affect is dependent on the same Spinozan parallelism as Damasio's, translate *affectio* as "affect." For Damasio, emotion is experienced bodily whereas feeling is conscious. Damasio's distinction between emotion and feeling therefore mirrors most affective critics' distinction between affect and emotion. See *Looking for Spinoza: Joy, Sorrow, and the Feeling Brain* (Orlando, FL: Harcourt, 2003).

25 See Brian Massumi, *Parables for the Virtual: Movement, Affect, Sensation* (Durham, NC: Duke University Press, 2002).

26 Sianne Ngai, *Ugly Feelings* (Cambridge, MA: Harvard University Press, 2004), 14. I discuss the relationship between cognitive mapping, affective mapping, and disorientation further in Chapter 3.

27 While I do not explore Badiou's work on affect here, there is broad consensus that it is a neglected dimension of his thought. The possible position of affect in Badiou's work has been taken up by Sam Gillespie, who argues that Lacanian psychoanalysis offers a necessary supplement to Badiou's lack of a theory of affect in *Being and Event*; Gillespie, *The Mathematics of Novelty: Badiou's Minimalist Metaphysics* (Melbourne: re:press, 2008). Badiou does offer a more thorough account of affect in *Logics of Worlds*, but the general criticism (offered by Peter Hallward and others) that Badiou does not account for the materiality of the subject who feels these affects remains ubiquitous in contemporary criticism. See Peter Hallward, *Badiou: A Subject to Truth* (Minneapolis: University of Minnesota Press, 2003); and Alain Badiou, *Logics of Worlds: Being and Event II*, trans. Alberto Toscano (London and New York: Continuum, 2009).

28 This satirical posture is amplified in Jess Walter's novel, *The Zero* (New York: HarperCollins, 2006), which, in departing from the realist mode that prevails in much 9/11 writing, offers a damning critique of the U.S. response to the tragedies.

29 Hunt acknowledges W. G. Sebald's *The Rings of Saturn* as a precedent and inspiration for his work, which is intended as "a book unlike one Sebald would have written … taking up and recasting his favorite themes and obsessions." Laird Hunt, *The Exquisite* (Minneapolis, MN: Coffee House Press, 2006), 245. Further references to *The Exquisite* will be cited parenthetically as *TE*.

30 The positioning of the September 11 attacks in *The Exquisite* differs from a range of novels that decenter the event historically or in terms of their plots. In *The Exquisite*, the attacks are unquestionably central to the novel, but they are never represented, unlike the occasional mention of the status of the ground zero grounds in Jennifer Egan's *A Visit from the Goon Squad*

(New York: Alfred A. Knopf, 2010), for instance, which figure material aspects of the attacks but pluralize the novel's contexts such that the novel does not read as being essentially about September 11.

31 That there is an intimate relationship between metaphor and other figurative language and affect is a contention that reaches back to I. A. Richards, *Practical Criticism* (New Brunswick, NJ: Transaction, 2004), 211.

32 This argument can be traced back to Philip Young's foundational work on Hemingway; see Young, *Ernest Hemingway: A Reconsideration* (University Park: Pennsylvania State University, 1966).

33 Ernest Hemingway, *In Our Time* (New York: Scribner, 1958), 133, 36, 55.

34 Ibid., 151.

35 The question of how to read the relationship between global capitalist crises and environmental crises has been taken up variously by scholars as diverse as Ulrich Beck, Ursula Heise, and Paul Virilio. See Ulrich Beck, *Risk Society: Towards a New Modernity* (Thousand Oaks, CA: Sage Publications, 1992); Ursula K. Heise, *Sense of Place and Sense of Planet: The Environmental Imagination of the Global* (Oxford: Oxford University Press, 2008), and Paul Virilio, *Unknown Quantity* (London: Thames and Hudson, 2003). I have found Virilio's work in particular useful for a project of considering ecological threat and neoliberalism together in an earlier essay, "Ecology beyond Ecology: Life after the Accident in Octavia Butler's *Xenogenesis* Trilogy," *MFS Modern Fiction Studies* 55 (2009): 545–65.

36 Mr. Kindt himself uncharacteristically references the classic environmentalist slogan, "touch one part of the web and the whole thing quivers," elsewhere in *The Exquisite* as he recalls his horror in seeing a fish gutted as a boy (*TE*, 83).

37 Massumi, *Parables for the Virtual*, 27.

3 Reading Like an Entrepreneur: Neoliberal Agency and Textual Systems

1 Fredric Jameson, "Cognitive Mapping," *Marxism and the Interpretation of Culture*, ed. Lawrence Grossberg and Cary Nelson (Urbana: University of Illinois Press, 1988), 349.

2 Ibid.

3 Jameson's concept of cognitive mapping recalls Georg Lukacs's interest in literature's ability to represent a social totality. In "Realism in the Balance" Lukacs praises the realist novel's achievement in "scrutinizing all subjective experiences and measuring them against social reality" (37). Unlike efforts among the expressionist avant-garde to transmit the immediacy of emotional experience, Lukacs's realist novelist "knows how thoughts and feelings grow out of the life of society and how experiences and emotions are parts of the total complex of reality" (36). As a result, whereas the anticapitalist force of the avant-garde is "purely aesthetic," the work of the realist gives readers the ability to "achieve a critical distance" from the world as it is, thus granting

them "freedom from the reactionary prejudices of the imperialist era" (36, 37). Jameson departs from Lukacs, however, in seeing this potential as existing within a range of forms, not only literary realism. See Theodor Adorno, Walter Benjamin, Ernst Bloch, Bertolt Brecht, and Georg Lukacs, *Aesthetics and Politics* (Brooklyn, NY: Verso, 2007).

4 In many theories of affect, the presence of emotion indexes the existence of structures that produce that emotion; emotions can therefore be used as touchstones for the discovery of larger systemic dynamics, whether psychological or sociopolitical. In these readings, interpretation of emotional states can allow for the development of reasoned distance from those states and the revelation of psychic or environmental conditions that give rise to them. Freud, for instance, describes the practice of psychoanalysis as the "means we possess for uncovering what is concealed, forgotten, and repressed in the mind [to bring] the pathogenic psychical material into consciousness [and] get rid of the ailments that have been brought about by the formation of substitutive symptoms." Analysis in this view functions analogously to ideology critique, revealing the fundamental material of consciousness and allowing for attention to be drawn to it rather than the emotional "substitutive symptoms" that cloak its actual function. See Sigmund Freud, *Five Lectures on Psychoanalysis*, electronic ed. (1909), http://www.anselm.edu/homepage/dbanach/h-freud-lectures.htm, accessed August 8, 2013.

5 Jonathan Flatley, *Affective Mapping: Melancholia and the Politics of Modernism* (Cambridge, MA: Harvard University Press, 2008), 80.

6 Ibid.

7 The liberal concept of agency is most commonly traced back to the work of John Locke in general and his *Second Treatise on Government* (1690) in particular. John Locke, *Second Treatise of Government*, ed. Dave Gowan (Project Gutenberg, 2005), http://www.gutenberg.org/files/7370/7370-h/7370-h.htm, accessed August 8, 2013.

8 Saba Mahmood, *The Politics of Piety* (Princeton, NJ: Princeton University Press, 2005), 11.

9 Ibid., 12.

10 Ibid.

11 John Locke, *Second Treatise on Government*.

12 Steven Shaviro, "The 'Bitter Necessity' of Debt: Neoliberal Finance and the Society of Control," 8. www.shaviro.com/Othertexts/Debt.pdf, accessed August 8, 2013.

13 Karl Marx, *Capital: A Critique of Political Economy, Volume One*, trans. Ben Fowkes (New York: Penguin Books, 1990), 875. I owe this reading of Marx to David Harvey's course on Volume One of *Capital* at the CUNY Graduate Center in 2002.

14 Shaviro, "The 'Bitter Necessity' of Debt," 8.

15 Harvey, *Brief History of Neoliberalism*, 5.

16 Ibid.

17 In a strange reflection on the relationship between free market ideology and the belief that human activity is based primarily on conscious choice, conservative commentator David Brooks recently acknowledged that his research into cognitive theories of embodied decision making made him "much more suspicious ... of the free market." David Burnett, "David Brooks Defines the New 'Social Animal,'" National Public Radio (March 7, 2011), http://www .npr.org/2011/03/07/134329412/david-brooks-defines-the-new-social-animal, accessed August 8, 2013.

18 The pursuit of freedom therefore acts as what Lawrence Grossberg calls an "affective epidemic." Grossberg explains that the theory of ideological structures "does not explain how people are called to these places, nor how they are 'trapped' within them despite their political and ideological disagreements." This explanation requires a theory of affective mobilization that produces "everyday life as a series of trajectories or mobilities which, while apparently leading to specific concerns, actually constantly redistribute and disperse investments." See Lawrence Grossberg, *We Gotta Get Out of This Place: Popular Conservatism and Postmodern Culture* (London and New York: Routledge, 1992), 283–4.

19 Wendy Brown, *Edgework: Critical Essays on Knowledge and Politics* (Princeton, NJ and Oxford: Princeton University Press, 2005), 41.

20 Sidonie Smith and Julia Watson see this as a form of preemption of the typical relationship between authentic memoir and skeptical criticism. See their "The Rumpled Bed of Autobiography: Extravagant Lives, Extravagant Questions," *Biography: An Interdisciplinary Quarterly* 24, no. 1 (2001): 8.

21 Ibid., 9.

22 Dave Eggers, *A Heartbreaking Work of Staggering Genius* (San Francisco, CA: McSweeney's, 2001), "Rules and Suggestions." Further references to *A Heartbreaking Work of Staggering Genius* will be cited parenthetically as *HW*.

23 There are also strong connections to Jonathan Franzen's concept of the Contract model. For more on the relationship between Contract reading and neoliberalism, see Chapter 1 of this study. For Franzen's articulation of the model, see Jonathan Franzen, "Mr. Difficult." *New Yorker* (September 30, 2002): 100–10.

24 Benjamin Widiss argues that the primary difference between Eggers's metacommentary and similar gestures in earlier works of literature lies in this persistence of emotional authenticity, which he locates in the work's implicit refusal to abide the "death of the author" paradigm of poststructuralism. See Benjamin Widiss, *Obscure Invitations: The Persistence of the Author in Twentieth-Century American Literature* (Stanford, CA: Stanford University Press, 2011).

25 Lee Konstantinou sees the paratextual elements of the memoir as "postironic": the devices are not, in his view, merely ironic. "Neither are they merely humorous devices, clever games for a special coterie of readers. Their purpose is, it seems apparent, to control interpretation and also to present Eggers's life as uncorrupted and exemplary." In "Wipe That Smirk Off Your

Face: Postironic Literature and the Politics of Character," PhD diss., Stanford University, 2010, 173.

26 A more radical form of audience participation is parodied in the paratextual material, when Eggers suggests that disenchanted readers might order a digital version of the book, which "will be interactive" so that "you'll have the option of choosing the protagonist's name" or even "change all the names within, from the main character down to the smallest cameos. (This can be about *you!* You and your pals!)" (*HW*, 27–8).

27 Dan Savage, "Brotherly Love," *Salon.com* (March 14, 2000), http://www.salon.com/2000/03/14/eggers_2/, accessed August 8, 2013.

28 Ben Marcus, *The Age of Wire and String* (Champaign, IL: Dalkey Archive Press, 2007), 3. Further references to *The Age of Wire and String* will be cited parenthetically as *AWS*.

29 As Peter Vernon writes, "In short this is a book that blocks interpretation by a constant series of definitions that are then constantly redefined." Peter Vernon, "Ben Marcus, *The Age of Wire and String*," *Yearbook of English Studies* 31 (2001): 120.

30 D. W. Daniels, "The World of Words: Ben Marcus' *The Age of Wire and String*," *Notes on Contemporary Literature* 33, no. 4 (2003): 6.

31 Vernon, "Ben Marcus, *The Age of Wire and String*," 121.

32 Vernon argues that Marcus's ability to "make language new" relies on a similar dynamic. He explains, "At almost every point he blocks the reader's expectations of logical discourse but, simultaneously, he enables the reader by opening up emotional lines of discourse which interconnect throughout this extraordinary book" (ibid., 124).

33 Dewey uses the term "emotion" to describe a kind of consciousness that precedes reflection. The experience he describes therefore comes closer to what other theorists call "affect."

34 John Dewey, *Art as Experience* (New York: Penguin, 1934), 12–13.

35 Ibid., 14. Emphasis mine.

36 Ibid.

37 Ibid., 18, 15.

38 Ibid., 18.

39 Baruch Spinoza, *Ethics* (Indianapolis, IN: Hackett, 1992), 103.

40 Jane Bennett, *Vibrant Matter: A Political Ecology of Things* (Durham, NC: Duke University Press, 2010), ix. Emphasis in original.

41 Ibid.

42 Bruno Latour, *Reassembling the Social: An Introduction to Actor-Network Theory* (Oxford and New York: Oxford University Press, 2005), 138.

43 Ibid.

44 Fredric Jameson, *Postmodernism, or, the Cultural Logic of Late Capitalism* (Durham, NC: Duke University Press, 1991), 54.

45 Latour, *Reassembling the Social*, 45.

46 Bruno Latour, "Why Has Critique Run Out of Steam? From Matters of Fact to Matters of Concern," *Critical Inquiry* 30 (Winter 2004): 227.

47 Bruno Latour, "An Attempt at a 'Compositionist Manifesto.'" *New Literary History* 41 (2010): 474–5.
48 Latour, *Reassembling the Social.*
49 Ibid., 82.

4 Ecology, Feeling, and Form in Neoliberal Literature

1 Billy Collins, "The Sandhill Cranes of Nebraska," *Harper's Magazine* (August 2011): 18.
2 This poem can therefore be seen as a correlation in the medium of poetry to the newest generation of nature documentaries. For both, the realm of the aesthetic allows for a sprawling account of nonhuman events that exceeds the perceptive capacities of any single individual. As Richard Beck argues of the mega popular television documentary series *Planet Earth*, the use of visual effects and seemingly impossible camera angles showcases expensive digital film technology as much as it does nature. Such techniques also serve to transform the series' "literal (but still Earth-bound) landscapes into alien worlds" such that "the world represented in *Planet Earth* is not one that we inhabit." In both Collins's work and these visual spectacles, the value of natural phenomena lies in their visibility. The work of art – whether a television show or a poem – conveys a vision of how the limited engagement with the natural world possible for an individual can be replaced with an impossibly grand perspective that necessarily constructs nature as something of value primarily for its representability. As Beck puts it, "At some point all nature films, either explicitly or implicitly, answer the question, 'What is nature good for? What is it worth?' The answer given by *Planet Earth*, over the course of its eleven episodes, is: 'Nature is good for looking at.' This makes for excellent television but questionable environmental advocacy." Costing Planet Earth," *Film Quarterly* 63, no. 3 (2010): 65; 63. See also Derek Bouse, "Are Wildlife Films Really 'Nature Documentaries'?" *Critical Studies in Media Communication* 15, no. 2 (1998): 116–40.
3 In an article on poetry and social consciousness, Brett Foster argues that the monotony of travel in the poem is "likely emerging from Collins' frequent travels to universities and libraries across the country where he reads his poetry to packed lecture halls." Read this way, the poem demonstrates the sad fact that "poets and poems often seem clueless about the embattled world around them." I see the very fact that Collins's speaker can be read either as a businessman or a poet as being fundamental to the neoliberal context of the work. As Collins's example suggests, there may be less and less of a distinction between entrepreneurs and poets, as both now lament but nevertheless abide the necessity of packed travel schedules. See Brett Foster, "Contemporary Poetry: Social Conscience? Not So Much," *Capital Commentary* (November 18, 2011), http://www.capitalcommentary.org/billy-collins/contemporary-poetry-social-conscience-not-so-much, accessed August 11, 2013.

4 Noel Castree outlines several conclusions that geographers have reached through empirical studies tracing neoliberalism as it is brought to bear on the biophysical environment. The activities he sees as commonly observed in such studies include privatization, or enclosure of previously common resources; marketization, or the institution of buying and selling of the bio-physical world; deregulation; "market-friendly reregulation" or the use of state-based apparatuses to guarantee the privatization and marketization of the biophysical world; and policies that emphasize what he calls "the creation of 'self-sufficient' individuals and communities" in regards to environmental practices. See Noel Castree, "Neoliberalism and the Biophysical Environment 3: Putting Theory into Practice," *Geography Compass* 5, no. 1 (2011): 35–49.

5 Vandana Shiva, *"Recovering the Real Meaning of Sustainability,"* ed. David E. Cooper and Joy A. Palmer (New York: Routledge, 1992), 191.

6 For an overview of these debates within Marxism, see Gerry Canavan, Lisa Klarr, and Ryan Vu's introduction to the *Ecology and Ideology* special issue of *Polygraph* (featuring contributions by Timothy Morton, John Bellamy Foster, and Slavoj Zizek). Gerry Canavan, Lisa Klarr, and Ryan Vu, "Introduction," *Polygraph* 22 (2010): 1–31.

7 Ecological form (as opposed to the literary representation of "environmental" or "animal" themes) has historically been marginalized in literary ecocriticism. Writing more than a decade before Morton, Karl Kroeber is one of the few critics of his time who issues a similar complaint, arguing the highly controver-sial point that "the most important ecological writing is un-Thoreauvian" in its ambitious scale and attention to the current state of ecological science (309). Citing Aldo Leopold, Rachel Carson, and others as exemplars of this un-Tho-reauvian strand, he argues that scholars of environmental literature who ignore attempts to take in complex ecological relationships that fall outside the limits of individual human perception risk missing "the complex implications of the evolutionary decentering of humankind" (312). Karl Kroeber, "Ecology and American Literature: Thoreau and Un-Thoreau," *American Literary History* 9, no. 2 (1997). Kroeber reviews Lawrence Buell, *The Environmental Imagination* (Cambridge, MA: Harvard University Press, 1995). For another key work in this vein, see Dana Phillips's ecological critique of what he sees as American ecocriticism's focus on works that seek mimetic relationships with the expe-rience of the natural world; in *The Truth of Ecology: Nature, Culture, and Literature in America* (Oxford and New York: Oxford University Press, 2003).

8 As Timothy Morton has argued, the focus on the local in environmental lit-erature can lead to "the kind of environmentalist ideology that wishes that we had never started to think – ruthlessly immediate, aggressively mascu-line, ruggedly anti-intellectual, afraid of humor and irony" (8). Morton iden-tifies commitment to local immediacy as the prevailing value in ecocritical approaches to literature, arguing that instead attention should be brought to "a counterstrain in literary 'green' writing that has not so much to do with hedgerows and birds' nests as it has to do with the planet Earth as a whole and the disorientation we feel when we start to think big" (15). He argues that the

positing of the "Universe's eye view" in Raphael's speech to Adam in Milton's *Paradise Lost* is the first of many instances of distanced ecological vision that allows humans to reflect "on their decentered place in the Universe – and on their inability to account for this disorientation" (22). As a result, Morton posits that "the 'impossible' viewpoint of space ... is a cornerstone of the ecological thought" (23). The distinction between the kind of flexibility we see in Collins's poem and the kind of distance that allows for a more thoroughgoing assessment of ecological interconnectedness is primarily a matter of formal effect. While the former envisions, and enacts through its form, a comfortable mastery over ecology, the latter envisions and formalizes the experience of displacement, disorientation, and decentering that may be provoked by such distant visions. In Morton's terms, the distinction can be summed up thusly: "Archimedes said, 'Give me somewhere to stand, and I shall move the Earth.' The ecological thought says, 'Give us nowhere to stand, and we shall care for the Earth'" (24). *Ecological Thought*. Qtd. John Milton, *Paradise Lost* (Harmondsworth, UK: Penguin, 2003), 7.617–25, 8.140–58.

9 Lydia Millet, *How the Dead Dream* (New York: Houghton Mifflin Harcourt, 2008), 3. Further references will be cited parenthetically as *HDD*.

10 In her review of *How the Dead Dream*, Carolyn Kellogg reads this line in conventional terms, arguing T. in this scene "is bewildered by the depth of his emotion: 'The fullness, the terrible sympathy!' This intensity fades, but the encounter is his first sign of compassion, a hairline fracture in his entrepreneur's shell." Carolyn Kellogg, "Money for Nothing," *Los Angeles Times* (January 27, 2008), http://articles.latimes.com/2008/jan/27/books/bk-kellogg27, accessed August 11, 2013.

11 See Patrick Ness, "How the Rich Live," *The Guardian* (October 10, 2008), http://www.theguardian.com/books/2008/oct/11/lydia-millet. See also "How the Dead Dream," *Publishers Weekly* (October 8, 2007), http://www.publishersweekly.com/978-1-59376-184-4, accessed August 11, 2013.

12 Joseph Conrad, *Heart of Darkness*, 4th ed., Norton Critical Editions (New York: W. W. Norton, 2005).

13 Ness, articulating the feelings of many critics of the novel, describes this episode as "a *Heart of Darkness* finale that I don't think Millet quite pulls off." Ibid.

14 I am indebted to Katie Muth for this insight.

15 *How the Dead Dream* is the first book in a trilogy that includes *Ghost Lights* (New York: Norton, 2011) and *Magnificence* (New York: Norton, 2012). But while T. appears at the margins of these works, he never reclaims narrative centrality.

16 For McKibben, this contamination verges on being total with the advent of climate change, whereby even the weather cannot be imagined to come from something outside the reach of human activity. See *The End of Nature* (New York: Random House, 2006).

17 McKibben, *The End of Nature*, 237; emphasis mine.

18 William Cronon, "The Trouble with Wilderness; or, Getting Back to the Wrong Nature," in *Uncommon Ground: Rethinking the Human Place in*

Nature, ed. William Cronon (New York: W. W. Norton, 1995), 88; emphasis in original.

19 Ibid., 89.

20 Ibid.

21 Ibid.

22 Ibid.

23 This was precisely the quandary that faced scholars of environmental literature at the turn of the millennium. Having only recently secured institutional support for the study of how literature represents the environment – ecocriticism as a field only coalesced in the late 1980s and early 1990s – ecocritics committed to the value of literature in representing the beauty and vulnerability of the environment were soon faced with critiques like Cronon's that emphasized the degree to which literary works do not represent so much as construct concepts of wild nature. Whereas for what Lawrence Buell defines as first-wave ecocritics writing in the late 1980s and early 1990s, "'environment' effectively meant 'natural environment'" and "the realms of the 'natural' and the 'human' looked … disjunct" (21); for the second-wave ecocritics writing in the mid- to late 1990s and early 2000s, "the prototypical human figure is defined by social category and the 'environment' is artificially constructed'" (23). On the level of thematics, Buell is correct in noting that for both types of scholarship "the understanding of personhood is defined for better or for worse by environmental entanglement. Whether individual or social, being doesn't stop at the border of the skin," there are still pronounced differences in what critics of each wave believe to be the role of the literary in addressing that entanglement (21). However, while first-wave critics might see literature as allowing readers to better understand and appreciate the degree to which humans interact with nonhumans, second-wave critics are likely to be attentive to how literature is one method among many by which humans inscribe nonhumans into human categories, producing understanding but also exercising discursive power. The motivating problem for first-wave critics is the marginalization of nonhuman nature; the motivating problem for second-wave critics is the violence of the forms of inscription we bring to bear on what we define as "nature." First-wavers fear the violence that results from ignorance; second-wavers fear the violence that results from incorporation. See Lawrence Buell, *The Future of Environmental Criticism: Environmental Crisis and Literary Imagination*, Blackwell Manifestos (Malden, MA: Blackwell, 2005).

24 Brian Massumi, *Parables for the Virtual: Movement, Affect, Sensation* (Durham, NC: Duke University Press, 2002), 39; emphasis in original.

25 Raymond Williams famously writes that "nature" is "perhaps the most complex word in the [English] language." In the historical span of its use, the word is most commonly used to indicate inherent qualities of a thing or to describe the whole of material existence. The notion of "nature" as meaning that which is not human should be understood as a minor definition even as it has become prevalent over the past century. *Keywords: A Vocabulary of Culture and Society*, rev. ed. (New York: Oxford University Press, 1985).

219. Also see the *Oxford English Dictionary*, *"nature, n."* (New York: Oxford University Press), http://www.oed.com.ezp.slu.edu/view/Entry/125353?rskey =8fbHbd&result=1&isAdvanced=false#eid, accessed August 11, 2013. For what is perhaps the most direct account of the problems with common uses of the term "nature," see Timothy Morton, *Ecology without Nature: Rethinking Environmental Aesthetics* (Cambridge, MA: Harvard University Press, 2007).

26 For a complex account of the affect of wonder's environmental dimensions, see Heather Houser's excellent essay on *The Echo Maker*, "Wondrous Strange: Eco-Sickness, Emotion, and *The Echo Maker*," *American Literature* 84:2 (2012): 381–408.

27 Kroeber, "Ecology and American Literature: Thoreau and Un-Thoreau," 310; emphasis in original.

28 Two key exceptions are Morton and Elizabeth Grosz; the latter engages with what it would mean to understand art as an evolved aspect of sexual selection in *Chaos, Territory, Art: Deleuze and the Framing of the Earth* (New York: Columbia University Press, 2008).

29 Powers is celebrated by neuroscientists as a novelist who takes great pains to get the science right – his appointment at the University of Illinois' Becker Institute and his work with the neuroscience research group there no doubt contribute to his knowledge of the cutting-edge brain research that provides the spine not only for *The Echo Maker* but for many of his other novels as well. On Powers's work with contemporary neuroscience in *The Echo Maker* see Charles B. Harris, "The Story of the Self: *The Echo Maker* and Neurological Realism," in *Intersections: Essays on Richard Powers*, ed. Stephen J. Burn and Peter Dempsey (Champaign, IL: Dalkey Archive Press, 2008). On cognitive science in Powers's earlier novels see Joseph Tabbi, *Cognitive Fictions* (Minneapolis: University of Minnesota Press, 2002). Because of his documented interest in neurological theories of cognition, I draw from Powers' own articulation of what affect is.

30 These are all writers of popular nonfiction books on neuroscience in the late twentieth and early twenty-first centuries. Weber is often directly compared to Sacks, whose *The Man Who Mistook His Wife for a Hat* (New York: Touchstone, 1998) appears in the novel when a man on a plane recognizes Weber and suggests that he is "The brain guy ... Sure. *The Man who Mistook His Life for a ...* " (449).

31 Richard Powers, *The Echo Maker* (New York: Picador, 2006), 106. Further references to *The Echo Maker* will be cited parenthetically as *EM*.

32 The notion that the drive to produce rational narratives, when detached from feeling, can lead to unreason is no surprise to Weber's wife, Sylvie, who responds wryly, "This just in: male scientists confirm the bleeding obvious," and it is true that, read one way, Weber's assessment of the dynamics of the brain only confirms what many critics of the hegemony of Western masculinist approaches to knowledge have known all along (*EM*, 106).

33 Harris points out that the gap between the impulses of Powers's characters and their conscious thoughts is at times so dramatic that "the reader must

often infer a focalizing character's motivation because the character lacks conscious access to that motivation, which springs from regions of the brain that lie far below the reach of the rational cortex" ("Story of the Self," 239).

34 *The Echo Maker* does with the human/animal divide what Powers's *Galatea 2.2* (New York: Harper Perennial, 1996) does for the human/machine divide. Similar ironic descriptions in which humans are almost, but not quite, aware of their machine-like qualities exist in *Galatea*.

35 This critique of sentimentalism is one of the reasons why I do not, as Joseph Tabbi does, read *The Echo Maker* as a "sentimental novel." "Afterthoughts on *The Echo Maker*," in *Intersections: Essays on Richard Powers.*, ed. Stephen J. Burn and Peter Dempsey (Champaign, IL: Dalkey Archive Press, 2008).

36 See T. M. Luhrmann, *When God Talks Back: Understanding the American Evangelical Relationship with God* (New York: Alfred A. Knopf, 2012), one of many works that see religious experience as the result of rigorous forms of affective training.

37 Richard Powers, "Making the Rounds," in *Intersections: Essays on Richard Powers*, ed. Stephen J. Burn and Peter Dempsey (Champaign, IL, and London: Dalkey Archive Press, 2008), 308.

38 Ibid.

39 Ibid., 309.

40 Ibid.

41 Lawrence Grossberg, *We Gotta Get Out of This Place: Popular Conservatism and Postmodern Culture* (London and New York: Routledge, 1992), 292.

42 See Henry David Thoreau, *Walden* (Boston, MA: Beacon Press, 1997), particularly the first chapter, in which Thoreau outlines the discrepancies between forms of capitalist production and forms of subsistence. Also see Wendell Berry, "Faustian Economics: Hell Hath No Limits," *Harper's Magazine* (May 2008), http://harpers.org/archive/2008/05/faustian-economics/, accessed August 11, 2013. These are, of course, just two examples of this tendency to emphasize limitation in environmental literature, a tendency that is ubiquitous throughout the history of nature writing.

43 A range of recent studies have argued that there is a crucial role for aesthetic work in representing ecological phenomena that are beyond the perceptive capacity of the individual. Evidence of recent interest in expansive temporal and spatial phenomena can be seen in the preponderance of critical works taking up theories of deep time, elemental time, and planetarity. The growth of these approaches attests to the commitment of contemporary scholars in a range of subfields to seeing environmental literature as reaching beyond the boundaries of a single, local perspective and instead engaging with global, interplanetary, and geological temporal and spatial scales. See among others Wai Chee Dimock and Lawrence Buell, eds., *Shades of the Planet: American Literature as World Literature* (Princeton, NJ: Princeton University Press, 2007); Wai Chee Dimock, *Through Other Continents: American Literature across Deep Time* (Princeton, NJ: Princeton University Press, 2006); Gayatri Chakravorty Spivak, *Death of a Discipline* (New York: Columbia University

Press, 2003); and Ursula K. Heise, *Sense of Place and Sense of Planet: The Environmental Imagination of the Global* (Oxford: Oxford University Press, 2008).

44 My immediate reference is to the title of Michael Pollan's early essay, "Playing God in the Garden," *New York Times Magazine* (October 25, 1998), http://www.nytimes.com/1998/10/25/magazine/playing-god-in-the-garden .html?pagewanted=all&src=pm, accessed August 11, 2013. Conceptually, I draw more substantively from Shiva's work on GMOs in *Biopiracy: The Plunder of Nature and Knowledge* (Cambridge, MA: South End Press, 1997).

45 Margaret Atwood, *Oryx and Crake* (New York: Anchor Books, 2004).

46 As I have emphasized throughout this study, neoliberal capitalism is not lais-sez-faire capitalism. The former sees state-based intervention as central to its operation. Indeed, neoliberalism can be defined in one sense as a form of capitalism that envisions itself as able to manage crises to the point where their effects (at least on the wealthy) are minimized. See Wendy Brown's argu-ment that neoliberalism sees itself as "achieved and normative" in American Nightmare: Neoliberalism, Neoconservatism, and De-Democratization," *Political Theory* 34, no. 6 (2006): 690–714.

47 Michael Warner, "Publics and Counterpublics," *Public Culture* 14, no. 1 (2002): 50.

48 Ibid., 56.

49 Ibid., 57–8; emphasis in original.

50 Ibid., 58.

Epilogue

1 In decline, perhaps, in terms of its cultural force, but not in terms of the sheer amount of reading that is taking place. Even Dana Gioia, who pre-sented the 2002 National Endowment for the Arts report "Reading at Risk," which was perhaps the most prominent example of doom-and-gloom fore-casts of literature's demise, introduced a much rosier report, "Reading on the Rise" in 2008. "Reading on the Rise" concludes that "for the first time in over a quarter-century ... literary reading has risen among adult Americans" and that "the most significant growth has been among young adults ... [a group which] has undergone a transformation from a 20 percent decline in 2002 to a 21 percent increase in 2008." Dana Gioia, "Preface," *Reading on the Rise: A New Chapter in American Literacy*, The National Endowment for the Arts (Washington, DC: The National Endowment for the Arts, 2008). See also *Reading at Risk: A Survey of Literary Reading in America*, The National Endowment for the Arts (Washington, DC: The National Endowment for the Arts, 2004).

2 This narrative of the trajectory of contemporary aesthetics is ubiquitous in assessments of so-called post-postmodern literature. See, for example, Stephen Burt's introduction to *Close Calls with Nonsense: Reading New Poetry* (Port Townsend, WA: Graywolf Press, 2009); Stephen J. Burn, *Jonathan Franzen*

at the End of Postmodernism (London and New York: Continuum, 2011); and Robert L. McLaughlin, "Post-Postmodern Discontent: Contemporary Fiction and the Social World," *Symplokē* 12, nos. 1–2 (2004). See also the tendency to praise compromise aesthetics in recent anthologies of poetry, including Paul Hoover, ed., *Postmodern American Poetry: A Norton Anthology*, Second Edition (New York and London: W. W. Norton, 2013) and Cole Swensen and David St. John, eds., *American Hybrid: A Norton Anthology of New Poetry* (New York and London: W. W. Norton, 2009).

3 See "Six Propositions on Compromise Aesthetics," forthcoming in *Postmodern/Postwar – and After*, ed. Jason Gladstone, Andrew Hoberek, and Daniel Worden (Iowa City: University of Iowa Press).

4 See Bruno Latour, *Reassembling the Social: An Introduction to Actor-Network Theory* (Oxford and New York: Oxford University Press, 2007).

5 For a related articulation of how literature works in a broader system consisting of both what lies within a given work and the human and nonhuman actors who engage with it, see Aaron Kunin, "Characters Lounge," *MLQ: Modern Language Quarterly* 70, no. 3 (2009): 291–317.

6 On the capacity for literature to reach beyond the prevailing assumptions of its historical context, see among others Rita Felski, "Context Stinks," *New Literary History* 42, no. 4 (2011): 573–91 and Caroline Levine, "Strategic Formalism: Toward a New Method in Cultural Studies," *Victorian Studies* 48, no. 4 (2006): 625–57.

Bibliography

Adams, Rachel. "The Ends of America, the Ends of Postmodernism." *Twentieth-Century Literature* 53, no. 3 (2007): 248–72.

Adorno, Theodor, Walter Benjamin, Ernst Bloch, Bertolt Brecht, and Georg Lukacs. *Aesthetics and Politics*. Brooklyn, NY: Verso, 2007.

Ahmed, Sara. *The Promise of Happiness*. Durham, NC: Duke University Press, 2010.

Allen, Brooke. "Review of *the Book of Illusions* by Paul Auster." *Atlantic Monthly* 290, no. 2 (2002): 154.

Anker, Elizabeth S. "Allegories of Falling and the 9/11 Novel." *American Literary History* 23, no. 3: 463–82.

Annesley, James. "Market Corrections: Jonathan Franzen and the 'Novel of Globalization.'" *Journal of Modern Literature* 29, no. 2 (2006): 111–28.

Atwood, Margaret. *Oryx and Crake*. New York: Anchor Books, 2004.

Auster, Paul. *The Book of Illusions*. New York: Picador, 2002.

Badiou, Alain. "15 Theses on Contemporary Art." *Lacanian Ink* 23 (2004), http://www.lacan.com/issue22.php, accessed August 13, 2013.

Logics of Worlds: Being and Event II. Translated by Alberto Toscano. London and New York: Continuum, 2009.

Banita, Georgiana. *Plotting Justice: Narrative Ethics and Literary Culture after 9/11*. Lincoln and London: University of Nebraska Press, 2012.

Beck, Richard. "Costing Planet Earth." *Film Quarterly* 63, no. 3 (2010): 63–6.

Beck, Ulrich. *Risk Society: Towards a New Modernity*. Thousand Oaks, CA: Sage Publications, 1992.

Beck, Ulrich, Anthony Giddens, and Scott Lash. *Reflexive Modernization: Politics, Tradition and Aesthetics in the Modern Social Order*. Stanford, CA: Stanford University Press, 1994.

Benjamin, Walter. "The Author as Producer." *New Left Review* 62, July–August (1970): 83–96.

The Work of Art in the Age of Its Technological Reproducibility, and Other Writings on Media. Edited by E. F. N. Jephcott. Cambridge, MA: Harvard University Press, 2008.

Bennett, Jane. *Vibrant Matter: A Political Ecology of Things*. Durham, NC: Duke University Press, 2010.

Bergson, Henri. *Matter and Memory*. Cambridge, MA: Zone Books, 1990.

Berlant, Lauren. *Cruel Optimism*. Durham, NC: Duke University Press, 2011.

The Female Complaint: The Unfinished Business of Sentimentality in American Culture. Durham, NC: Duke University Press, 2008.

Berry, Wendell. "Faustian Economics: Hell Hath No Limits." *Harper's Magazine* (May 2008), http://harpers.org/archive/2008/05/faustian-economics/, accessed August 11, 2013.

Bewes, Timothy. "Against the Ontology of the Present: Paul Auster's Cinematic Fictions." *Twentieth Century Literature* 53, no. 3 (2007): 273–97.

Bogost, Ian. *Alien Phenomenology, or What It's Like to Be a Thing*. Minneapolis: University of Minnesota Press, 2012.

Bouse, Derek. "Are Wildlife Films Really 'Nature Documentaries'?" *Critical Studies in Media Communication* 15, no. 2 (1998): 116–40.

"The Brain Is the Ultimate Storytelling Machine, and Consciousness Is the Ultimate Story." Interview with Alec Michod, *The Believer* (February 2007), http://www.believermag.com/issues/200702/?read=interview_powers, accessed August 11, 2013.

Brecht, Bertolt. "On Chinese Acting." *The Tulane Drama Review* 6, no. 1 (1961): 130–6.

Brown, Wendy. "American Nightmare: Neoliberalism, Neoconservatism, and De-Democratization." *Political Theory* 34, no. 6 (2006): 690–714.

Edgework: Critical Essays on Knowledge and Politics. Princeton, NJ and Oxford: Princeton University Press, 2005.

"Neo-Liberalism and the End of Liberal Democracy." *Theory & Event* 7, no. 1 (2003), http://muse.jhu.edu.ezp.slu.edu/journals/theory_and_event/v007/7.1brown.html, accessed August 11, 2013.

Bryant, Levi. *The Democracy of Objects*. London: Open Humanities Press, 2011.

Buell, Lawrence. *The Environmental Imagination*. Cambridge, MA: Harvard University Press, 1995.

The Future of Environmental Criticism: Environmental Crisis and Literary Imagination. Blackwell Manifestos. Malden, MA: Blackwell, 2005.

Buell, Lawrence, and Wai Chee Dimock, eds. *Shades of the Planet: American Literature as World Literature*. Princeton, NJ: Princeton University Press, 2007.

Burn, Stephen J. "Don DeLillo's *Great Jones Street* and the Science of the Mind." *MFS: Modern Fiction Studies* 55, no. 2 (2009): 349–68.

Jonathan Franzen at the End of Postmodernism. London and New York: Continuum, 2011.

Burnett, David. "David Brooks Defines the New 'Social Animal.'" National Public Radio (March 7, 2011), http://www.npr.org/2011/03/07/134329412/david-brooks-defines-the-new-social-animal, accessed August 8, 2013.

Burt, Stephen. *Close Calls With Nonsense: Reading New Poetry*. Port Townsend, WA: Graywolf Press, 2009.

"Review of *Smokes*, by Susan Wheeler." *Boston Review* (Summer 1998), http://www.bostonreview.net/BR23.3/burt.html, accessed August 11, 2013.

Butler, Judith. *Frames of War: When Is Life Grievable?* New York: Verso, 2009.

    Precarious Life: The Powers of Mourning and Violence. New York: Verso, 2004.

Canavan, Gerry, Lisa Klarr, and Ryan Vu. "Introduction." *Polygraph* 22 (2010): 1–32.

Caruth, Cathy. *Unclaimed Experience.* Baltimore, MD: Johns Hopkins University Press, 1996.

Castree, Noel. "Neoliberalism and the Biophysical Environment 3: Putting Theory into Practice." *Geography Compass* 5, no. 1 (2011): 35–49.

Chabon, Michael. "After the Apocalypse." *New York Review of Books* (February 15, 2007), http://www.nybooks.com/articles/archives/2007/feb/15/after-the-apocalypse/?pagination=false, accessed May 23, 2013.

Clough, Patricia Ticineto. *The Affective Turn: Theorizing the Social.* Durham, NC: Duke University Press, 2007.

Clover, Joshua. *1989: Bob Dylan Didn't Have This to Sing About.* Berkeley and Los Angeles: University of California Press, 2009.

Clune, Michael. "Responses to *Neoliberal Aesthetics.*" *nonsite.org*, issue 2 (2011). http://nonsite.org/issues/issue-2/responses-to-neoliberal-aesthetics, accessed May 13, 2013.

Collins, Billy. "The Sandhill Cranes of Nebraska." *Harper's Magazine* (August 2011): 18.

Connolly, William. *Neuropolitics: Thinking, Culture, Speed.* Minneapolis: University of Minnesota Press, 2002.

Conrad, Joseph. *Heart of Darkness.* 4th ed. Norton Critical Editions. New York: W. W. Norton, 2005.

Cronon, William. "The Trouble with Wilderness; or, Getting Back to the Wrong Nature." In *Uncommon Ground: Rethinking the Human Place in Nature.* Edited by William Cronon. New York: W. W. Norton, 1995: 69–90.

Cullum, Charles. "The Blue Stone, Heidegger, and 'I': The Issue of Identity in Paul Auster's *The Book of Illusions.*" *EAPSU Online: A Journal of Critical and Creative Work* 5 (2008): 36–44.

Cvetkovich, Ann. *An Archive of Feelings: Trauma, Sexuality, and Lesbian Public Cultures.* Durham, NC: Duke University Press, 2003.

Damasio, Antonio. *Looking for Spinoza: Joy, Sorrow, and the Feeling Brain.* Orlando, FL: Harcourt, 2003.

Daniels, D. W. "The World of Words: Ben Marcus' *The Age of Wire and String.*" *Notes on Contemporary Literature* 33, no. 4 (2003): 6–8.

Danta, Chris. "'The Cold Illucid World': The Poetics of Gray in Cormac McCarthy's *The Road.*" In *Styles of Extinction: Cormac McCarthy's The Road.* Edited by Julian Murphet and Mark Steven. London and New York: Continuum Books, 2012.

Deleuze, Gilles. *Bergsonism.* Translated by Hugh Tomlinson and Barbara Habberjam. Cambridge, MA: Zone Books, 1990.

    Cinema 1: The Movement-Image. Minneapolis: University of Minnesota Press, 1986.

Expressionism in Philosophy: Spinoza. Translated by Martin Joughin. Cambridge, MA: Zone Books, 1992.

Nietzsche and Philosophy. Translated by Hugh Tomlinson. New York: Columbia University Press, 2006.

Spinoza: Practical Philosophy. Translated by Robert Hurley. San Francisco, CA: City Lights Books, 1988.

Deleuze, Gilles, and Félix Guattari. *What Is Philosophy?* New York: Columbia University Press, 1994.

DeLillo, Don. *Falling Man.* New York: Simon & Schuster, 2007.

Derrida, Jacques. "Signature, Event, Context." *Limited, Inc.* Chicago, IL: Northwestern University Press, 1988: 1–23.

Dewey, John. *Art as Experience.* New York: Penguin, 1934.

D'hoker, Elke. "Theorizing the Middlebrow: An Interview with Nicola Humble." *Interférences littéraires/Literaire interferenties* 7 (November 2011): 259–65.

Dillard, Annie. "The Wreck of Time: Taking the Century's Measure." *Harper's Magazine* (January 1998): 51–6.

Dimock, Wai Chee. *Through Other Continents: American Literature across Deep Time.* Princeton, NJ: Princeton University Press, 2006.

Donohue, Julie M., et al. "A Decade of Direct-to-Consumer Advertising of Prescription Drugs." *New England Journal of Medicine* 357, no. 7 (2007): 673–81.

Egan, Jennifer. *A Visit from the Goon Squad.* New York: Alfred A. Knopf, 2010.

Eggers, Dave. *A Heartbreaking Work of Staggering Genius.* San Francisco, CA: McSweeney's, 2001.

Eisenstein, Sergei. *Film Form.* Translated by Jay Leyda. New York: Harcourt, 1977.

Eliot, George. "The Natural History of German Life." *Westminster Review* 66 (July 1856): 51–79.

Eliot, T. S. *The Sacred Wood: Essays on Poetry and Criticism.* New York: Alfred A. Knopf, 1921.

Farrell, Kirby. *Post-Traumatic Culture: Injury and Interpretation in the Nineties.* Baltimore, MD: Johns Hopkins University Press, 1998.

Felman, Shoshana, and Dori Laub. *Testimony: Crises of Witnessing in Literature, Psychoanalysis and History.* New York: Routledge, 1991.

Felski, Rita. "Context Stinks." *New Literary History* 42, no. 4 (2011): 573–91.

Flatley, Jonathan. *Affective Mapping.* Cambridge, MA: Harvard University Press, 2008.

Foer, Jonathan Safran. *Extremely Loud and Incredibly Close: A Novel.* New York: Mariner Books, 2006.

Forster, E. M. *Aspects of the Novel.* Electronic ed. New York: RosettaBooks, 2002.

Foster, Brett. "Contemporary Poetry: Social Conscience? Not So Much." *Capital Commentary* (November 18, 2011), http://www.capitalcommentary.org/billy-collins/contemporary-poetry-social-conscience-not-so-much, accessed August 11, 2013.

Foucault, Michel. *The Birth of Biopolitics*. Edited by Michel Senellart, Francois Ewald, and Alessandro Fontana. Translated by Graham Burchell. *Lectures at the College De France*. New York: Palgrave Macmillan, 2008.

The History of Sexuality. Volume One: An Introduction. Edited by Robert Hurley. New York: Random House, 1978.

Franzen, Jonathan. "Mr. Difficult." *New Yorker* (September 30, 2002): 100–10.

The Corrections. New York: Farrar, Straus & Giroux, 2001.

Freud, Sigmund. *Five Lectures on Psychoanalysis*. Electronic ed. 1909, http://www .anselm.edu/homepage/dbanach/h-freud-lectures.htm, accessed August 8, 2013.

Fried, Michael. *Absorption and Theatricality: Painting and Beholder in the Age of Dierot*. Chicago, IL: University of Chicago Press, 1988.

Friedman, Milton. *Capitalism and Freedom*. Chicago, IL: University of Chicago Press, 2002.

Fukuyama, Francis. *The End of History and the Last Man*. New York: Free Press, 1992.

Gee, Maggie. "Review: Fiction: The Book of Illusions by Paul Auster." *Sunday Times* (October 20, 2002), http://www.thesundaytimes.co.uk/sto/culture/ books/article55211.ece, accessed May 23, 2013.

Gillespie, Sam. *The Mathematics of Novelty: Badiou's Minimalist Metaphysics*. Melbourne: re:press, 2008.

Gray, Richard. "Open Doors, Closed Minds: American Prose Writing at a Time of Crisis." *American Literary History* 21, no. 1 (2009): 128–51.

Grossberg, Lawrence. *We Gotta Get Out of This Place: Popular Conservatism and Postmodern Culture*. London and New York: Routledge, 1992.

Grosz, Elizabeth. *Chaos, Territory, Art: Deleuze and the Framing of the Earth*. New York: Columbia University Press, 2008.

Gurr, Martin Butler, and Jens Martin. "The Poetics and Politics of Metafiction: Reading Paul Auster's *Travels in the Scriptorium*." *English Studies* 89, no. 2 (2008): 195–209.

Hallward, Peter. *Badiou: A Subject to Truth*. Minneapolis: University of Minnesota Press, 2003.

Harman, Graham. *Guerilla Metaphysics: Phenomenology and the Carpentry of Things*. Chicago, IL: Open Court, 2005.

Harris, Charles B. "The Story of the Self: The Echo Maker and Neurological Realism." In *Intersections: Essays on Richard Powers*. Edited by Stephen J. Burn and Peter Dempsey. Champaign, IL: Dalkey Archive Press, 2008.

Harvey, David. *A Brief History of Neoliberalism*. New York: Oxford University Press, 2005.

Heidegger, Martin. *Being and Time*. Translated by Joan Stambaugh. Albany: State University of New York Press, 1996.

Heise, Ursula K. *Sense of Place and Sense of Planet: The Environmental Imagination of the Global*. Oxford: Oxford University Press, 2008.

Heller-Roazen, Daniel. *The Inner Touch: Archaeology of a Sensation*. Brooklyn, NY: Zone Books, 2007.

Hemingway, Ernest. *In Our Time*. New York: Scribner, 1958.

Hoberek, Andrew. "Cormac McCarthy and the Aesthetics of Exhaustion." *American Literary History* 23, no. 3 (2011): 483–99.

Hoover, Paul, ed. *Postmodern American Poetry: A Norton Anthology*, Second Edition. New York and London: W. W. Norton, 2013.

"How the Dead Dream." *Publishers Weekly* (October 8, 2007), http://www.publishersweekly.com/978-1-59376-184-4, accessed August 11, 2013.

Hunt, Laird. *The Exquisite*. Minneapolis, MN: Coffee House Press, 2006.

Hutchinson, Colin. "Jonathan Franzen and the Politics of Disengagement." *Critique: Studies in Contemporary Fiction* 50, no. 2 (2009): 191–207.

James, Henry. "The Art of Fiction." In *The Norton Anthology of Theory and Criticism*. Edited by Vincent B. Leitch. New York and London: W. W. Norton, 2010: 744–59.

The Portrait of a Lady. New York: Random House, 1966.

James, William. *The Principles of Psychology*. Vol. 2. New York: Dover, 1918.

Jameson, Fredric. *Brecht and Method*. London and New York: Verso, 1998.

"Cognitive Mapping." In *Marxism and the Interpretation of Culture*. Edited by Lawrence Grossberg and Cary Nelson. Urbana: University of Illinois Press, 1988.

Postmodernism, or, the Cultural Logic of Late Capitalism. Durham, NC: Duke University Press, 1991.

Kakutani, Michiko. "A Man, a Woman and a Day of Terror." *New York Times*, May 5, 2007, http://www.nytimes.com/2007/05/09/books/09kaku .html?pagewanted=all, accessed August 13, 2013.

Kaplan, E. Ann. *Trauma Culture*. New Brunswick, NJ: Rutgers University Press, 2005.

Kauffman, Linda S. "The Wake of Terror: Don Delillo's 'In the Ruins of the Future,' 'Baader-Meinhof,' and *Falling Man*." *MFS: Modern Fiction Studies* 54, no. 2 (2008): 353–77.

Kellogg, Carolyn. "Money for Nothing." *Los Angeles Times*, January 27, 2008, http://articles.latimes.com/2008/jan/27/books/bk-kellogg27, accessed August 11, 2013.

Klein, Naomi. *The Shock Doctrine: The Rise of Disaster Capitalism*. New York: Continuum, 2007.

Konstantinou, Lee. "Wipe That Smirk Off Your Face: Postironic Literature and the Politics of Character." PhD diss. Stanford University, 2010.

Kravitz, Richard L., et al. "Influence of Patient's Requests for Direct-to-Consumer Advertised Antidepressants: A Randomized Controlled Trial." *Journal of the American Medical Association* 293, no. 16 (2005): 1995–2002.

Kroeber, Karl. "Ecology and American Literature: Thoreau and Un-Thoreau." *American Literary History* 9, no. 2 (1997): 309–28.

Kunin, Aaron. "Characters Lounge." *MLQ: Modern Language Quarterly* 70, no. 3 (2009): 291–317.

Kunsa, Ashley. "Maps of the World in Its Becoming: Post-Apocalyptic Naming in Cormac McCarthy's *the Road*." *Journal of Modern Literature* 33, no. 1 (2009): 57–74.

Latour, Bruno. "An Attempt at a 'Compositionist Manifesto.'" *New Literary History* 41 (2010): 471–90.

"The Promises of Constructivism." In *Chasing Technoscience: Matrix for Materiality*. Edited by Don Ihde. Indiana Series for the Philosophy of Science. Bloomington: Indiana University Press, 2003: 27–46.

Reassembling the Social: An Introduction to Actor-Network Theory. Oxford and New York: Oxford University Press, 2005.

"Why Has Critique Run Out of Steam? From Matters of Fact to Matters of Concern." *Critical Inquiry* 30 (Winter 2004): 225–48.

Lee, Sue-Im. "'We Are Not the World': Global Village, Universalism, and Karen Tei Yamashita's *Tropic of Orange*." *MFS Modern Fiction Studies* 52, no. 3 (2007): 501–27.

Levine, Caroline. "Strategic Formalism: Toward a New Method in Cultural Studies." *Victorian Studies* 48, no. 4 (2006): 625–57.

Levine, Stacey. "An Inter(e)view with Ben Marcus." *electronic book review* (December 15, 1998). http://www.electronicbookreview.com/thread/wuc/disruptive.

Leys, Ruth. *Trauma.* Chicago, IL: University of Chicago Press, 2000.

"The Turn to Affect: A Critique." *Critical Inquiry* 37, no. 3 (2011): 434–72.

Locke, John. *Second Treatise of Government.* Project Gutenberg, 2005, http://www.gutenberg.org/files/7370/7370-h/7370-h.htm, accessed August 8, August 2013.

Love, Heather. *Feeling Backward: Loss and the Politics of Queer History.* Cambridge, MA, and London: Harvard University Press, 2007.

Luhrmann, T. M. *When God Talks Back: Understanding the American Evangelical Relationship with God.* New York: Alfred A. Knopf, 2012.

Mahmood, Saba. *The Politics of Piety.* Princeton, NJ: Princeton University Press, 2005.

Marcus, Ben. *The Age of Wire and String.* Champaign, IL: Dalkey Archive Press, 2007.

"Why Experimental Fiction Threatens to Destroy Publishing, Jonathan Franzen, and Life as We Know It: A Correction." *Harper's Magazine* (October 2005): 39–52.

Martin, Randy, *The Financialization of Daily Life.* Pennsylvania: Temple University Press, 2002.

Marx, Karl. *Capital: A Critique of Political Economy, Volume One.* Translated by Ben Fowkes. New York: Penguin, 1990.

Massumi, Brian. *Parables for the Virtual: Movement, Affect, Sensation.* Durham, NC: Duke University Press, 2002.

McCarthy, Cormac. *The Road.* New York: Random House, 2006.

McGee, Micki. *Self-Help, Inc.: Makeover Culture in American Life.* Oxford and New York: Oxford University Press, 2005.

McGurl, Mark. *The Program Era: Postwar Fiction and the Rise of Creative Writing.* Cambridge, MA: Harvard University Press, 2009.

McHale, Brian. *Postmodernist Fiction.* London and New York: Routledge, 1987.

McKibben, Bill. *The End of Nature.* New York: Random House, 2006.

McLaughlin, Robert L. "Post-Postmodern Discontent: Contemporary Fiction and the Social World." *Symplokē* 12, nos. 1–2 (2004): 53–68.

Michaels, Walter Benn. "Neoliberal Aesthetics: Fried, Ranciere and the Form of the Photograph." *nonsite.org*, issue 1 (2011). http://nonsite.org/issues/issue-1/neoliberal-aesthetics-fried-ranciere-and-the-form-of-the-photograph, accessed May 13, 2013.

The Shape of the Signifier. Princeton, NJ: Princeton University Press, 2004.

Millet, Lydia. *How the Dead Dream*. New York: Houghton Mifflin Harcourt, 2008.

Milton, John. *Paradise Lost*. Edited by John Leonard Harmondsworth. New York: Penguin, 2003.

Monbiot, George. "The Road Well Travelled." *The Guardian* (October 30, 2007), http://www.monbiot.com/2007/10/30/the-road-well-travelled/, accessed May 13, 2013.

Moraru, Christian. *Cosmodernism: American Narrative, Late Globalization, and the New Cultural Imaginary*. Ann Arbor: University of Michigan Press, 2010.

Morton, Timothy. *The Ecological Thought*. Cambridge, MA: Harvard University Press, 2010.

Ecology without Nature: Rethinking Environmental Aesthetics. Cambridge, MA: Harvard University Press, 2007.

Mukherjee, Siddhartha. "Post-Prozac Nation." *New York Times Magazine*, April 19, 2012, http://www.nytimes.com/2012/04/22/magazine/the-science-and-history-of-treating-depression.html?pagewanted=all&_r=0, accessed May 13, 2013.

"Nature, N." Oxford English Dictionary, http://www.oed.com.ezp.slu.edu/view/Entry/125353?rskey=8fbHbd&result=1&isAdvanced=false#eid, accessed August 11, 2013.

Nealon, Jeffrey. *Post-Postmodernism: Or, the Cultural Logic of Just-in-Time Capitalism*. Stanford, CA: Stanford University Press, 2012.

Ness, Patrick. "How the Rich Live." *The Guardian* (October 10, 2008), http://www.theguardian.com/books/2008/oct/11/lydia-millet, accessed August 8, 2013.

Ngai, Sianne. *Our Aesthetic Categories*. Cambridge, MA: Harvard University Press, 2012.

Ugly Feelings. Cambridge, MA: Harvard University Press, 2005.

Nussbaum, Martha. *Poetic Justice: The Literary Imagination and Public Life*. Boston, MA: Beacon Press, 1997.

O'Hagan, Andrew. "Racing against Reality." *New York Review of Books* (June 28, 2007), http://www.nybooks.com/articles/archives/2007/jun/28/racing-against-reality/?pagination=false, accessed August 11, 2013.

Peacock, Jim. "Carrying the Burden of Representation: Paul Auster's *The Book of Illusions*." *Journal of American Studies* 40 (2006): 53–69.

Phillips, Dana. *The Truth of Ecology: Nature, Culture, and Literature in America*. Oxford and New York: Oxford University Press, 2003.

Pollan, Michael. "Playing God in the Garden." *New York Times Magazine* (October 25, 1998), http://www.nytimes.com/1998/10/25/magazine/playing -god-in-the-garden.html?pagewanted=all&src=pm, accessed August 11, 2013.

Powers, Richard. *The Echo Maker*. New York: Picador, 2006.

    Galatea 2.2. New York: Harper Perennial, 1996.

    "Making the Rounds." In *Intersections: Essays on Richard Powers*. Edited by Stephen J. Burn and Peter Dempsey. Champaign, IL, and London: Dalkey Archive Press, 2008.

Protevi, John. *Political Affect: Connecting the Social and the Somatic*. Minneapolis: University of Minnesota Press, 2009.

Quart, Alissa. "Networked: Don Roos and 'Happy Endings.'" *Film Comment* (July/August 2005): 48–51.

Read, Jason "A Geneaology of Homo-Economicus: Neoliberalism and the Production of Subjectivity," *Foucault Studies* 6 (2009): 25–36.

Reading at Risk: A Survey of Literary Reading in America. The National Endowment for the Arts. Washington, DC: The National Endowment for the Arts, 2004.

Reading on the Rise: A New Chapter in American Literacy. The National Endowment for the Arts. Washington, DC: The National Endowment for the Arts, 2008.

Reber, Dierdra. "Headless Capitalism: Affect as Free Market Episteme." *differences: A Journal of Feminist Cultural Studies* 23, no. 1 (2012): 62–100.

Richards, I. A. *Practical Criticism*. 1929. Reprint, New Brunswick, NJ: Transaction, 2004.

    Principles of Literary Criticism. 1924. Reprint, London and New York: Routledge, 2002.

    Science and Poetry. New York: W. W. Norton., 1926.

Rody, Caroline. "The Transnational Imagination: Karen Tei Yamashita's *Tropic of Orange*." In *Asian North American Identities: Beyond the Hyphen*. Edited by Eleanor Ty and Donald C. Goellnicht. Bloomington: Indiana University Press, 2004: 130–48.

Sacks, Oliver. *The Man Who Mistook His Wife for a Hat*. New York: Touchstone, 1998.

Savage, Dan. "Brotherly Love." *Salon.com* (March 14, 2000), http://www.salon .com/2000/03/14/eggers_2/, accessed August 8, 2013.

Savu, Laura. "Souls Shifted Sideways": The Ethics and Aesthetics of Affect in Post-9/11 Narrative." *Studies in American Culture* 35, no. 1 (2012): 31–58.

Sedgwick, Eve Kosofsky, and Adam Frank, "Shame in the Cybernetic Fold: Reading Silvan Tomkins," *Critical Inquiry* 21, no. 2 (1995): 496–522.

Shaviro, Steven. "The 'Bitter Necessity' of Debt: Neoliberal Finance and the Society of Control," www.shaviro.com/Othertexts/Debt.pdf, accessed August 8, 2013.

Sherry, Vincent B. *The Great War and the Language of Modernism*. New York: Oxford University Press, 2004.

Shiva, Vandana. *Biopiracy: The Plunder of Nature and Knowledge.* Cambridge, MA: South End Press, 1997.

"Recovering the Real Meaning of Sustainability." In *The Environment in Question: Ethics and Global Issues.* Edited by David E. Cooper and Joy A. Palmer. New York: Routledge, 1992: 187–93.

Smith, Rachel Greenwald. "Ecology beyond Ecology: Life after the Accident in Octavia Butler's *Xenogenesis* Trilogy." *MFS Modern Fiction Studies* 55 (2009): 545–65.

"Postmodernism and the Affective Turn. *Twentieth-Century Literature* 57, nos. 3–4 (2011): 423–46.

"Six Propositions on Compromise Aesthetics," *Postmodern, Postwar, and After.* Ed. Andrew Hoberek, Daniel Worden, and Jason Gladstone. Iowa City: University of Iowa Press, in press.

Smith, Sidonie, and Julia Watson. "The Rumpled Bed of Autobiography: Extravagant Lives, Extravagant Questions." *Biography: An Interdisciplinary Quarterly* 24, no. 1 (2001): 1–14.

Spinoza, Baruch. *Ethics.* Indianapolis, IN: Hackett, 1992.

Spivak, Gayatri Chakravorty. *Death of a Discipline.* New York: Columbia University Press, 2003.

Swensen, Cole, and David St. John, eds. *American Hybrid: A Norton Anthology of New Poetry.* New York and London: W. W. Norton, 2009.

Tabbi, Joseph. "Afterthoughts on *The Echo Maker.*" In *Intersections: Essays on Richard Powers.* Edited by Stephen J. Burn and Peter Dempsey. Champaign, IL: Dalkey Archive Press, 2008.

Cognitive Fictions. Minneapolis: University of Minnesota Press, 2002.

Tanenhaus, Sam. "Peace and War." *New York Times* (August 19, 2010), http://www .nytimes.com/2010/08/29/books/review/Tanenhaus-t.html?pagewanted=all, accessed May 13, 2013.

Terada, Rei. *Feeling in Theory.* Cambridge, MA: Harvard University Press, 2003.

Thatcher, Margaret. "Press Conference for American Correspondents in London." *Thatcher Archive: COI Transcript* (June 25, 1980), http://www.mar-garetthatcher.org/document/104389, accessed May 23, 2013.

Thrailkill, Jane F. *Affecting Fictions: Mind, Body, and Emotion in American Literary Realism.* Cambridge, MA: Harvard University Press, 2009.

Thoreau, Henry David. *Walden.* Boston, MA: Beacon Press, 1997.

Uexkull, Jacob von. *A Foray into the Worlds of Animals and Humans.* Minneapolis: University of Minnesota Press, 2010.

Vernon, Peter. "Ben Marcus, *The Age of Wire and String.*" *Yearbook of English Studies* 31 (2001): 118–24.

Verslys, Kristiaan. *Out of the Blue: September 11 and the Novel.* New York: Columbia University Press, 2009.

Virilio, Paul. *Unknown Quantity.* London: Thames and Hudson, 2003.

Wallace, David Foster. "E Unibus Pluram: Television and U.S. Fiction." *Review of Contemporary Fiction* 13, no. 2 (1993): 151–94.

Infinite Jest. New York: Little, Brown, 1996.

Walter, Jess. *The Zero*. New York: HarperCollins, 2006.

Warner, Michael. "Publics and Counterpublics." *Public Culture* 14, no. 1 (2002): 49–90.

Watt, Ian. *The Rise of the Novel: Studies in Defoe, Richardson and Fielding*. Berkeley and Los Angeles: University of California Press, 1957.

Wertheimer, Linda. "Paul Auster and Salman Rushdie Discuss Reimagining the Shape of the World since September 11th." *All Things Considered*. National Public Radio, September 8, 2002.

Widiss, Benjamin. *Obscure Invitations: The Persistence of the Author in Twentieth-Century American Literature*. Stanford, CA: Stanford University Press, 2011.

Williams, Raymond. *Keywords: A Vocabulary of Culture and Society*. New York: Oxford University Press, 1985.

Marxism and Literature. Oxford: Oxford University Press, 1978.

Wimsatt, W. K., and Monroe C. Beardsley. *The Verbal Icon: Studies in the Meaning of Poetry*. Lexington: University Press of Kentucky, 1954.

Woloch, Alex. *The One and the Many: Minor Characters and the Space of the Protagonist in the Novel*. Princeton, NJ: Princeton University Press, 2003.

Wood, James. "Human, All Too Inhuman." *New Republic* 223, no. 4 (2000): 41–5; http://www.newrepublic.com/article/books-and-arts/human-all-too-inhuman#, accessed May 13, 2013.

"Shallow Graves: The Novels of Paul Auster." *New Yorker* (November 30, 2009), http://www.newyorker.com/arts/critics/books/2009/11/30/091130crbo_books_wood, accessed May 23, 2013.

"Tell Me How Does It Feel?" *The Guardian* (October 6, 2001), http://www.theguardian.com/books/2001/oct/06/fiction, accessed May 13, 2013.

"What the Dickens." *The Guardian* (November 9, 2001), http://www.guardian.co.uk/books/2001/nov/09/fiction.reviews, accessed May 13, 2013.

Yamashita, Karen Tei. *Through the Arc of the Rainforest*. Minneapolis, MN: Coffee House Press, 1990.

Tropic of Orange. Minneapolis, MN: Coffee House Press, 1997.

Young, Philip. *Ernest Hemingway: A Reconsideration*. University Park: Pennsylvania State University Press, 1966.

Zunshine, Lisa. *Why We Read Fiction: Theory of Mind and the Novel*. Columbus: Ohio State University Press, 2006.

Index

Lightning Source UK Ltd.
Milton Keynes UK
UKHW010433120821
388723UK00008B/64